MAIN STREET IN CRISIS

The Great Depression and the Old
Middle Class on the Northern Plains

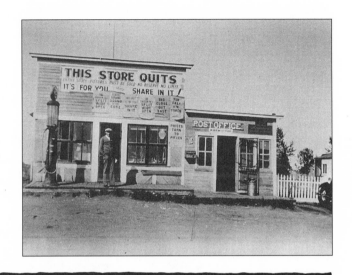

MAIN
STREET
IN CRISIS

CATHERINE McNICOL STOCK

The University of North Carolina Press   Chapel Hill & London

© 1992

The University of

North Carolina Press

Manufactured in the

United States of America

The paper in this book meets

the guidelines for permanence

and durability of the Committee

on Production Guidelines for

Book Longevity of the Council

on Library Resources.

96   95   94   93   92

5   4   3   2   1

Library of Congress Cataloging-in-Publication Data

Stock, Catherine McNicol.

   Main street in crisis : the great depression and the old middle class on the northern plains / Catherine McNicol Stock.

      p.   cm.

   Includes bibliographical references and index.

   ISBN 0-8078-2011-3 (alk. paper)

   1. South Dakota—Social conditions. 2. North Dakota—Social conditions. 3. Middle classes—South Dakota—History—20th century. 4. Middle classes—North Dakota—History—20th century. 5. Depressions—1929—South Dakota. 6. Depressions—1929—North Dakota.   I. Title.

HN79.S83S76 1992

305.5′5′09783—dc20   91-32613

                                      CIP

RUTH

McNICOL

FINCH

1902–1985

In Her Memory

With All My Love

CONTENTS

MAPS & ILLUSTRATIONS

ACKNOWLEDGMENTS

I owe thanks to many people in many places for helping me see this project through to its completion. In my years as a student, for example, I was fortunate to attend two remarkable schools and to learn from a large number of gifted teachers. At Northrop Collegiate School (subsequently known as the Blake Schools) in Minneapolis, Janet and Lee Woolman, Ann Hutchins, Barbara Reynolds, Ina Jeanne Strong, Jane Rice, Rodney Anderson, and John Hatch taught me how to write about culture before I knew that was what I was doing. At Yale College, I wandered into several classes in the American Studies program and gradually came to realize that I had found a uniquely vital center of scholarship. Between 1977 and 1985, Elliot Gorn, Ann Fabian, William Ferris, Richard Fox, Alan Trachtenberg, Nancy Cott, William Cronon, Cary Carson, Richard Brodhead, David Brion Davis, and David Montgomery greatly furthered the interests first nourished in my midwestern hometown. When I turned my attention to a dissertation, Kai Erikson, Jean-Christophe Agnew, and Robert Westbrook all thought and read and talked more about the northern plains than they ever knew possible—to my immeasurable benefit. Each of their intellectual imprints is easy to find on the pages that follow. Finally, as the project's director, Howard R. Lamar maintained the reputation for wise, kind, and interested counsel that has made him the undisputed leader of his field.

A number of my peers did their share of teaching as well. First, I owe a large debt of thanks to the members of my dissertation study group—Mary Dudziak,

Sarah Wilson, Kathryn Oberdeck, and Jacqueline Dirks. Scott Casper, Glenn Wallach, and Stephen Lassonde likewise listened patiently to my ideas in less formal settings. Research done by Louisa Gerritz and Barbara Lassonde was of extraordinary assistance at two critical moments in writing and revising. Special thanks go to Regina Kunzel, without whose abiding friendship and keen observations on the social dynamics of the Great Depression I may neither have begun nor completed this work.

As I traveled around the northern plains doing research, I received help from many regional historians and archivists. Many thanks go to Joseph Cash, Herbert Hoover, and Leonard Brugier of the South Dakota Oral History Project at the University of South Dakota in Vermillion for allowing me complete access to tapes and transcripts, an office, and a typewriter. Elizabeth Lang was exceptionally generous with materials at the University's Richardson Archives, as was LaVera Rose with photographs from the South Dakota Historical Society in Pierre. Frederick Manfred, Joseph Amato, William Pratt, and Richard Lowitt guided my thoughts and ideas at the project's earliest stage. To Frederick Luebke of the Center for Great Plains Studies in Lincoln go innumerable thanks for the simple suggestion that I leave the study of Nebraska in the 1930s to another traveler. Daniel Rylance, John Bye, Gregory Camp, Todd Strand, Patricia Jessen, and L. Martin Perry of the University of North Dakota, the North Dakota Institute for Regional Studies, and the State Historical Society of North Dakota were all very helpful with materials for and comments about my work. Larry Remele was perhaps the most generous and encouraging of all; his sudden, early death in 1988 was a terrible loss for all historians of the northern plains.

This project has also been supported by several grants. The Woodrow Wilson Foundation, the Mrs. Giles Whiting Foundation, and the Yale American Studies Graduate Student Travel Fund enabled its completion. Several outside readers encouraged and criticized the work as it was in formation. I am indebted for the time taken by David Danbom, Alan Brinkley, Richard Fox, Christopher Lasch, David Noble, and various readers for the *Western Historical Quarterly* and the University of North Carolina Press. At the Press, Kate Torrey led the way in her inimitably kind but firm manner; it would not be a book if not for her.

Lastly, I want to thank my family. My mother and father, Barbara Finch Stock and Arthur J. Stock; my parents-in-law, Lois M. and Peter E. Lefeber; and my grandfather, H. Thompson Stock, have helped in ways they know and remember all too well. The amount of help my wonderful husband, Peter J. Lefeber, has given me, however, I fear he does not even suspect. Others—Grace Campbell, Janet Olson, Jill and Bill Robbins, Patricia D. and C. Camak Baker, Jr., and Catherine C. and Harold B. Finch, Jr.—have lent their ears, not to mention food and shelter, as I came through town. Bogumila Zielinski has helped me care for my children as long as this book has been underway. But my greatest debt must be paid to my grandmother, Ruth McNicol Finch, originally of Grand Forks, North Dakota. Her idea for an undergraduate seminar paper in 1978 started this project that she did not live to see completed. I wrote it to make her proud of me.

INTRODUCTION

In a recently republished collection of short stories, Lois Phillips Hudson recalled a humiliating experience from her childhood near Eldredge, North Dakota, in the 1930s. One day at school, two of Lois's friends noticed that she did not have anything to eat for lunch. When they asked her why her family did not go on relief, however, Lois would not reply. She knew that her father, a merchant whose store had failed, had been told to lie about his income, "to say we were even poorer than we were," to qualify for government assistance. He had refused and said that he "would rather starve." Like her father, Lois was "really proud" that she had no lunch pail, even if it meant pretending to her friends that she was not hungry.[1] This book examines the basis of Lois's pretension: the moral economy of the old middle class on the northern plains during the Great Depression.

The story of America's "hard times" has been told again and again, but never quite this way. In the 1930s an ecological disaster on the Great Plains accompanied the economic upheavals of the Great Depression. Throughout the nation's vast midsection, drought and dust ruined the land and drove thousands of families from their homes. Since then, historians have traveled to the southern plains to examine the ecological and social effects of the Dust Bowl.[2] Few have ventured to the equally devastated sections of the northern plains. There, however, a drama unfolded that went well beyond economics and demographics and that more completely involved those who stayed behind than the better-known migrants who headed West. In North and South Dakota, farmers, shopkeepers, artisans,

1

and independent professionals battled not just to save their land but also to maintain a complex way of life. For them, the Great Depression marked a liminal moment in the ongoing struggle to protect the authority and the viability of their culture.

The number of minority groups that have been underrepresented in the canons of American scholarship and misunderstood by the American public is nearly too many to count. But the rural petite bourgeoisie, or what C. Wright Mills more aptly called the "old middle class," is undoubtedly the group of people Americans think they understand best but in fact know the least.[3] As a midwestern farmer suggested in 1937, when the owners of small property in rural communities—family farmers, corner-storekeepers, country doctors, small-town preachers, and teachers—"break into the New York headlines it means one of two things has happened. Either we have suffered an act of God or else we have made fools of ourselves."[4] In the 1980s, too, the public read gripping tales of farm crisis, drought, and disaster—or Garrison Keillor's best-selling comic portraits of "Norwegian bachelor farmers." The truth is, whether Americans send their pity, their laughter, or their tax dollars to the hinterland, very few have ever met a real farmer or thought to listen to what he or she might have to say.

For their own quite different reasons, American historians have played a part in the invention and persistence of the dissonance whereby rural people have become objects rather than subjects of contemporary thought. The new social history and its progeny, the new labor and the new rural history, abound with compelling images of and provocative debates about nineteenth-century "producerism"— the ideology that celebrated workers as the makers of useful things and the owners of labor power, not simply the recipients of hourly wages. Likewise, historians as diverse but as equally well-respected as Gordon Wood, David Montgomery, and Sean Wilentz have explored the concept of "republicanism"—the notion that the virtue of a nation rises and falls with property-owning citizenry—in an effort to understand both how these ideals inspired the making of the American Constitution and how they influenced the making of the American working class. Most relevant to the region studied here are the continuing his-

Map 1. The Dakotas

toriographic debates about populism. Long understood either as an anxious, potentially antidemocratic lot or as the failed forerunners of New Deal liberalism, Populists now are seen by many as proud, resistant, radical producers, perhaps the last of their kind.[5]

Little of this scholarly interest, however, extends to the century following the debacle of 1896. Serious and rich historical accounts of the lives of small producers after 1900 barely fill one library shelf.[6] Ironically, this disinterest is but the obverse side of the interest described above. That is, most studies of producerism have been done by those, like Herbert Gutman, for example, who have set out in search of the nineteenth-century working class. In "immature" capitalism, the lines between the old middle class, artisans, and wage-workers were often blurred. It was not unusual, for example, for shopkeepers to ally with workers against capital during strikes in certain towns. Thus historians have found it necessary to discuss the ideals that linked such diverse occupational groups.[7] Following the rationalization of the economy, the formal inauguration of the labor movement, and the realliance of small with big capital, however, these lines became much more distinct. The relevance of the petite bourgeoisie to the working class (and to their historians) thus greatly diminished.[8]

In the place of serious social history remain the uniformly uncomplimentary images of the "village rebels"—social critics like Thorstein Veblen and Sinclair Lewis, who in the 1920s took on all the inadequacies of small-town America. In some of America's most widely read works, writers described America's Main Streets as "place[s] of spite, frustrated lives, conformist, middle-class morality."[9] According to Richard Pells, these intellectuals believed that "nineteenth-century values had lingered on into the modern world, thereby freezing America in attitudes totally inappropriate to twentieth-century conditions."[10] The result has been a remarkably thin and ahistorical image, shared by many Americans to this day. Instead of Mary Ryan's organizing mothers, for example, we have Sinclair Lewis's gossiping gaggle of clubwomen. Instead of John Faragher's neighborly Sugar Creek, we have Veblen's contentious Country Town. Instead of Lawrence Goodwyn's radical democrats, we have Norman Thomas's proto-Fascists.[11]

What actually befell the old middle class between 1820 and 1920, and how it has since become an unpopular, even untouchable, historical subject, are separate questions. The answers to both of them, however, are based in the maturation of industrial capitalism. In what has now become a classic analysis, Robert Wiebe explained that before the Civil War rural towns stood like "island communities" on the social landscape. The people who lived in them retained a large measure of independence in their working lives and had local control over the affairs of their communities: they were the rank-and-file of antebellum American society. After Appomattox, however, the incorporation of American business, the expansion of national transportation systems, the bureaucratization of government, and the professionalization of many occupations began to change all that. By 1920, farmers, shopkeepers, and artisans had to negotiate their daily affairs with others: big business, labor, and some new faces—the white-collar workers of a "new" middle class. In short, they had to share their lives with Americans who had left the world of producerism far behind.[12]

It is not just these events but what, in theory, they have portended for small producers that have shaped our historical images of these men and women. To most social theorists on the left, the maturation of industrial capitalism guaranteed not just the separation of the old middle class from the working class but also the eventual dissolution of the old middle class—just as the growing power of large firms overwhelmed the hegemonic authority, not to mention the capital, of small ones. As Karl Marx and Friedrich Engels put it, the petite bourgeoisie was nothing but a "transitional class" caught between two more powerful groups (labor and capital) and doomed to "disappear in the face of modern industry."[13] As such, it would try to save itself, to "roll back the wheel of history," by adopting politically conservative, even reactionary, positions. In short, not only would most small producers disappear from modern capitalist society, but those who survived also would go bad.[14]

This automatic link between class status and political position has led to controversial historical analyses by Marxists and non-Marxists alike. Richard Hofstadter's well-known argument that it was the "status anxiety" of American farmers that led them to foment antidemocratic ideals in the Populist party, for example, moved Goodwyn and others to revise the history of the Farmers' Alliance.[15] But the most influential work on petit bourgeois politics is that which evaluates the rise of Adolf Hitler in Germany. Scholars from Theodor Geiger to William Allen Sheridan have argued that the German lower middle class provided Hitler's grass-roots support, and that it did so because it believed he could restore the political and cultural authority it had lost to big business, labor, and the new middle class.[16] A dying and desperate group, petty producers in Germany were naturally inclined to anti-intellectualism, anti-Semitism, and fascism.[17] By the late 1930s, influential social critics in America wondered whether such a reaction might not also "happen here."[18]

Only recently have some historians and sociologists revised these ideas and launched a campaign to broaden our understanding of petty producerism in the twentieth century. In 1982, for example, Richard Hamilton demonstrated that, at least in urban areas, the major support for Hitler may not have come from the petite bourgeoisie after all.[19] Further, Alan Brinkley has suggested that the American followers of Huey Long and Charles Coughlin—purported by many in the 1930s to be the American equivalents of Europe's Fascist demagogues—were not attracted by antidemocratic rhetoric but by their "urge to defend the autonomy of the individual and the independence of the community against encroachments from the modern industrial state."[20] More generally, scholars have warned against any reductive approach that automatically links class location with political position, particularly in a field that has been long on theory and short on empirical evidence.[21]

Finally, the new students of the petite bourgeoisie—Christopher Lasch being the most recent and most provocative—have begun to ask what the experience of petty producers in the twentieth century reveals, not about politics strictly defined, but about modern capitalist society as a whole. All predictions to the contrary, independent producers have not disappeared but in the 1970s and 1980s have actually increased in number.[22] Also, as Lasch contends, the ideals and ways of life that small producers represent may be more important to explore than ever, as both liberal and conservative visions of "progress" have in no way prepared Americans for the "world of limits" we must now inhabit.[23] Whether one agrees with Lasch that the petite bourgeoisie wholeheartedly rejected the progressive vision or that they indeed constituted a "whole world of heroes," this much is true:[24] many of the ideals and strategies of the old middle class have been relegated to the scrap heap of politically incorrect historiography. Digging them out can help us better understand how traditional ways have persisted in modern society, what functions they serve, and what meanings they hold for the future.[25] Moreover, they can help us understand the ways in which industrial capitalism and the modern state have affected— often adversely—all manner of people in the world, even those who would never have predicted it. The task is to examine petty producers "on their own terms," acknowledging that, at the very least, their perplexing persistence warrants a new approach.

For all the not-so-benign neglect of the old middle class, my analysis of their experience on the northern plains in the Great Depression did not appear out of thin air but has its roots in several classic works of sociology and history. It was Robert and Helen Lynd, of course, who first wondered how the depression and the New Deal had affected the people of the Middle West.[26] In many ways, I pose the same question that they did sixty-five years ago. Further, C. Wright Mills's *White Collar* lends this book its basic terminology as well as its hypothesis that the transformation of America into a "mass society" is at odds with the traditional worldview of the small producer.[27] Since Mills's main objective is to condemn the new middle class, however, his "old middle class entrepreneurs" act as foils and are no more complex than are the village rebels' monochromatic "booboisie." Still, by identifying the differences between "old" and "new" middle classes and by locating much of their interaction in the early twentieth century, Mills sets the stage for further research.

Until now, there have been two sorts of historical studies of the Dust Bowl experience. The first shares Mills's presumption that class is a fundamental structural component of American society but does not extend this analysis from the old to new middle class. The second ignores class entirely. Donald Worster's *Dust Bowl*, for example, is a brilliant critique of the impact of the "maximizing creed" (read greed) of capitalist agriculture and mass culture on rural society. But Worster takes much of his analysis of the social life of Haskell County, Oklahoma, and Sublette, Kansas, directly from New Deal government documents, without the least acknowledgment of the cultural politics encoded in them.[28] Likewise, Richard Hofstadter was correct to say that postwar midwestern conservatism developed from the "sense of powerlessness" and "resentment" felt by many farmers and townspeople toward the people and policies of the New Deal.[29] But Hofstadter was so impressed by and allied with New Deal liberals that he failed to consider the possibility that this resentment might have been well-placed. At the very least, it was the outcome of an interaction vastly more complex than that between good-hearted reformers and ungrateful clients.

Robert Athearn comes closer than any other historian to understanding these complex cultural dynamics. He suggests, for example, that the New Deal "intelligentsia" believed the "dreaming was over" in the West and that, as a result, New Deal programs were often at odds with Westerners' "basic [optimistic] cultural make-up." He even recognizes that most recipients of New Deal largess in the West want nothing better today than to forget about the whole thing.[30] Still, the language of class is altogether missing from Athearn's work, perhaps because it is so antithetical to the culture of the people he describes and from whom he himself descended. It is, I admit, problematic to adopt an explanatory strategy that one's subjects would wholeheartedly reject. Without it, however, Athearn is left "explaining" his subjects' ambivalence to the New Deal as "political schizophrenia" and not as the logical outcome of the contradictions inherent in their precarious class position.[31] For historians, the challenge is not just to tell a tale as well as possible, aided by the tincture of time, but to bring to that story whatever analytic concepts might help reveal its every nuance, whether or not those concepts were available to the subjects under consideration. In this case, old-middle-class culture rested upon ideals of equality of opportunity that required a denial of class conflict. As historians, we can acknowledge that denial and perhaps even sympathize with it, without accepting it as our own.

Three scholars have succeeded in combining analyses of the old middle class with empirical evidence from the 1930s. Warren Susman, in *Culture as History*, identifies the 1920s and 1930s as a critical moment in "the struggle between two cultures—an older culture, often loosely labeled [a] Puritan-republican, producer-capitalist culture, and a newly emerging culture of abundance."[32] Moreover, he locates expressions of this conflict in unusual sources, from Babe Ruth to Mickey Mouse. As we have seen, Alan Brinkley discusses the expression of the same conflict in the alternative politics of the 1930s.[33] Two essays by Lawrence Levine, however, best introduce the era's deep complexities and critical transformations. "We must try to comprehend the Great Depression as a complex, ambivalent, disorderly period," he writes, "which gave witness to the force of cultural continuity even as it manifested signs of deep cultural change."[34] Best of all, Levine suggests that this complexity (if not the class analysis he brings to it) was understood not only by social critics and other intellectuals but also by everyday people living everyday lives.[35] It is everyday people who reveal much of the story that follows, however much they might not agree with the way I tell it.

North and South Dakota in the Great Depression provide a nearly perfect laboratory for the study of the old middle class and its persistence in the twentieth century. The states were settled in large part by rural Americans and northern Europeans who owned productive property, or hoped to. Moreover, as late as 1925 nearly 65 percent of all workers there still called themselves "boss."[36] As late as 1930, owning property remained an important priority for those without it.[37] Most Dakotans remained wedded to the ideals customarily associated with petty production—faith in hard work, individuality, autonomy, and progress, coupled with loyalty to home, family, community, state, and country. The *Fargo Forum*'s 1924 "Creed of Good Citizenship" listed these devotions and one more: loyalty to "our fellow man." Editor Charles Anderson urged all Dakotans to "adopt the teachings of the Golden Rule and do [your] best to live up to it. . . . Be neighborly and friendly with rivals and competitors. Speak ill of no man."[38]

Deeply rooted as the culture of petty producerism was on the northern plains, it was also very frail. One challenge to its strength from the 1880s through the 1920s was familiar, if not yet fully potent: the ever-increasing authority of "postproducerist" America, including the experts and officials of the new middle class. But an equally serious threat originated within Dakota culture from the internal social conflicts and the fundamental contradictions of its beliefs. Unlike Steven Hahn's upcountry Georgia yeomen who, he contends, could from time to time be "in" but not "of" the market, the people of the Dakotas actively participated in the market and in the philosophy of growth and progress that made it possible.[39] In other words, most Dakotans—like most of their fellow Americans—were not unhappy with the fundamental tenets of capitalism. They sought to make a profit and did what was required to do so, whether that meant raising cash crops, plowing virgin grassland, or promoting small-scale industrialization in their communities.[40] At the same time, however, they relished many of the timeworn ways of village life. To be a Dakotan, then, meant balancing fundamentally contradictory, but equally heartfelt, impulses: loyalties to individuality and community, to profit and cooperation, to progress and tradition. Facing the devastations of the Great Depression, the people of the northern plains were armed with the weapons of a common culture. Even so, they were not as well protected as they imagined.

The depression challenged the economic foundations, social structures, and fundamental values of old-middle-class culture. Drought, dust, wind, pests, and oppressive heat ruined crops, bankrupted local organizations, forced the curtailment of community rituals, and overturned accustomed social relations. Even more significantly, however, it brought the New Deal, with its new-middle-class agents, agencies, ethos, and a host of other representatives of mass society. These men and women offered Dakotans a "choice" between their customary "pride in independence" and local control and survival itself.[41] At bottom, the depression and the New Deal upset the fragile balance of contradictory beliefs that lay at the heart of old-middle-class culture. In the 1930s, Dakotans discovered that, to survive, they had to live without many of the notions that helped them make sense of life.

In this study I make a number of assumptions that I should explain in the introduction. The most apparent is my decision to use the cumbersome term "old middle class" (and, for variety's sake, "petty producer," "petty proprietor," and "small producer"). Strictly speaking, the definitions of "old middle class" and "petite bourgeoisie" are the same: men and women who own the means of production on a small scale; who retain control over physical capital, money capital, and labor; and who continue to extract their own surplus labor value.[42] For this work, however, I prefer the term old middle class for three reasons. Again adhering to Mills's conception, old middle class generally refers to small-property owners in rural areas, whereas petite bourgeoisie evokes artisans and shopkeepers with origins in eighteenth- and nineteenth-century European cities. More importantly, however, the term *old* middle class presupposes the formation and development of the *new* middle class—men and women of great significance to Dakotans in the 1930s. Finally, I shy away from the term "petite bourgeoisie" because of the conflation so often implied between the twin meanings of "petite" and "petty." These people were the owners of small and relatively unimportant property. They were not small or unimportant people.

I have also chosen to use "Dakota" to describe the vast region that today, of course, encompasses two separate states. I am well aware of the many differences between North and South Dakota, the most relevant being a more successful tradition of farm radicalism in Bismarck, North Dakota, than in Pierre, South Dakota. There are also significant differences between the ranching, spring wheat, Red River Valley, corn-hog, and mixed-cropping areas, as there are between the "east river" and "west river" sections of both states.[43] When these differences have been important to my argument, I have tried to point them out. Still, I think that the similarities between the states during the Great Depression vastly outweigh the differences. It was, after all, only forty years before the onset of the drought that the Dakota Territory had been divided into two states at the forty-sixth parallel.[44] Moreover, North and South Dakota were affected by the Great Depression in very similar ways. According to federal researchers Francis Cronin and Howard Beers, no other pair of states on the plains were so thoroughly ruined by the drought and dust (see Map 2).[45]

Although it is more complicated to do so, I also believe it is appropriate to speak of Dakotans as one people. The vast majority of the white people of North and South Dakota shared common work experiences and common ideas about their community lives. It was the

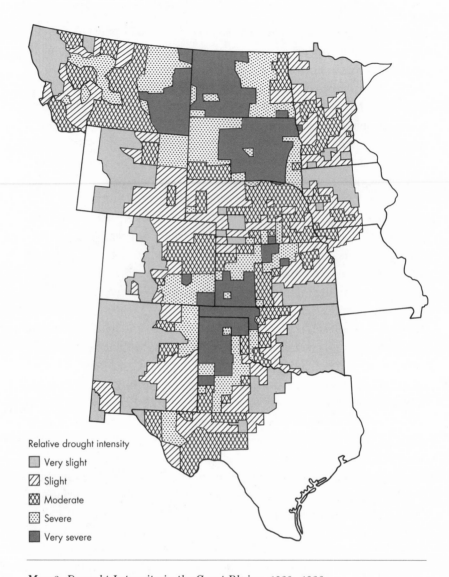

Relative drought intensity

▨ Very slight

▧ Slight

▩ Moderate

░ Severe

■ Very severe

Map 2. Drought Intensity in the Great Plains, 1930–1936

promise of independence in the workplace and "neighborliness" in the community that brought pioneers to the Dakotas, and, even for those who had not attained it, it was what kept them there. Most Dakotans would never have spoken the language of class, but they were nevertheless "aware" of the special nature of their way of life and through a number of diverse political movements sought to protect it. Most of all, however, Dakotans shared a hegemonic culture; that is, the values and ideals associated with small production were the "common sense" notions of everyday life. No one had to tell a Dakotan that it was better to work than not to work, better to be "on your own" than to work for somebody else, better to be a good neighbor than a bad one. What Dakotans shared most needed to be expressed least.[46]

For all their bonds, however, Dakotans were anything but exactly alike. Indeed, the differences between and among Dakotans were as essential a part of their culture as were their similarities. Although they shared ideas about work and community, Dakotans were also split into a panoply of different religious, political, occupational, and ethnic groups.[47] In most towns, an elite group of bankers and businessmen—usually Yankee or Scandinavian, Protestant, and Republican—presided over the comings and goings (and sometimes the fates) of smaller shopkeepers, artisans, employees, and farmers—some of whom were Catholic, German-Russian, Democrat, "Leaguer," or even Socialist. Intraclass conflict, as we shall see, became one of the hallmarks of life in these "quiet" country towns. Nevertheless, in community ritual and rhetoric these diverse peoples decidedly and emphatically celebrated their unity.

There were, however, men and women in the Dakotas who were not included in such celebrations at all. "Common laborers" and other workers who seemed to aspire to little else than wage-labor, tenant farmers who would never "make good," drunks, drifters, prostitutes, peddlers, troublemakers, and other "riff-raff" all helped define membership in the communities of the plains. Most completely excluded were the tens of thousands of Native Americans who in the early twentieth century were literally wasting away on federal reservations. In these years, white Dakotans felt they had nothing whatsoever in common with their Indian neighbors and made no mention of the fact that, west of the Missouri River, many Dakotans held their land in direct violation of official government treaties. Just as African Americans in the South, Native Americans in the West served to determine a bottom line of cultural "belonging" for whites. Unlike their southern counterparts, however, Dakotans did not often share community space with Native Americans, and thus, however unfortunately, Native Americans remain outside this analysis as well.

Dakota women occupied a highly ambiguous place within the old middle class and, perhaps as a result, a quite central place in this narrative. On one hand, the old middle class was something like a "family class," where men and women shared in the tasks of production, whether that was on a farm or in a "Mom and Pop" grocery store. On the other hand, women did not own equally the means of that production, nor did they share equally in the major decisions about the distribution of its profits. Moreover, when they were gainfully employed, Dakota women were far less likely than Dakota men to be independent entrepreneurs, farmers, or professionals.[48] Finally, even as women's work was defined by class, it was also defined by gender. Dakota women worked in the home as well as the barns; they worried about nurture as well as nature; they tended baby girls and boys as well as baby fillies and colts.[49] Women of the old middle class, then, sometimes had a great deal more in common with each other than they did with the men with whom they lived and worked.

Dakota women also experienced old-middle-class community in different ways than Dakota men. For men, community was based in organizations: bands, lodges, clubs, political organizations, and church boards, some of which specifically excluded women and reinforced male dominance. Even so, the kind of community men idealized in their organizations was that which women realized in their daily lives. It was women who tended to laboring mothers when the doctor did not arrive; took in strangers for a meal or a night's rest; gathered around a quilt, a taffy pull, or a harvest meal to "visit" with one another. In short, it was women who were on the community's "front lines" and who produced and reproduced most directly its forms and functions. It was women who were fluent in the ways and attuned to the nuances of their world.

Perhaps because they stood both inside and outside their class, Dakota women are both integrated into the whole of this narrative and segregated from it in the form of a separate chapter. Wherever they appear, however, women's voices and understandings resound. True, they do not overtly speak the language of class. But women's voices nonetheless reveal much of what the Depression was all about. Ruth Carothers tells what it took to be successful in the early days; Grace Martin Highley suggests what federal programs really cost their beneficiaries; Ann Marie Low details the ways drought could devastate lives as well as land. Without those women who, despite their urge to forget, recorded their thoughts and ideas for others to read or hear, this study could not have been written. This is a work of cultural history and historical sociology. It is also a history told largely by women.

Finally, a word about my sources. For reasons I hope to make clear in the body of the text, I felt it was best to rely whenever possible on indigenous sources: letters, diaries, memoirs, oral histories, newspaper accounts, autobiographies, and manuscript collections from the northern plains. I have likewise tried whenever appropriate to illustrate the text with photographs taken by Dakotans, for the images recorded by the Farm Security Administration (FSA) photographers are new-middle-class documents like myriad others on file in federal and state repositories. I have relied on New Deal publications, reports, correspondence, and photographs, however, for supplementary evidence and for my analysis of new-middle-class culture. This is especially important to chapters 1, 4, and 5. But cultural bias exists, of course, even in indigenous sources. Newspaper editors in Dakota were, for example, often more conservative politically than their readership. Also, letters and interviews overrepresent those who survived until the late 1970s, when this and other preservation projects were begun. Additionally, memories are not the same in all cases as facts. Some of these difficulties are simply part and parcel of historical research. I have tried to overcome them when possible by supplementing traditional written sources with documentation from popular culture and the built environment. Much of the story of the Dust Bowl on the northern plains, I believe, is reflected in Bismarck's skyscraper capitol, the Pioneer Family statue that sits to its front, and the countless billboards advertising "Free Ice Water" at Wall Drug Store.

This work sets out to accomplish four things: to reconstruct in detail the culture of petty producerism on the northern plains, its strengths and its weaknesses; to examine the effects of the depression on that society and culture; to explore the strategies Dakotans adopted in order to survive this crisis; and, finally but much more briefly, to examine the long-term costs of these adjustments to the people who have remained. The old middle class has survived on the northern plains, but it has hardly thrived. Since the 1930s, it has been supported and reproduced in large measure because other Americans want to see it so. In many respects, "hard times" continue for Dakotans even to this day.

1   THE HARDEST TIMES

Few settlers, if any at all, had come to Dakota Territory expecting life there to be easy. Profitable, plentiful, exciting, invigorating—these things they had heard—but not easy. Breaking prairie sod was back-wrenching labor; making a home on a quarter- or a half-section of land miles from the nearest neighbor tried the heartiest pioneer spirit. Even the landscape portended struggle: flat and treeless east of the Missouri River, rugged and arid west of it, and everywhere raked by a relentless, dry wind. Settlers and their children confronted the rigors of heat and cold and the terrors of tornado, prairie fire, ice, hail, and blizzard. And they became accustomed to less natural kinds of disasters as well—times when the national economy, through inflation, recession, or depression, made the fruits of their dangerous labors hardly worth the time they put into them. In the late 1880s and 1890s and in the early 1910s, economic distress brought "hard times" to Dakota men and women who, by most standards, had known little else.

Still, neither the challenges of pioneer life nor the vagaries of the agricultural economy prepared Dakotans for what came to pass in the 1930s. In those years, an unprecedented drought and an unprecedented depression met at a crossroads on the northern plains and created havoc for all living things. Year after year, Dakotans watched new records set for the longest, hottest, driest, lowest, worst, and least—only to see them broken once again. By 1940, one-third of all farmers who owned their land had lost it to foreclosure; tenancy had risen to nearly 50 percent; more than 150,000 people had left the region forever; and the federal government had spent $400 million to help those who stayed behind. This story of hardship was the story of the Dust Bowl on the northern plains. It had much in common with the disaster on the southern plains immortalized in John Steinbeck's novel, *The Grapes of Wrath*. In the Dakotas, though, conditions were even worse.[1] On 9 November 1933, Lorena Hickok wrote to New Deal administrator Harry Hopkins from Pierre, South Dakota. "This is the 'Siberia' of the United States," she said. "A more hopeless place I never saw."[2]

Although the majority of Americans recognized "Black Thursday," 24 October 1929, as the first day of the Great Depression, the people of North and South Dakota could not say exactly when their troubles had begun. The Dust Bowl crisis there, as elsewhere, was made up of two concomitant catastrophes: a worldwide collapse in farm prices and a devastating drought. Neither problem had followed the stock market crash, but both had commenced in the early 1920s. In fact, by 1929, life in the Dakotas was already so difficult that October's "big event" seemed curiously irrelevant. Writing in the diary she would keep until 1937, young Ann Marie Low mused that "there seems to be quite a furor in the country over a big stock market crash that wiped a lot of people out. We are ahead of them. The hailstorm in July of 1928 and bank failures that fall wiped out a lot of people locally. As far as that goes, most of North Dakota was hard hit last year."[3]

Many factors contributed to the agricultural crisis of the 1920s, but overproduction of foodstuff and overextension of farm credit during World War I were the most important.[4] The war had stimulated demand for farm products in Europe and in the United States and had motivated farmers on the northern plains to try to "cash in" on good times. With help from government-sponsored price supports, they increased their acreage, updated their equipment, and planted as many acres as possible in cash crops—especially wheat. For a time, the gamble paid off; in July 1920, wheat sold at the Minneapolis Grain Exchange for $2.96 a bushel—a price that would mark the peak of prosperity on the plains for years to come. At the same time, however, mortgage indebtedness increased to 70 percent in North Dakota and 55 percent in South Dakota, making farmers there even more vulnerable to a downswing in the market.[5] When, in 1921, that downswing came more drastically and sooner than expected, Dakota farmers were in deep trouble.

The trouble came this way: throughout the 1920s, farmers' costs (taxes, mortgage payments, and prices for feed, seed, and consumer goods) stayed constant or increased, while prices for their products decreased and the declining value of their land impaired their credit. The ensuing loss of income led farmers to plant more, but more crops on the market only further decreased prices. This cycle had a debilitating effect on the individual farm family's purchasing power at a time when many other Americans could afford to spend more, not less, on consumer goods. D. Jerome Tweton estimates, for example, that a suit that cost a Dakota wheat farmer twenty-one bushels of grain in 1913 cost him thirty-one bushels in 1923.[6] As the price for wheat fluctuated between $.97 and $1.20 throughout the decade, Dakota farmers fought off tax delinquency, foreclosure, and tenancy. Many did not succeed. In 1927, William Lemke (at the time a North Dakota attorney) wrote, "The farmers have never been as hard up as at present."[7]

As "hard up" as Dakota farmers were in 1927, they had seen nothing yet. Soon after the stock market crashed, its relevance became perfectly clear: farm prices and land values both hit new record lows. The average acre of farmland in South Dakota, for example, valued at $71.39 in 1920 and $35.24 in 1930, was worth only $18.65 in 1935.[8] Oats, barley, corn, and hogs all sold for prices at or below their costs of production.[9] The nadir came in 1932: "two dollar wheat" sold for fifty cents in Minneapolis and as little as twenty-five cents at some local elevators. Many farmers, like the Vaagens of Taylor, North Dakota, had harvested a bumper crop that year for the first time since 1925 but found local elevators full and the cost of shipping more than the price they would receive for it at the end of the line. Despite reports of widespread hunger—even starvation—in America's cities, the Vaagens had to leave their wheat in big piles on the farm and watch wild animals fatten on it until it spoiled.[10]

Like many other Americans who had tried to reap the benefits of prosperity, the people of North and South Dakota suffered dearly when the economy failed. Nevertheless, low prices, low wages, and unemployment were but one part of the nightmare on the northern plains. Accompanying the depression was a drought so severe that it literally tore, cracked, and ruined the earth. Moreover, it brought unspeakable suffering to both the animals and the human beings who lived upon that land. It was this drought, not the depression alone, that made the Dust Bowl.

The way South Dakota rancher Richard Mansfield recalled it, the great drought of the 1930s was like a slow, tortuous degeneration: "The depression came out and every year it got worse," he said. "It started to get dry [in 1930] and '31 was drier than that and '32 was drier than that, and '33 was drier than that. Every year it got worse."[11] In fact, between 1927 and 1938 there were two wet years, but all the rest were dry, and two—1934 and 1936—were the driest years Dakotans had ever known. Between 1930 and 1934, North Dakota accumulated a rainfall *deficiency* of 16.5 inches; most Dakota counties did not even get half of the moisture they expected.[12] Wells, springs, prairie potholes, and even some lakes went dry. Animals, gardens, and households alike were parched. As Lois Phillips Hudson recalled, water was recognized in those years for what it had been all along—something that could bring people without it to their knees: "There was, after all, nothing anyone could barter for water."[13]

Severe drought conditions made bringing a crop to maturity nearly impossible. Between 1930 and 1936, a familiar pattern developed. After a bitterly cold and snowy winter, a late chinook (quick thaw) filled rivers and streams but left little moisture in the frozen soil. Perhaps a few spring showers came, but the summers saw hardly a drop of moisture. If rain did come (as in 1935), it was accompanied by damaging cloudbursts, hailstorms, or tornadoes.[14] Farmers broke their backs to plant the little seed they had saved from the previous harvest, only to watch the shoots "turn yellow, then brown, then black."[15] In July 1933, one newspaper man in Cavalier County, North Dakota, reported, "Things are not good [but they might still] be looking up." In the fall, however, he wrote simply, "No bumper crop here."[16] The 1936 harvest

North Dakota farmer Fritz Frederick shows how high his wheat would grow if there were no drought, Grant County, North Dakota, July 1936 (Rothstein-FSA, courtesy National Archives)

was the worst of all: land that had produced wheat as far as the eye could see yielded as little as five bushels per acre. In some areas west of the Missouri River, like Williams County, North Dakota, the harvests were "a total failure."[17]

If any plants survived the drought, they were threatened by plagues of grasshoppers that hatched quickly in the dry, windy climate. In 1933, more than two-thirds of North Dakota was heavily infested with grasshoppers, and conditions in South Dakota were as bad or worse.[18] Althia Thom remembered that when grasshoppers hit "it would look like the ground was moving with those things. . . . It was enough to drive anyone buggy. Be sure everything was buttoned up tight and there'd be four grasshoppers."[19] Try as farmers and their wives might to save them, gardens, corn fields, and even clotheslines were stripped clean. Stories of "hopper" infestation became local legend. In Mott, North Dakota, the bugs were so thick in August 1933 that town offi-

Aftermath of a grasshopper infestation and poisoning near Pierre, South Dakota, in 1933 (courtesy South Dakota Historical Society)

cials turned on the streetlights during the day and built huge fires at the street corners.[20] In Killdeer, someone dared to measure them; locusts lay in piles four inches deep on city streets.[21]

With the drought came not just pests but also oppressive heat. For days and weeks at a time, particularly in the summers of 1931, 1934,

1935, and 1936, Dakotans did not see the thermometer fall much below 100°. A new record—as yet unbroken—was set in Steele, North Dakota: 121° on 6 July 1936. Most other towns were not much cooler.[22] In Grafton, North Dakota, two girls grilled a cheese sandwich on the sidewalk outside the drugstore where they worked, "proving that they did not need a toaster."[23] Intense heat only aggravated the drought by evaporating the tiny bit of moisture left in the subsoil. In eastern North Dakota, an Agricultural Extension Service agent estimated that 15 percent of local crops were ruined in the first two days of a heat wave and 65 percent were ruined after one week.[24] Cattle and horses wandered the fields in search of food and water, "dropping dead in their tracks from the heat."[25] A few human creatures (especially the elderly and the newborn) also died those summers, but most just struggled to work during the day and to rest at night. For Lois Hudson, each night she spent trying to find "every unslept-on cooler piece of sheet" was "like the worst two days of the measles."[26]

Once drought had dried the land, hoppers had emptied it, and heat had seared it through, the dust began to blow. As early as 1878, John Wesley Powell recognized the danger of exposing delicate prairie sod to humid-area cultivation techniques. Instead of the traditional 160 acres of land offered for settlement, he recommended that beyond the 100th meridian the plains be settled only in allotments of 2,560 acres and reserved for livestock.[27] More popular among homesteaders and government officials, however, was the notion that "rain would follow the plow" to create a garden in what early-nineteenth-century explorer Stephen Long had dubbed "the Great American Desert."[28] Even in the 1930s, many Dakota farmers clung to this belief. After all, between 1900 and 1916 they had recorded above-average rainfall in all but three years.[29] Moreover, dry spells had come and gone before. Even "dust storms are not new," argued a columnist for the *Dakota Farmer* in 1937.[30] But, in the early years of settlement, much less land had been under cultivation, and thus dust storms had been relatively isolated and manageable. By the 1930s, however, every county in both states was being "dry-farmed"—plowed up, planted, and subjected to the winds. Without the strongly rooted prairie grasses, nothing remained to stop the storms' devastating course.

Dust storms, like the drought itself, developed recognizable patterns.[31] Early in the morning, a hot wind would begin to blow, becoming increasingly strong as the day went on, until by midday it could knock down a school-aged child or move a car across a road. At the same time, the air became thicker and thicker, darker and darker, with blowing dirt. Sometimes, a great black cloud appeared on the dim horizon. It was not the thunderhead prayed for but a "black blizzard" that darkened the day and "swept away the spring." When the cloud struck, the day became as black as night. Often the dust did not settle until sundown.

Probably the best-known Dakota dust storm struck on "Black Sunday," 9 May 1934. Beginning in Montana but gathering strength in North and South Dakota, 350 million tons of Great Plains topsoil blew eastward toward urban America. Twelve million tons of dust settled on Chicago that same day; more sprinkled down on Boston and New York two days later and on ships 300 miles off the Atlantic Coast two days after that.[32] Although it was the only storm covered extensively by the national media, this famous calamity was neither the first nor the last for the people of the Dakotas. In the terrible summers of 1934 and 1936, storms in some counties were almost continuous. A week after Black Sunday, Adams County auditor L. M. Howell wired Senator Gerald Nye in Washington, D.C.: "Drought situation critical. No moisture in ground. Dust storms almost daily. Soil drifting like snow."[33]

Worse, if possible, than dust storms when they struck were dust storms when they stopped. Cattle, drifting blindly over the fields, had hides filled with dirt, digestive tracts coated with mud. Weaker and smaller animals like calves and piglets suffocated unless farmers had hung muslin bags over their snouts.[34] Inside the house, dirt stood inches thick on everything: every cup, every saucer, every counter, every cupboard, every bed, every piece of clothing. If a farm woman, perhaps a bit "too eager . . . for spring," had just whitewashed her kitchen, the "foul darkening streaks on the wall" would be left for the rest of the year.[35] Scrubbing and cleaning was a job that had to be done not once or twice, but again and again. On 6 July 1936, it was more than 110° in the Stony Brook country of central North Dakota and the dirt had flown all day. That evening, sixteen-year-old Ann Marie Low wrote, "I'm writing this on the living room floor, dripping sweat, and watching the dirt drift in the windows and across the floor. I've dusted this whole house twice today and won't do it again."[36] Like many other Dakotans, Ann Marie Low had had enough.

The conditions of the Dust Bowl did not merely threaten the viability of land, crops, and livestock but deeply affected the lives of the men and women who struggled against them. Soon enough they discovered that their ability to earn a living, to support a family, and to participate in the community had dried up with the soil. It was this very real human suffering that, before long, brought the problems of the Dust Bowl to the attention of the federal government, the national media, and the world at large.

The Dust Bowl affected the lives of Dakota farmers and their families most drastically because they were directly dependent upon the land. In 1937 Works Progress Administration (WPA) researchers Francis Cronin and Howard Beers bluntly summarized the situation: after six years of drought, Dakota farmers could not grow food, could not produce a crop, and could not adequately feed their animals. The reasons why were equally simple: 34 of 54 counties in North Dakota and 47 out of 69 counties in South Dakota had produced less than 60 percent of their normal crop between 1930 and 1935; these were the lowest figures for any two states in the nation.[37] Similarly, 100 percent of North Dakota and 81 percent of South Dakota counties had less than 54 percent of normal pasture conditions.[38] As a result, the two states also lost more cattle than any others.[39] When Cronin and Beers combined all indices of drought, they reported that 104 of 122 counties in North and South Dakota qualified as "areas of intense drought distress."[40] In 1939, the federally sponsored Northern Great Plains Committee called the situation "the most difficult agricultural problem of its kind in the United States."[41]

These stark statistics suggested even starker living conditions for farm families. Between 1932 and 1937, North Dakota per capita income was only 47 percent of the national average; in 1933, most families had only $145 to spend for the entire year.[42] There was abject poverty—real hunger and cold—in a land once likened to a "golden bowl."[43] Men and women parceled out food, clothing, and fuel, finding

Three girls near Fort Yates, North Dakota, with the Russian thistles, or tumbleweeds, they had collected (courtesy South Dakota Historical Society)

new ways to make a pound of flour, a bit of meat, a gallon of gasoline, or a pair of shoes last just a little while longer. In Kidder County, North Dakota, Pearl Wick visited a woman who had nothing but flour and lard baked into pie crusts to last four days until surplus commodities arrived.[44] Presumably she, like other women, found her children's hunger even more difficult than her own to endure. "The hardest thing in my life that I ever had to do," Mrs. Orren Merritt of Salem, South Dakota, recalled years later, "was to have the kids say, 'Mama, how many pieces of this can I have?' or 'How many spoonfuls of that can I have?'."[45]

On her tour of the drought states in the late fall and early winter of 1933, journalist Lorena Hickok saw the conditions of life on the northern plains. Between the drought and the hoppers, few farmers had harvested a crop the previous summer, and those who did had gotten "almost nothing" for it. As winter set in, farmers harvested what hay they could salvage to feed their livestock and supplemented it with Russian thistle, a harsh prairie shrub Hickok compared to barbed wire.[46] Some families, however, did not even have this much. In Williston, she spoke to a farmer who was taking turns with his eldest son wearing a set of clothes and to another who began to cry when asked about his supply of food for the winter.[47] Again, the source of the problem was self-evident. In Dickinson, an elderly German farmer reported that he had harvested only 150 bushels of wheat from 800 acres of land.[48]

Hickok found the harshest conditions of all in Bottineau County, close to the Canadian border. On a visit to one of the "better relief homes," she saw a house patched together with pieces of tin, old license plates, and flattened cans. Outside, it was -20°. Inside,

> two small boys . . . were running about without a stitch save some ragged overalls. No shoes or stockings. Their feet were purple with cold. Their mother—barelegged, too, although she had some ragged sneakers on her feet—is going to have another baby in January. . . . [Upstairs they had] one bed. A filthy, ragged mattress. Some dirty pillows. [The mother] said the last of her sheets and pillowcases gave out two years ago. Over the bed two worn and dirty flannel blankets, just rags, that was all. "So you and your husband and the children all sleep together?" the investigator asked. "We have to," she replied simply, "to keep warm."[49]

Hickok estimated that in Bottineau County alone families needed 5,000 suits of underwear, 5,000 pairs of shoes and socks, 20,000 yards of dress material, 1,500 heavy quilts, and 1,000 blankets—"RIGHT AWAY."[50]

Like their farming neighbors, Dakota townspeople were devastated by the depression and drought. Shopkeepers and their employees, for example, were dependent on the agricultural economy; the lower the farm income, the lower their own. For many people, "making do" meant doing without all but the most basic store-bought items. To make matters worse, when shopkeepers could not collect on long-term accounts, they lost not only current but also past business. Julius Albrecht, owner of an automobile garage in Freeborn, South Dakota, remembered a man who came into his store in the 1930s to buy a tire: "He was not much good. I knew he was not much good . . . [so] I told him how much I got [how much it cost]. 'Oh, that's so much,' [he said again and again] and kind of made me sore a little bit, and I said, 'Well, what's the difference how much I charge, you won't pay anyway.' And he said, 'Well, but if you don't charge that much you won't lose that much.'"[51] For George Costain, the owner of a music business in Huron,

One Dakota shopkeeper expresses both exasperation and defeat, Krem, North Dakota, fall 1928 (courtesy State Historical Society of North Dakota)

this sort of negotiation often ended abruptly, as did his business in 1933. "In those black thirties, a good many farmers just pulled out and left [their] piano in the house. I got several letters saying, 'George, I promised I'd never do this but everybody's jipping me and . . . I'm pulling out. . . . You [just] go out and pick [the piano up yourself].'"[52]

It was not just doing business but owning a business that became burdensome in the depression. With no income, shopkeepers had no way of paying wholesalers to restock their shelves. Moreover, they could not lower their prices sufficiently to keep customers from traveling to chain stores in larger trading areas. And, finally, they could not sell out or get help from the government. Lorena Hickok explained the problem to Harry Hopkins: "Real estate in [these] towns is nothing but a liability. You can't sell it—you couldn't give it away. [Many] people who should have relief . . . aren't strictly eligible because they have unencumbered real estate. Why, unmortgaged real estate in one of [these] towns isn't a resource, it's a liability. You couldn't raise five cents at a bank on any of it. All you do is pay taxes."[53]

Because they had considerably less capital invested in their work,

Dakota professionals were not tied down to particular communities as Dakota shopkeepers were, but their working lives were disrupted by the economic crisis nonetheless. To start with, they were rarely if ever paid in cash. Doctors, dentists, veterinarians, and even some teachers learned to live on the chickens and eggs they received as payment-in-kind, if they were lucky. Moreover, the drought exacerbated those aspects of their callings that had always been difficult. When Mrs. Gene Whiting was giving birth to her third child, for example, her doctor was not fighting a blizzard (as he had come to expect) but a raging dust storm. When he finally arrived, both mother and child were near death.[54] Similarly, teachers—when they could get jobs at all—were sometimes assigned to counties whose commissioners could barely afford coal or wood, to say nothing of books, pencils, or slates.[55] Perhaps the most difficult professional work of all, however, fell to the Dakota clergy. Struggling to keep churches alive and flocks together, they also had to try to account for the disaster. "I spent most of my time assuring my people that things would get better and that God would answer their prayers," recalled Reverend Peter Larson of Minot, North Dakota. "By 1936 it was hard to get them to believe either. I had doubts myself."[56]

With Dakota farmers and townspeople living so near the edge, local towns and villages began to suffer, too. In 1937, Donald Hay of North Dakota State University published a study of the rate of persistence and decline of social organizations in North Dakota since 1926. Page after page documented the basic trends. Organizations supported by private donations suffered the most. Between 1926 and 1936, for example, there were 175 fewer churches, 397 fewer lodges, 17 fewer men's clubs, 13 fewer women's clubs, 269 fewer pool halls, and 18 fewer dance halls in North Dakota.[57] On the other hand, youth organizations and farmer's clubs that were funded and organized by the government increased in number.[58] The remaining private organizations just barely hung on, forgoing new paint, free lunches, and even membership dues.

What happened to community organizations in the 1930s happened to towns and villages as a whole. In counties where as many as 75 percent of all residents were tax delinquent, funds for the traditional rituals of community life were hard to find. Here and there, town leaders had to cancel some of their best-loved fairs, parades, and festivals. Similarly, officials put off again and again the necessary maintenance of public buildings. While she traveled about South Dakota, Lorena Hickok noticed the demise of these small towns. "I visited three towns where I lived as a child," she reported, "Milbank, Summit, and Bowdle. They were all the same size as they were when I left Dakota 25 years ago! Hardly a new house. On the main street of Bowdle there was a big gap where there were no buildings at all. Someone said they'd had a fire there fifteen or twenty years ago. The buildings had never been replaced."[59]

As it turned out, Hickok's three hometowns were among the lucky ones: between 1930 and 1945, twenty-three towns in South Dakota were simply abandoned.[60] In those places, the eerie emptiness bespoke an interdependence of land and community underestimated even by the people who had claimed to love them both so much. If the Great Earth perished, the human landscape was sure to succumb as well.[61]

The job of rescuing the land, the animals, the people, and the communities of the northern plains fell almost immediately to governments—first to county and state organizations, then to the Herbert Hoover administration, and finally to Franklin D. Roosevelt's New Deal. At each stage it was a Herculean task; the severity of the drought and depression was reflected in the unprecedented and ever-increasing amounts of money officials spent trying to soften its blows. Much of the money spent was literally invaluable. For many Dakotans, federal relief meant the difference between saving or losing their farms or businesses. For some, it also (presumably) meant the difference between saving or losing their lives. At the very least, federal funds vastly improved the facilities of public life on the northern plains, as work crews built new courthouses, libraries, swimming pools, roads, and bridges and brought electricity to even the tiniest hamlets. Nevertheless, many Dakotans did not accept federal largess altogether eagerly, nor did they live with its legacy very easily once prosperity returned to the plains.

When prices started to fall and the drought began, Dakotans turned for help to traditional sources of aid to the poor—private charity and county commissioners' funds.[62] For the most part, private organizations gave up large-scale work by 1930, but the county commissioners continued to do their part as best they could. In South Dakota, aid from counties increased every year (except 1935) throughout the Great Depression, totaling in 1934, for example, more than $1.5 million.[63] While aid greatly expanded, the counties continued their traditional role of caring for widows, children, and the unemployable.[64] The problem was that, in drought country, almost every citizen was in a very real sense unemployable and thus qualified for emergency relief. The county funds were simply not enough.

Even before 1930, some Dakotans had begun to demand federal assistance for agriculture. Beginning in the early 1920s, for example, farmer leaders from several midwestern states had advocated passage of the McNary-Haugen Act, which would have raised prices for farm goods through a combination of marketing quotas and increased exports. So controversial was the very idea of farm relief, however, that it took Dust Bowl conditions (and a Democratic majority) to initiate concerted action from Congress.[65] Meanwhile, two other organizations provided stopgap relief. In 1931 and 1932, the American Red Cross mobilized local agencies in the Dakotas to distribute approximately $660,000 worth of food, clothing, and livestock feed.[66] In September 1932, the Hoover administration authorized the Reconstruction Finance Corporation (RFC) to allocate money for public works programs. During the nine-month period between September 1932 and June 1933, the RFC spent $1.8 million in South Dakota and $500,000 in North Dakota.[67] These expenditures, though unprecedented at the time, were still woefully inadequate. It would take a new president's new ideas about relief to make a dent in the drought emergency.

Over the years, historians have categorized and interpreted the programs of the New Deal in a variety of ways. From the point of view of farmers and townspeople on the northern plains, the majority of the programs fell into three groups: the emergency relief that immediately followed Roosevelt's famous "hundred days" of legislation and the works programs that eventually took its place; the Agricultural Adjustment Act (AAA) programs of crop reduction and livestock sale administered by Secretary of Agriculture Henry Wallace; and the "second New Deal" programs that emphasized soil and water conservation, rural rehabilitation, electrification, and submarginal land adjustment and were influenced by a more radical cohort within the United States Department of Agriculture (USDA). No Dakotan was supported by all of these programs. Some, in fact, were directly supported by none of them. Nevertheless, so pervasive were they in the reconstruction of the economy that not a single man, woman, or child who survived the drought did so without the government's intervention. As D. Jerome Tweton discovered in nearby Otter Tail County, Minnesota, checks from one New Deal program alone contributed $44,000 per month to Main Street economies.[68]

Getting cash into the hands of the people most in need was the driving force behind Roosevelt's initial legislative proposals. In March 1933 the new president called for "action and action now," and only two months later Congress allocated $500 million to the Federal Emergency Relief Administration (FERA) to assist individual states with emergency relief cases.[69] Under Harry Hopkins's supervision, the aid came in two forms: matching funds (one federal dollar for every three state/local dollars); and $250 million in discretionary funds for states whose resources were depleted.[70] North and South Dakota qualified for both kinds of relief. In South Dakota, for example, 9,900 families received relief in the first month of FERA distributions; nearly seven times that many received relief nine months later.[71] Hickok estimated that 1,000 families were already on relief in Morton County, North Dakota, in October 1933, and seven new applications were coming in every day. In one township in Bottineau County, every family but one was on the rolls.[72]

As soon as he could, however, Roosevelt hoped to replace the direct payment programs like FERA with works programs like the tiny but popular Civilian Works Administration (CWA) and Public Works Administration (PWA). Hopkins likewise believed that works programs gave unemployed men and women something socially useful to do, thus uplifting their spirits while they improved public facilities.[73] Such a program, if implemented nationwide, would require many times more money than had been allocated for direct relief. Thus it was not until the huge Emergency Relief Appropriation Act of 1935 that Roosevelt received the nearly $5 billion the plan required. When he did, however, he inaugurated one of the best-remembered pro-

WPA *workers on a road near New Salem, North Dakota*
(courtesy State Historical Society of North Dakota)

grams of the New Deal—the Works Progress Administration (WPA).

Under the WPA, unemployed men (and eventually women and young people) signed on to do appropriate work in their own communities for a monthly stipend. The kind of work varied according to the people available to do it. Teachers and other professionals, for example, repaired books at local libraries, served lunches at local schools, compiled state guides, and organized the manuscripts of hundreds of county archives. Farmers and unemployed workers built, repaired, or improved countless numbers of public facilities. In South Dakota, for example, the WPA spent more then $35 million to complete 131 buildings and to refurbish 250 others, among many other projects.[74] In North Dakota between 1935 and 1942, the WPA built over 20,000 miles of new streets, 721 bridges, 166 sidewalks, 15,000 culverts, 503 new buildings, 680 outdoor recreation facilities, 809 water wells, and 2 irrigation projects.[75] Not surprisingly, the works programs found their rolls particularly full in 1934 and 1936. At the peak of the works program's lifetime, 53,000 North Dakotans were earning $40 per month in the WPA.[76]

Also approved in the 1935 allocation were monies for a program designed to help young men across the nation—the Civilian Conservation Corps (CCC). In the Dakotas as elsewhere, the CCC sought to aid young men between the ages of seventeen and twenty-five who, despite their ages and abilities, were still financially dependent on their parents. Kenneth E. Hendrickson, Jr., has contended that, in the Dakotas, CCC boys generally came from populated areas, not farms in the open country where they were still needed at home.[77] Even so, nearly 3,600 young men per year per state left home to work on reforestation, irrigation, and wildlife preservation projects in camps like those in Custer and Sturgis, South Dakota, and Mandan and Wishek, North Dakota.[78] Like freshmen in college or young recruits in the army, the CCC boys signed up eagerly, if with some trepidation, and often complained about the food. None of them, however, reported being idle. In 1938 alone, CCC boys in North Dakota planted 364,000 trees, constructed 99 dams, built 500 wildlife shelters, collected 150 tons of seed, and "rid over 844,000 acres of harmful rodents."[79]

The experience of a single Dakota town gives a precise illustration of the permanent contributions made by the various works projects described above. Interviewed in the 1970s, Henry Timm—the mayor of Wishek, North Dakota, in the 1920s and 1930s—told about the town park he and others had tried in vain to build just before the depression began. They had selected an acre of flat and treeless prairie near the center of town and planted sixty Chinese Elms by hand, only to watch them die for lack of water. In the 1930s, however, they authorized WPA workers to build a swimming pool and tennis court complex for the city near that site, to help CCC boys cut a drainage sluice through the park for irrigation, and to plant 500 more seedlings. These all survived. Next, they set WPA and PWA workers to constructing a large city auditorium. "Every rock [was] cut and chiseled by local people who needed enough [money] to buy groceries," Timm recalled. The total bill to the town for these three major municipal improvements—plus a few miles of new roads—came to merely $18,000.[80]

As important as the FERA and WPA programs were to the drought relief emergency, the AAA was even more critical. Assisted by Secretary Wallace, Roosevelt believed that farmers needed much more than relief, emergency or otherwise; they needed a permanent solution to the debilitating cycle of falling prices, increasing production, and decreasing land values. The first AAA, passed by Congress in May

1933, thus had three related objectives: first, to stimulate prices of seven basic commodities by reducing their production; second, to return those prices to the same level of purchasing power or "parity" that they had commanded between 1909 and 1914; and, third, to provide cash-in-hand to stricken farmers.[81] The first AAA was ruled unconstitutional in 1936 and replaced by a variety of crop and land programs, but before that time it had made significant inroads into the farm economy on the northern plains. By February 1936, the first AAA had spent $65 million in North Dakota alone.[82]

The AAA had slightly different programs for the two major commodity groups produced on the northern plains—wheat and corn/hogs—because they had slightly different growing schedules. While the bill was being hammered out in Congress in 1933, for example, no reduction of the wheat crop was attempted. In the fall of 1933, however, a grass-roots education program was put into full swing. County agents from the Agricultural Extension colleges, allied with the AAA, were sent to lecture farmers on the new program and to enroll them in it. After several meetings, the farmers voted and chose a township advisory committee; then those who had decided to participate submitted acreage proposals based on their own production histories.[83] All over the Dakotas, farmers overwhelmingly approved the AAA plan; well over 70 percent joined up in every county. In the end, wheat reduction was estimated at 15 percent for 1934 and 10 percent for 1935. Farmers received "benefit checks" of approximately $.29 a bushel in 1934 and $7.09 an acre in 1935.[84] These costs were passed on to wheat processors (General Mills and Pillsbury in Minneapolis, for example), who in turn passed them on to consumers.

The corn/hog plan was also based on the idea of production reduction, but its administration was somewhat different. Because the 1933 birthing season passed before the bill itself did, AAA officials immediately initiated a hog-killing program in order to reduce the overall population by 10 to 15 percent. The smaller pigs, mostly newborns, were processed into fertilizer; the larger ones, mostly brooding sows, were processed into food for the Surplus Commodities Corporation. In the spring, farmers agreed to cut hog production even further and to reduce corn acreage by 20 percent.[85] Like wheat prices, corn/hog prices rose considerably in 1934 and 1935—due, in part, however, to the drought. One North Dakota editor called this "Mother Nature's program of crop reduction . . . in a big way."[86]

In "west river" counties, the most important AAA programs were the emergency livestock purchase programs of the Drought Relief Service, passed in June 1934. With cattle literally dying on the hoof for lack of feed and water, many ranchers, like David Haxby, could no longer care for their herds and were considering "letting them loose for the winter and just seeing what happened."[87] Under the emergency plan, farmers could sell to the government any cattle they could not provide for themselves, at a price between $4 and $12 for diseased animals and $12 and $20 for healthy ones. In South Dakota alone, more than 900,000 cattle were sold, of which 87,000 were condemned as unfit for human consumption. The rest were processed at local slaughterhouses and, like the hogs, distributed to people on relief through the Surplus Commodities Corporation.[88] Although many farmers lost their entire herds, except for a breeding unit, and none received anything near what they had paid for them, most supported the buy-out program.[89] If nothing else, they were spared the agony of seeing livestock die a slow and ghastly death. At the same time, they could spend the money they received trying to save their remaining animals.

The third and final group of programs that affected Dakota farmers and shopkeepers was also designed to stem the agricultural crisis. After the Supreme Court ruled the first AAA unconstitutional in 1936, Congress passed a second set of farm bills. These reinforced the acreage allotment plans incorporated in the first AAA but, in view of the drought, added new emphases. The programs instituted under the second AAA—the Resettlement Administration (which later became the Farm Security Administration, or FSA), and the Soil Conservation Service—focused not just on reducing production but also on taking some acres out of production altogether and, finally, on adjusting the farming practices of all those who remained on the land. As Richard Lowitt has contended, these programs were poorly administered and ill-defined at best; nevertheless, in watered-down form, some of these new programs and the ideas behind them made their way to the northern plains.

The report of the Great Plains Committee in 1936 outlined in blunt terms what new administrators Rexford Tugwell and Jerome Frank believed to be the problems facing the drought regions and the new programs that would correct them. At bottom, they argued, "even [a] relatively small population cannot be sustained adequately under present conditions."[90] The reason was twofold: the land itself, arid and semiarid, at one time covered with wild grasses and deep sod, was not suitable for cultivation and certainly not for the cash-crop, intensive-farming methods presently employed; and the people of the plains, whose parents and grandparents had initiated these "destructive techniques," shared "controlling attitudes of mind" that helped to perpetuate the same "maladjustments."[91] In short, the rehabilitation of the Great Plains would require not just the rehabilitation of the land but also the reeducation of the people who lived upon it.

The recommendations of the Great Plains Committee were never followed to the letter. Political and ideological conflicts within the USDA itself did not allow for a unified approach to drought relief in the second New Deal.[92] At any rate, some programs did come to the northern plains and, as we shall see later, a handful of them became the best-known and most controversial of all the New Deal reforms.[93] In general, the new policies emphasized participation in water and soil conservation districts, where committees aided by technicians from the state set goals for crop reduction, resources conservation, mortgage and debt adjustment, and tenant ownership or relocation. For example, in Ward County, North Dakota, local residents initiated several programs to rehabilitate stricken farmlands. Beginning in 1937, a planning committee made up of local farmers, AAA officials, and county agents studied county land practices in order "to encourage good land use and farming systems and in some cases discourage undesirable land use and farming practices." Then they planned to readjust debts, reassess taxes, and reorganize the school system. The county was also the site of one of several migratory-waterfowl refuges constructed by the FSA on submarginal farmlands.[94] Meanwhile, in nearby Burleigh County, the Bureau of Reclamation was researching and planning a pumping and irrigating system on the Missouri River that would cost $600,000.[95]

Two other aspects of the farm bills had a long-lasting impact on everyday life and work in the Dakotas. First was the establishment of the Farm Credit Administration (FCA) under Title 2, the Emergency

Farm Mortgage Act of the first AAA. To help stave off foreclosures (and, some historians think, the radical politics that foreclosures engendered), the Roosevelt administration reorganized all the institutions of farm credit into a single agency under the supervision of Henry Morgenthau.[96] Thereafter, the FCA refinanced farm mortgages, adopted new terms for second mortgages, and eventually organized regional banks authorized to make a variety of farm loans. Additionally, through the Bankhead-Jones Farm Tenancy Act of 1937, the government was authorized to provide low-interest loans to tenants who were trying to buy property. In other words, in the 1930s the federal government became a major player in establishing fiscal policy over farmland. Long an owner of public land, now the government became a lender, and sometimes a re-owner, for privately held land as well.

At the same time, the Rural Electrification Administration (REA) attempted to significantly improve the quality of farm life. Although it was slow getting started, the REA eventually helped to bring electricity to the vast majority of rural Americans. The problem getting electricity in North and South Dakota, as in other states, was simply its cost: the expense of running utility lines to isolated farmsteads was more than most electric companies would assume. Thus in 1936 the REA began to provide loans to private cooperatives or other organizations for the purpose of constructing electric lines. By 1938 three South Dakota and two North Dakota REAs had borrowed over $1 million from the government and had run 800 miles of line to 3,000 customers.[97] By 1954, 90 percent of North Dakota farms had electricity.[98]

Altogether, by 1939, the Roosevelt administration had spent more money in North and South Dakota than had all the preceding administrations combined: $185 million in the north, $172 million in the south. Indeed, the federal government spent more money per capita in the Dakotas than in all but six other states.[99] For all that, however, its record of success was rather mixed. New Deal programs put cash into the hands of thousands of Dakotans who literally could not have done without it. There is no question that programs like the WPA, CCC, AAA, and REA vastly improved local facilities and suggested to many Dakotans that in their darkest hour "their government had not forgotten them."[100] Moreover, crop and land values all rose slightly

Abandoned farm near Beach, North Dakota
(FSA, courtesy National Archives)

over the period. No year was ever again as dismal as 1932. And yet, it was not until the heavy rains of 1937 and 1938, and the demands of war in the early 1940s, that good times prevailed on the plains again.[101] By then, more than 86,000 people had left North Dakota and 103,000 had left South Dakota, some for places as far away as they could find.[102] This massive out-migration was one of the many "adjustments" Dakotans made to the imperatives of life in an arid environment—but its human cost was dear nonetheless. For many transplanted Dakotans living in Arizona, California, or the Pacific Northwest, memories of life on the northern plains are not just bitter, but repulsive.[103]

But the New Deal amassed a mixed record in ways that were at once more subtle, more fundamental, and arguably more important than these strictly economic or demographic adjustments. Even though they voted for Roosevelt in 1932 and 1936 and thought of his aid as a "Godsend," most Dakotans never fully embraced the means and ends of the New Deal. In the north, for example, farmers and townspeople elected

Roosevelt by large majorities, but very few state politicians fully backed his policies.[104] At the same time, Republican and Democratic newspapers alike questioned the philosophies behind some reformist programs. The emergence of several alternative political movements, like the Farmers' Holiday Association, suggested that individuals, too, were seeking a better way. Finally, despite the monies that continue to support the agricultural economy in the United States, many Dakotans today recall the problems—and few the benefits—of federal intervention during the crisis, and some refuse to recall the period at all. According to sociologist Inda Avery, many Dakotans are "reluctant to admit that they themselves received [assistance]."[105] Althia Thom, for example, did not "think they [even] had welfare in those days."[106] In fact, the entire decade seems to have become a piece of Dakota history that its survivors do not care to remember. It is the rare centennial history publication that devotes more than a tiny percentage of its space—3 pages out of 528 in Grant County, South Dakota's, edition, for example—to the "Dirty Thirties."[107]

Reactions that range from troubled ambivalence at the time to convenient forgetfulness today suggest that the Dust Bowl era was "dirty" in more ways than one. They suggest, in fact, that the depression and New Deal in some way deeply affected the most fundamental values and ideals of Dakota society. Understanding the meaning of their experience, then, depends first upon understanding the common bonds and common problems they brought with them to the Dust Bowl and then exploring the ways their common culture shaped and in turn was shaped by the crisis. But to do this—to reconstruct Dakota culture—means leaving the dust in its place for a moment. It means returning to the late nineteenth and early twentieth centuries and examining the culture that was planted on the plains, eventually to sprout forth verdant and strong in its hegemonic authority. It means returning to less desperate times.

2   COMMON CHORDS

The Old Middle Class on the

Northern Plains, 1889–1925

In the years after World War II, when Dakota "old-
timers" began to think back on the society they had
built at the turn of the century, they spoke of places
where people knew each other well and got along
easily. "We had more fun [than you can imagine],"
Rueben Taralseth of Landa, North Dakota, recalled in
1976. "You know, we were all in the same boat. Everybody was alike back then."[1] Writing at the University
of North Dakota, Elwyn Robinson argued that this
golden age had a logical historical explanation. The diverse people of the plains had been joined, he contended, by the common bonds of the pioneer experience. Thus they shared certain inalienable "pioneer
virtues": "courage, optimism, self-reliance, aggres-
siveness, loyalty, and an independent cast of mind and
spirit." In short, most Dakotans had been "workers
and stickers," not "'shirkers and quitters' . . . natural
pioneers, born to conquer the land."[2]

When Robinson and other Dakotans recalled the
early years of the twentieth century as a time of ex-
ceptional cultural unity, they were not just imagining
things. Despite important ethnic, religious, political,
and class divisions, in those years Dakotans were as
much alike as they were different. Their "independent

cast of mind and spirit" had not been forged merely from the hardships of pioneering, however. In an era when "workers" in New York outnumbered "proprietors" by nearly three to one, in the Dakotas the opposite was true (see Appendix). As late as 1925, more than 60 percent of rural Dakotans worked for themselves on family farms or in small-town businesses. Moreover, many tenants, clerks, and laborers aspired to do the same.[3] Yet the most crucial bond Dakotans shared was the worldview associated with small-scale, rural production. Between the time of settlement and 1925, Dakotans built a society in which the ideals of making things and making a home, of getting by and getting along, were the stuff of common sense, so much a part of everyday life as to be nearly taken for granted.

However important the pioneer experience may have been, then, these adventures cannot tell us everything we need to know about the people who faced the Great Depression. Instead, the history of the small producer in the twentieth century should reveal much more. Sadly, though, this history has hardly ever been told. American historians, even those who practice the "new" western and the "new" rural history, have paid little attention to producerism after the Populist debacle of 1896. For that matter, they have paid little attention to class relations of any sort in the settled West.[4] Limited access to faraway libraries, together with people who are best known for their uninteresting and potentially undemocratic lives, have left the experience of small producers in the twentieth-century West virtually an untouched field.

Touched but briefly, however, a rich and complex society comes to light. Between the time of statehood (1889) and the Great Depression, Dakota culture had two main focal points: ideals about work and individual success and ideals about community and the common good. Although they rarely agreed on the means—to the contrary, political divisions were often violently expressed—for most Dakotans the end was the same: a rural society filled with self-sustaining and hardworking men and women who, while they strove for individual success, shared a cooperative vision of community life. This ideal was reinforced by social organizations and public rituals that emphasized equality, fraternity, charity, loyalty, and faith. Theirs was, in short, a vision of a society where individualism and even capitalism were tempered by "neighborliness."

The story of old-middle-class hegemony in North and South Dakota began with and was sustained by three major migrations of small producers to the area officially designated as Dakota Territory in 1861. From throughout the eastern United States, from some parts of the middle South, and from western and northern Europe they came—first by horse, ox cart, and covered wagon, and finally by steamship, ocean liner, railroad, and automobile. The first period of migration (1878–87), often referred to as the "great Dakota Boom," was stimulated by the decision of several railroads to extend their lines westward into Dakota.[5] The Northern Pacific Railroad, for example, sold huge tracts of land in northern Dakota to individuals who wanted to set up "bonanza farms." George Cass and Benjamin Cheney purchased 13,000 acres at the equivalent of $.60 per acre and set up a huge factory for the production of wheat. Of the 150,000 people who came to northern Dakota between 1875 and 1890, however, only 91 had enough capital to set up farms larger than 3,000 acres. The average farmer's holdings were 296 acres.[6] Moreover, the bonanza farms themselves did not last long, breaking up under the strain of tax policies and the deaths of the original owners. Many more of the small owners—classic American homesteaders—had come to stay.[7]

The division of Dakota Territory into two states in 1889, and the completion of railroad lines into the interior of the northern plains, encouraged a second, and eventually a third, wave of migration. Between 1890 and 1915, nearly 500,000 people came to settle the lands east of the Missouri River and, beginning in the 1910s, the newly opened "Indian lands" to the west. These migrations, like the first, were renowned for the "suitcase farmers" and land speculators, men (and a remarkable number of women) who claimed a homestead to make a profit, to rent to others, or simply to have an adventure.[8] But, again, it was small producers—those who had come to stay—who dominated early Dakota political, social, and cultural life. In the main, the migrants to North and South Dakota were members of the old

Mr. and Mrs. Edward Kezar and two sons outside their sod house near Belvidere, South Dakota, 1906 (courtesy South Dakota Historical Society)

middle class and its aspirants, people who had come seeking "free land," with all its burdens and responsibilities.[9]

Numbers and figures reinforce the broad outlines of these movements and their impact on the construction of local society. A study of settlers completed in 1941, for example, suggested that, at least in western North Dakota, most pioneers had been small producers before they arrived on the prairie.[10] Rural sociologists reported that, of all those settlers who took up claims, 75 percent had been farm operators, shopkeepers, or artisans and only 25 percent had been agricultural or industrial wage-laborers. They noticed, however, that many of these settlers had come not because their businesses had been successful but because their viability had somehow been threatened or compromised. Senator Usher Burdick's father left Minnesota for eastern North Dakota, for example, because he feared he might never pay off his mortgage.[11] Similarly, many Norwegian peasants came because they had no more land to leave to their children as inheritance.[12] These desires to "start over in a new country" did not indicate that settlers had given up on their dreams of independence. To the contrary, they suggested a desire to defend this independence even more tenaciously.[13]

Despite what was nearly always an arduous journey, and conditions that were far from homey, pioneer settlers in the Dakotas found that getting established "on their own" was relatively easy. They could purchase land from the railroads, who needed settlers to live along their major routes, from the federal government, or through the Homestead and Timber Culture acts. As the pioneers commonly put it, Uncle Sam bet any farmer "160 acres of land that he could not live on it for five years without starving." But, as South Dakota rancher David Haxby remembered, many settlers came to start businesses, not farms. "You could start out here as a young man even in my time [and] if, say, you wanted to become a grocery man or you wanted to run a clothing store, you could go to work for somebody and by working faithfully and saving what you could, you might be able to . . . save $1,500 and start."[14] Jacob Eisenmenger was one of those who got his start near Haxby's ranch. A young lawyer from Sioux City, Iowa, Eisenmenger came to Milbank, South Dakota, to "get some experience [and] start from scratch." To do so, he (along with seven others) hung out a shingle and slowly but surely made a living.[15]

Settlers like Eisenmenger discovered that capital was sometimes not the most important thing they needed to get established. In Aberdeen in the late 1890s, for example, what Carl Swanson had "needed to get started was a good reputation." Having that, he proceeded to "borrow a horse here, a horse there . . . put five of them together and start farming."[16] According to Ruth Carothers, the key to starting up in North Dakota thirty years later was much the same. It was a question of character and skill, not good fortune or privilege. "To make it . . . [in North Dakota]," she recalled in 1978, "wasn't a matter of being in the right place at the right time, like it was out East. It was having the courage to consider the risks and the chances and then make a decision and stick to it. It was courage and responsibility both."[17]

Even though acquiring a business or a piece of land was usually easy enough, "not starving" on it was another thing altogether. Almost every homesteader on the plains experienced considerable deprivation in the first years, hardships that ranged from inadequate shelter and food to increased infant and maternal mortality to farm and home accidents.[18] Barns, sod houses ("soddies"), and shops were burned by prairie fires, toppled by tornadoes, and overtaken by pests. Every year, families who had believed in their chance to make it on their own headed out again. Sometimes, John Hudson has told us, entire towns, like Firesteel, South Dakota, disappeared when the land gave out or the railroad chose another place to stop.[19]

Before the Dust Bowl, the hardest times were in the late 1880s and 1890s, when the people of the northern plains found themselves caught in their first severe period of drought. To make matters worse, many were also financially overextended, and all were trapped in a stranglehold of federal monetary policy and corporate exploitation.[20] As Herbert Schell put it, "When the farmers realized that transporting their wheat to the large commercial mills was costing them half the value of the product, their earlier patronizing attitude toward the railroads turned into resentment."[21] Even these terrible years were not a complete loss for Dakotans, however. As we shall see, the memory of human suffering and popular political resistance provided a usable, if extraordinarily controversial, heritage for Dakota men and women in the years to come. If in the 1890s the Dakota statehouses were filled with Alliancemen and Populists, in the 1930s they would be teeming with their "hell-raising" children and grandchildren.

Although settlers had come to the Dakotas with high hopes, not everything had worked out the way they had planned. Throughout the early twentieth century, Dakotans remained uncomfortable with the states' "colonial" dependence on outside capital for internal development and were angry at the power corporate "middlemen" still had to dictate success or failure. Until the "Revolution of 1906," even the states' own political representatives seemed to care more about outside interests than they did about their own people.[22] But most disappointingly, many individuals were less independent than they had imagined they would be. With every decade after 1890, for example, farm tenancy increased, until in 1920 it neared 40 percent.[23] Similarly, competition from Rural Free Delivery, the ubiquitous Sears and Roebuck catalogue, and an increasing number of chain stores threatened the viability of many small businesses. Nevertheless, the people of North and South Dakota still believed that a society of independent enterprise was possible for them, both individually and collectively. Even in the drought year of 1930, 93 percent of tenant farmers believed that they would soon till land of their own.[24] And throughout the first decades of this century, political movements from progressivism to the Nonpartisan League sought, albeit with different and even opposing strategies, to preserve that possibility.

In 1925, the state census of South Dakota reflected in two ways that—despite the trials of settlement—Dakotans had succeeded in creating a society of small producers on the northern plains. The first measurement it provided was quantitative. The census revealed that, outside of Minnehaha and Pennington counties, family farms, small businesses, and shops literally dotted the landscape. In rural Day County, for example, only 500 men and women were reported as "laborers," while there were approximately 2,000 farmer-operators, 6 bakers, 21 bankers, 48 carpenters, 2 harness makers, 8 painters, 61 merchants, 12 doctors, and 1 architect. Altogether, 65 percent of the officially employed population were their own bosses.[25]

But the census revealed something about its authors' values and abilities. When director Doane Robinson and the staff of the state census bureau created their occupational categories, they undoubtedly picked and chose from those used by federal authorities in 1920. In making their selections, however, they not only anticipated the numerical preponderance of independent concerns, but they also revealed that the state valued those occupations over all other kinds. Of the sixty-six occupations they listed, more than forty-eight were likely to be old-middle-class, nine working-class, and nine white-collar wage-labor. More importantly, however, the independent occupations listed were extremely specific—Robinson made room for everything from bookbinders to undertakers—while the categories of dependent occupations were extremely general. The people the census called "clerks," "salesmen," "factory operatives," and "common laborers" may well have done many different kinds of work. Nevertheless, they were not considered important enough for the state to enumerate precisely.[26]

The 1925 South Dakota census suggested that the men and women who settled the Dakotas had reproduced the cultural as well as the economic dynamics of petty production. Still, neither the census nor any other set of statistics can tell us exactly what that worldview entailed or, moreover, how it maintained its hegemonic authority. It cannot tell us, for example, what kind of "reputation" it was that Carl Swanson had needed in Aberdeen, or what kind of community it was where character seemed to count at least as much as capital. To understand what the people of North and South Dakota believed, and how their society reflected and reinforced those values, we must rely not just on numbers but on the words of the people themselves.

When Helen and Robert Lynd visited Muncie, Indiana, in the 1920s, they found that the best way to understand the character of "modern American culture" was to understand the work that modern Americans did.[27] So, too, with understanding the culture of petty production on the northern plains. As we have seen, most Dakotans engaged in the common labors of independent proprietorship, either as land-owning farmers, small shopkeepers, artisans, or professionals. But bound to the specific nature of their work were specific ideas about the personal and social value of work in general. As it had been in mid-nineteenth-century northern America, "work was the core of the moral life" in twentieth-century North and South Dakota.[28] In other words, it "defined the soul of the worker," predicted success or failure, and influenced the overall health of the local community.

It was fortunate, in a sense, that work was so central to the world-view of most Dakotans because they worked extremely hard. To begin with, their lives were dominated by the endless and timeless tasks of cultivation. In the "busy season," a farmer (whether owning or renting land) might work sixteen or eighteen hours a day in hot fields or stifling barns. And, despite this overtime, nature granted only partial vacations. Even in the dead of winter, farmers had stock, equipment, and outbuildings to tend. Every Dakota farmer knew the agony of slowly and carefully following a clothesline from the house to the barn in the midst of a howling blizzard.

Farm women may have known the constancy and monotony of farm labor even more intimately than their husbands did. From the earliest days of settlement well into the twentieth century, Dakota farm women handled such diverse tasks as gardening, dairying, spinning, weaving, soap-making, and meat-processing, not to mention the endless rounds of washing, cleaning, cooking, and diapering that accompanied caring for their families of six, eight, or more children.[29] And, as

One farmer's wife, Rachel Cole Katterjohn, at work in the barnyard
(Dakota Farmer, *courtesy Intertec Publishing Corporation*)

Alice Conitz of Bluegrass, North Dakota, remembered, all this work expanded geometrically at threshing time. On those days, women rose well before dawn so the threshing crews could have breakfasts of pancakes, bread, oatmeal, eggs, bacon, and baked beans at 5:30 A.M.[30] Over and again, the imperatives of farm labor took precedence over all other kinds. Jim Shikany's mother rose from her bed three hours after bearing him, her first child, to milk a freshening cow.[31]

The rhythms of work in Dakota towns and villages were also influenced by the task orientation of agricultural life. Many stores and shops that served farmers—general stores, repair shops, farm equipment stores, livery stables, and blacksmiths, for instance—opened for work at 7:00 A.M. and closed at 9:00 P.M. Monday through Friday. And these were their short days. On Saturdays during the summer, Mittelstaedt's Store in Milbank, South Dakota, stayed open until 11:00

*Shopkeepers at the Beaudry store in Hoven, South Dakota, 1922
(courtesy Hoven Centennial Committee)*

P.M., and even then the workday was not done. Arthur Mittelstaedt, the owner's nephew and a young clerk in the 1910s, remembered that:

> [On Saturday nights] there was always a last minute scramble while customers' bundles were carried out, egg cases picked up, and butter jars replaced. After [that], the doors were locked and the shades pulled down. Sweeping compound was sprinkled on the hardwood floor and the push brooms were brought out to sweep behind the counters and along the aisles. . . . By this time it was a half-hour after closing-time, meaning that, on Saturdays the men worked until 11:30 . . . "on the floor" for 14 hours . . . [and] there were no coffee breaks.[32]

Young Arthur's experience suggests that another reason Dakota petty producers worked so hard was directly related to the fact that they *were* petty producers. Unlike the owners of big corporations, who only managed or oversaw production, the majority of the "surplus labor value" extracted by a small producer was his own or that of a member of his immediate family. In other words, if a farmer or shopkeeper was his own boss, he was also his own employee. As the clerks were cleaning up Mittelstaedt's Store, Uncle Harold was undoubtedly counting the day's receipts and waiting to lock the door behind them.

Country doctors knew best of all what life was like under the working conditions of petty proprietorship. Family members could not take over for them, of course, and a farm accident, a severe illness, or the birth of a baby could happen at any time of the day or night. Many knew the hardships of travel on a frigid evening as they hurried to save a patient or to arrive moments too late. Dr. Leonard Tobin accepted primitive conditions as an inevitable, albeit frustrating, part of his calling: "You didn't think about the clock in those days," he remembered. "[You] just thought, well, here's another one. Let's see if we can pull this one through. . . . [Sometimes] I [would go] out to the cemetery and [take] a look at the graves out there and say . . . God, if we could have been there a little bit more you might not be here."[33] In later years, Dakota doctors would recall with pride their willingness to serve their patients, no matter the circumstance. Dr. M. G. Flath of Stanley, North Dakota, for example, delivered 2,900 babies before the local hospital opened. "I never refused anybody," he contended. "When they called I went, day or night! I wouldn't say, 'Wait till morning,' or [some such]! I'd go right away!"[34]

But, like other small proprietors, Dakota doctors worked hard not just because they enjoyed it or because conditions required it; in the worldview of Dakota farmers and townspeople, hard work promised important personal and social rewards. Daniel Rodgers has explained that the American middle-class "work ethic" had roots in the Protestant Reformation and "branches" of it that extended to a wide variety of social, political, and ethnic groups.[35] On the northern plains in the twentieth century, however, this work ethic had been trimmed down to two related ideas—that work was good for the individual (and the pocketbook) and that it was instrumental to the overall health of the community. Together, these ideals motivated the people of North and South Dakota to work hard, or, as one of them put it, "to pour [their] souls into the work they feel to be a very part of [their] existence."[36]

Central to Dakota ideals about work was the (originally) Protestant notion that hard work in and of itself was a good thing. Many Dakotans remember their parents encouraging them to work just so they would learn how. Ruth McNicol of Grand Forks recalled, for example, that her mother "never allowed me to go outside before I had finished [embroidering] one end of a dish cloth. . . . And, you know, she never looked at the front side, which was always nice, but headed straight for the underside to see if it were neat too. . . . [If it wasn't], she would always say, 'When a task is once begun, never leave it until it's done. Be it great or be it small, do it well or not at all.'"[37] Ruth's sister Geraldine contended that even this strict regimen did not satisfy her parents. She remembered being sent to a nearby farm every summer, "so we could *really* learn how to work."[38]

Alice and Harry McNicol undoubtedly believed that hard work, whether at home or on the farm, was good for their daughters' characters. Throughout the 1920s, Charles Day of the *Sioux Falls Argus-Leader* was among the region's most outspoken social "moralists," and, as such, he wrote often about this critical connection. "Work is the great schoolmaster of the nation," he contended in 1925. "[It] teaches patience, forbearance, perseverance, and application."[39] Complaining that too many young people tended to look for unchallenging jobs, he argued, "Sooner or later we all have to get down to this sweat-of-thy-brow stuff . . . [and] the sooner we do the sooner we absorb the hard knocks that eventually better us into something worthwhile."[40]

What did it mean to be a "worthwhile" worker in the Dakotas? Dakota newspapermen offered a potpourri of different, but essentially related, answers in their writings from the mid-1920s. According to John Simon at the *Bismarck Tribune*, for example, a good worker was persistent (someone who "knew that a diamond is just a piece of coal that stuck to the job") and practical ("not the kind of man who sits around and dreams").[41] For Charles Anderson at the *Fargo Tribune*, the key was aggression, the desire to "tackle every job that came along."[42] Critical to Day was competitiveness, self-reliance, and an ability to think independently.[43] Above all else, however, the editors agreed that a successful Dakotan believed in the "inevitable progress of man and society." As the editor of the *Mitchell Gazette* put it, "There is a cash value in optimism. . . . It is the person who thoroughly believes in himself, in his fellow man, and in the opportunities of life that enjoys the public esteem and draws the check that never goes to protest."[44]

In a speech given to the South Dakota Independent Farm Implement Retail Association, C. R. Peters summarized the qualities of mind and character that together produced the "ideal businessman." At his very core, Peters began, the ideal businessman must have a desire to make money. He must "value a profit even more than a deal."[45] To do so, however, he must also believe in progress and keep "up-to-date" with developments in his field, including organizational systems, employee relations, and advertising. Ambition and ability still meant little, however, if they were not accompanied by a good reputation. Finally, the ideal "dealer practices strict honesty with his customers and with the manufacturers with whom he deals. He does not oversell his goods. His warrantee is good. His service is prompt and efficient. . . . His motto is 'No man shall be disappointed who relies on my word.' . . . Even his competitors admire him for he is always ethical in all his transactions. He does not cut his prices in his own territory and in no case would do so in another's territory."[46] As much as he was driven to succeed, then, the ideal Dakota businessman was also "considerate to others and a gentleman to all."[47]

It was hardly a coincidence that, as most Dakotans saw it, people who did good work and had good character also deserved to make good money. The American work ethic both reflected and reinforced the ideals of capitalist success, and no "right-thinking" Dakotan had anything against moderate financial gain. Still, Dakotans believed that "fortune" had to be won "fair and square" and put to use in moderation. Just as they believed that competition could and should be honest, they believed that prosperity could and should be prudent. "There is a limit to the amount [of money] a man can make wholesome use of," Day wrote in 1925. "Too much wealth brings ease, selfishness, indulgence, flabbiness of spirit, and final decadence."[48]

In sum, the people of North and South Dakota saw work as a forum for individual effort and gain within the inherited structures of capitalism: profit, competition, and growth. They believed that "progress" could bring good things to a hard-working society. At the same time, however, they tempered their aggressive instincts with concern for good character. As important as they were, individual success, personal gain, and social progress were not Dakotans' only goals, and thus they were not the only reasons they worked so hard. The people of

Main Street, White River, South Dakota, in 1912, with a bank, café, general store, and four hotels (courtesy South Dakota Historical Society)

North and South Dakota also worked hard because they believed they had a responsibility to their communities to do so. As Althia Thom recalled it, "In those days you worked, everybody worked, you learned to work. . . . You did your share."[49]

When, in 1927, the Greater South Dakota Association asked the editors of local newspapers to tell them "why South Dakota is a Great Place for Home-Seekers and Home-Builders," they received the same two answers again and again. The first was predictable enough: editors described in lusty detail the huge tracts of land available for settlement and the big money that (in a good year) a settler could make from them. But most of the editors told the association about a unique quality of local society as well. As Allen Brigham of the *Alpena Journal* put it, "The neighborliness found in the cities and especially the rural communities of the state is one of the really fine things in the life of our people. And this neighborliness is extending to a greater social communion between cities and rural districts. . . . The state [is becoming] one big community."[50]

It may not have mattered much to potential investors, but to the people of North and South Dakota "social communion" was a critically important part of life on the northern plains. Rural society in the Dakotas had long been more than a group of "frontier individualists" who happened to own contiguous property. Although some moved in and out, most pioneers came to the northern plains to stay, making new homes and establishing the familiar structures of community life.[51] For them, like others around the world, community connoted membership, the idea that the whole was greater than the sum of its parts. It was, in their words, a grand kind of neighborliness, a way of staying true to the "homeplace," its people, and its problems in the midst of an ever-changing world.[52]

Dakota ideas about community began with a notion based first in the world of work: equality of opportunity. "The wage earner of today is the employer of tomorrow," wrote Day. "In no other country is it so easy for men to improve their conditions by honest effort. . . . America is essentially a land where opportunity awaits around the corner for every man with the initiative to use it."[53] Not all Dakotans, of course, agreed with Day that the ideal of equal opportunity was in fact a reality; many believed that large corporations and middlemen were destroying the autonomy of the small producer and that, with every passing year, it was getting harder and harder to survive. Nevertheless, all agreed that everyone deserved a "fair chance" to make it. Ruth Carothers was one Dakotan who was lucky enough to take opportunity "for granted." Riding on a train to school as a girl, she would "look north to the whole stretch of the horizon" and "know that [she] could put the whole world in her pocket."[54]

When expressed in the community, the ideal of social equality took on the form and the language of Christian benevolence. As most Dakotans saw it, all human beings were equally created in God's image and thus deserved to be served equally. "I would be brother to the meanest clod, knowing that he too is born on the dream of God," Grace Campbell remembered her aunt singing.[55] In practice, the ideal of Christian benevolence took many forms. At its root, however, were individual acts of charity. Ada Engsten's mother, for example, would go anywhere at any time to "help a soul in need . . . never saying a thing about it, just putting on a clean apron and going."[56] Sometimes, the ideal of charity compelled women to overcome even their deepest

Members of the Smith family of Pembina, North Dakota, working and visiting over a quilt, ca. 1888 (courtesy State Historical Society of North Dakota)

fears. Ruth Carothers's widowed mother once invited "an Indian she had found sleeping on her porch" in for breakfast, even though she felt she might "die of fright" the entire time he stayed.[57]

Together, the ideas that everyone was essentially equal in God's sight and that everyone had an equal chance for success in the market-place forged the most important assumption of Dakota community life—the notion that, although people were different, no one group of people had more authority than any other in the community at large. In small towns this idea was generally expressed in the politically neutral language of "good will," "hospitality," "equality," and "fraternity."[58] But, in cities, it often assumed the more explicit rhetoric of "classlessness." Lydia Eastwood of Watertown, South Dakota, boasted, for example, that "a spirit of good will prevails among the laboring classes [here]. . . . There has never been a strike or dissension to leave its ugly scars."[59] Charles Day opposed the very notion of class difference. "The tendency toward class distinctions is an importation from effete Europe," he argued. "It has no place in America . . . and can never be fixed on

Community band in Eckman, North Dakota, 4 July 1912
(courtesy State Historical Society of North Dakota)

the people of the United States. . . . The nation will endure . . . so
long as [we] avoid class distinctions."[60]

The people of North and South Dakota not only had ideas about
society and how it should work, but they also had activities created for
the expression of those ideals. Some, like neighborliness, were rooted
in the traditional "habits of mutuality" generally associated with pre-
industrial village life.[61] Throughout the first part of the twentieth century, for example, women's quilting bees, cooperative harvest work,
neighborhood picnics, parades, and barn-raisings were still popular in
Dakota townships.[62] An even more traditional custom was called "visiting." In the lonely winter months, or whenever a friend needed another pair of hands, one woman would go to "visit" for a week or so in
exchange for a return visit from her friend later in the year.[63]

Community rituals in the Dakotas could be born of a more modern
sensibility as well. The community band, for example, was a fad that

swept the plains in the early twentieth century and was forever immortalized in Meredith Willson's story, *The Music Man*. Unlike those in River City, Iowa, however, Dakotans who supported local bands wanted more than a way to "keep their children moral after school." To their minds, the quality, size, and skill of a band was critical to a town's "self-image" and was one way of advertising their community.[64] The band was, then, one of many booster activities that merged recreation for the public with public relations. Others included town-slogan and limerick contests, community clean-up projects, and "crazy-days" sidewalk sales. The North and South Dakota regional and state fairs were the biggest orgies of togetherness of all, promoting social communion just as vigorously as corn, wheat, and cattle.[65]

In the era of "joinerism," however, it was not the activities as much as the social organizations of Dakota towns and villages that reflected and reinforced these ideals about community life. Dakota towns were filled with organizations for worship, recreation, education, and political action that "offered a communion of cultural values" to the community at large.[66] In each of these small communities, common lessons of service and sameness were taught, albeit in different ways. It was, in fact, through small groups that Dakotans learned the ideals and practiced the skills that they brought to the community as a whole.

The most influential of all Dakota social organizations were the local churches. In both states, missionaries had preceded settlers to the plains and left indelible marks on village landscapes—usually small, white, frame buildings surrounded by humble "soddies." Nevertheless, it was a rare town that had but a single steeple to mark its moral center. As rural sociologists discovered—to their horror—in the 1930s, most towns had many different churches with very small congregations. In North Dakota, for example, they counted forty-five different denominational groups, or an average of one church for every 350 men, women, and children.[67] Some of these were mainline Yankee Protestant groups like the Presbyterian, Congregational, and Methodist churches. But many others were the sects that immigrants had brought with them from Europe. In North Dakota, twelve different branches of Lutheranism had arrived with settlers from Finland, Denmark, Norway, Sweden, Germany, and German-settled Russia.[68]

In reports sponsored by the Works Progress Administration, the sociologists concluded that the sheer number of churches in the Dakotas, together with the significant doctrinal differences among them, severely threatened the quality of community life in rural towns and villages.[69] For all their careful observations, however, they did not see the many ways in which those churches also *added* coherence to Dakota society. At the very least, the sheer number of churches reflected the prominent place of sacred belief within the culture. Dakotans did go to many different churches, but at least the majority of them attended one or another. Thus the notion that "going to church was a good thing to do" was utterly taken for granted by most Dakotans.

Perhaps more importantly, however, the common teachings of the churches added coherence to the moral universe of Dakota community life. Despite their differences, Dakota churches generally agreed on several fundamental articles of faith and practice. Most broadly, of course, nearly all Dakota churches were Christian, despite the existence of a few isolated Jewish settlements. But they all taught the importance of traditional morality as well. With the exception of some German and German-Russian churches, for example, Dakota churches discouraged the use of alcohol and tobacco. Others, like the Methodists and Baptists, frowned on Sunday activities and movies; the Evangelical Lutherans forbade card-playing and dancing. Most commonly, however, the churches encouraged the practice of traditional sexual morality and gender roles, thus offering, in John Faragher's words, "a communal mainstay of the traditional family order."[70]

Finally, churches offered coherence to Dakota communities by providing a location for the teaching and expression of its most fundamental tenet—the equality of individuals and the importance of service to others. Each church had its own version of a Ladies' Aid Society, for example, where women gathered to sew, quilt, or cook for a congregant in need. These social activities served a number of functions in their members' lives, from the chance to escape the isolation of the home or farmstead to the opportunity for leadership in otherwise male-dominated churches. At the same time, however, they (along with men's church groups) reflected and reinforced the notion that all members of the group were worthy of Christian charity.

Churches sometimes sought only to serve their own flocks, but clubs, lodges, and political organizations served themselves and the larger community, too. There were four kinds of clubs in Dakota towns and villages—altogether more clubs than churches. Although each kind had a distinct history, purpose, and structure, and some competed with others for members, by the 1920s they all had dedicated themselves to serving, improving, or promoting the community. As such, they became the primary location for expressions of community loyalty, or what has been known as "boosterism."

The oldest and most popular clubs in the Dakotas were secret fraternal organizations and their women's auxiliaries. According to the (again horrified) sociologists, there were ten different "lodges" in North and South Dakota, and sometimes more than one in the tiniest villages.[71] The best-known and most prestigious of them all were the Masons and the Eastern Star, organizations with roots in England and the antebellum Northeast. But there were other lodges, too, some of which were tied to ethnic groups. In Webster, South Dakota, with a population of 2,033, Masons were accompanied by OddFellows, Woodmen, Rebekkah, Knights of Pythias, Catholic Order of Foresters, Royal Neighbors, and A.O.U.W.[72] Like the churches, these organizations provided benefits, such as life insurance, to members only. At the same time, however, they extended their philanthropic efforts to the community at large. In Hope, North Dakota, the Masons brought bags of groceries to the homes of poor widows every week throughout the 1920s; in cities like Fargo and Grand Forks, they sponsored major scholarships for the universities.[73]

Around the turn of the century, two other kinds of clubs appeared. First came women's clubs, study groups, book clubs, dramatic clubs, and other social groups. These were accompanied by the emergence of men's luncheon clubs—the Kiwanis, Lions, Rotary, and other business groups that were primarily devoted to improving civic affairs. Often, women's and men's clubs were even more selective than the lodges were, and they provided their members with privileges in less "secret" but equally effective ways. Nevertheless, they were also even more devoted to promoting and improving the community as a whole. Mrs. J. M. Featherstone of Valley City, North Dakota, for example, believed that women's clubs could help the community pull together in times of trouble. "In this time of unrest, discontent, criticism, and doubt, we need to cultivate neighborliness," she told the annual meeting of the North Dakota Federation of Women's Clubs in 1927. "[This can be accomplished] by a picnic in some convenient and lovely place—a good program, a good visit, and a good lunch, everyone providing their own."[74]

The clubs with the broadest scope but, arguably, the greatest dedication to service were Dakota political clubs. Strictly speaking, the Republican, Democratic, Populist, Nonpartisan, and Socialist parties were not social clubs, but they did serve a social function. Radical farm organizations, in particular, were well known for their abilities to combine picnics and parades with speeches and debates in the style of nineteenth-century popular politics.[75] Likewise, their overall goal was improvement of life in the community and in the nation as a whole. A logical extension of loyalty to the hometown, loyalty to the nation was the final mainstay of Dakota culture. Although they expressed it in many ways—from support for World War I and "100 percent Americanism" in the 1910s and 1920s to fervid isolationism in the late 1930s, and from a dedication to laissez-faire economics to attempts at state control of major industries—Dakotans were ardently patriotic and demonstrated it through lively and rich political activities.

They approached the task in different ways, but the myriad clubs in North and South Dakota towns agreed on one thing: that promotion of and service to community affairs were among the most important tasks of life. Since the 1920s, historians and social critics alike have denigrated this tradition of community service by calling it foolish boosterism or simple-minded "babbitry." Although perhaps it was unsophisticated, boosterism was nevertheless an expression of the sincere commitment to community life that lay at the heart of old-middle-class culture. The *Fargo Tribune* included "loyalty to my hometown" in its 1924 "Creed of Good Citizenship," contending that a good citizen should pledge "to stay loyal to my hometown, giving my ear to its problems, my hand to others. . . . I should live by the side of the road and be a friend to man."[76] That same year, Charles Day put the same sentiment in a less graceful but equally heartfelt way. He advised all "one hundred percent good sports [to] say 'I like Sioux Falls because it's my home!'"[77]

The ideals, rituals, and organizations of Dakota community life provided a cornerstone just as important to Dakotans' culture as their ideas about work. The community was a place to belong, support, and defend, a place where everyone should be on equal terms and have an equal opportunity to succeed, a place where the common good should come first and ultimately reinforce individual success. Put this way, petty producerism provided Dakotans with a way to live within market capitalism that seemed above reproach or challenge. As they saw it, if every man and woman in Dakota stayed true to "home, school, town, charity, God, state, and government," they could easily fulfill the promise of their settled land.[78]

Dakotan social ideals, like most ideals, were just that, however— values and aspirations firmly believed but often unrealized. As anywhere else, people *were* different in the Dakotas: they were both men and women; they came from different religious and ethnic backgrounds; they did different kinds of work and made different amounts of money; and they held strikingly different political views. Moreover, they were not treated equally but sorted out and categorized in ways that helped individual members and the old middle class as a whole define and retain its power. Most significantly of all, however, the two groups of ideals upon which Dakotans had built their society— loyalties to a progressive and modern, if somewhat tempered, capitalism and to a traditional, faithful, and neighborly community—were often utterly unreconcilable. To understand their culture more fully, we must go beyond Dakotans' dreams and examine the everyday workings of their society.

3 COMMON DISCORDS

Conflict and Contradiction in

Old-Middle-Class Culture

Most days at the bank in Garretson, South Dakota, where Benjamin Wangsness worked for his father, Tom, were typical small-town banking days, quiet and uneventful. One day in the 1910s, however, Benjamin overheard a conversation between his father and a potential client that was so remarkable he remembered it all his life. Like other Dakotans, bank president Tom Wangsness cared deeply about his work and about his community, but by all outward appearances he cared about character most of all. As his son put it, he was a true "gentleman" in all his affairs, "an impeccably honest businessman and a church and civic leader." He held others to similar standards. "His major requirement for granting a loan," for example, "was good character." Thus he carried over any farm family whom "he considered . . . worthy in trying to do their best." No matter what his ultimate decision about a client, however, he gave everyone who walked in the door "a respectful hearing."

One client pushed the banker's respect to its limit. The town drunk in Garretson was a man known simply as "Mike." Mike came into the bank that day "in his usual condition" and asked Wangsness "for a loan of ten dollars." According to Benjamin, "Dad strung him along for a while and finally asked him if he really needed the money. Mike, trying to straighten up, said, 'No, I just wanted to know how it feels to owe Tom Wangsness ten dollars.'" At this, the banker's son could hardly contain himself; moreover, he remembered that the conversation had "amused Dad as much as it did the rest of us in the office."[1]

Not nearly so funny was what another man in a similar condition said to the president of the First National Bank of Pierre, South Dakota. Like Tom Wangsness, Walter Burke looked for loan applicants who were both solvent and "worthy" of his investment. Still, he tried to treat all his clients fairly. Then, one morning—and it was a particularly busy morning, he recalled later—a very drunk man approached him and said, "I want a hundred dollars. I want to borrow a hundred dollars. . . . Make me out a note." When Burke suggested that he come back when he was sober, he "started staggering out, and he got clear out to the door, and he turned around and, in a loud voice, he [said], 'Everybody in this goddamn bank, kiss my ass!'" Rather than laugh, Burke called the chief of police in Pierre and told him to catch the man and "give him the works." By noon, the would-be customer was a prisoner.[2]

It is no wonder that Benjamin Wangsness and Walter Burke found these incidents so memorable. Mike, by admitting that he wished he knew how it felt to owe money, had put into words something that most sober Dakotans knew went without saying. In the communities of the northern plains, where the rhetoric of equality and neighborliness mattered so much, differences counted as much as similarities in the daily lives of residents. Some people (like Tom Wangsness) had a great deal of local power, others (like his customers) had access to that power, and a small number (like Mike) were shut out altogether. Still, by revealing his place in Dakota society in the self-effacing way he did, Mike did little more than embarrass himself; he did little more than add one more story to those already told about him around town and over dinner. What the drunk man in Pierre did was much more serious. When he said "Kiss my ass" to Walter Burke, he breached his role in society by deeply embarrassing someone whose business was staked on maintaining a trustworthy, honorable, unflappable persona. It should not surprise us, then, that Burke considered the drunk's behavior to merit a brief stay in jail. Dakota communities were places where the common ideals that bonded most men and women together could also be used as social artillery against those who chose to dissent. They were places known as much for controversy and discord as for consensus and communion.

The paradox at the heart of old-middle-class culture—the rhetoric of equality and the reality of inequality—was first described by Robert Lynd, Carl Withers, W. Lloyd Warner, and other sociologists who studied American communities in the 1920s and 1930s.[3] Again and again, they reported the same phenomenon: community members would claim that everyone in their town was equal but then proceed to distinguish between different groups of their neighbors with no sense of contradiction. These early observers never agreed on how many social groups made up the typical small town (in the Lynds' "Middletown," there were two groups, in Carl Withers's "Plainville," three, and in Lloyd Warner's "Yankee City," six) nor on what to call them. They had nevertheless discovered "the small town's dirty little secret"—that within a culture that deified equality and fraternity "a discrimination system of enormous complexity" structured both the present realities and the future possibilities of every community member.[4]

The factors that tore Dakota communities, as others, apart were but the obverse sides of those that brought them together—loyalty to churches, clubs, political groups, and shared ideals. Despite their blind spots, the Works Projects Administration (WPA) researchers who studied Dakota social life in the 1930s were not all wrong. When a tiny community had a panoply of social organizations, it was in effect split into many different pieces. Nevertheless, in the Dakotas these pieces did not cause community conflict simply because they existed, as the sociologists thought, but because those members of the community with the most local power and authority valued the organizations differently. In most towns in the 1910s and 1920s—other than German-Russian enclaves—a Yankee and/or Scandinavian, Protestant elite handled most important economic transactions and civic affairs and controlled the membership of the most prestigious clubs and lodges. Like Tom Wangsness and Walter Burke, they used the rhetoric of character to make their evaluations, but often their economic power was enough actually to determine character itself. In other words, these men—and their wives and families—articulated the values of community at the same time as they used them to defend their own positions at the head of the class.

Not surprisingly, it was anti-Catholicism that most apparently undermined Dakotan ideals of equality and community. That Protestants and Catholics could not (and should not) get along was one of many "common sense" notions for rural Americans in the early twentieth century, and Dakotans were no exception. Ruth Finch recalled, for example, that her mother, Alice, had a "black and white" policy about dating: "City or farm boy, she didn't think about that. . . . Mother only forbade me to step out with a Catholic."[5] Ironically, Alice's unabashed anti-Catholicism was hardly based in ignorance: her own mother had married a Catholic man, much to the horror of their parents. But, because the newlyweds themselves believed that the two religions could never really be mixed, they raised their daughters in the Protestant church and their sons in the Catholic church. As an adult and a devout Presbyterian, Alice considered the majority of her brothers to be "ne'er-do-wells" who drank heavily, used foul language, and had immoral sexual habits. When her father died and Alice was asked to hold a wake, she put an end to the traditional celebration before it had even begun. As Ruth recalled, "She simply sent [my uncles] home, blew out the candles, and we all went upstairs to bed."[6]

When put into action outside the home, attitudes like Alice's fostered a social climate in many Dakota communities that in the 1920s made them perfect breeding grounds for the resurgent Ku Klux Klan. The Klan first appeared in South Dakota in 1921, when a national organizer came to Sioux Falls. From there, the Klan grew rapidly. Between 1922 and 1928, Catholics throughout South Dakota, but particularly in the west-river mining towns of Spearfish, Sturgis, Rapid City, Lead, and Marcus, were plagued by cross- and circle-burnings, tar-and-featherings, and mass rallies and parades, including one attended by nearly 8,000 people.[7] As elsewhere, some Dakota Catholics were members of the agricultural or industrial working class, but others were land-owning farmers and small shopkeepers. The membership of the Klan in the Dakotas, however, was not nearly so heterogeneous.

Members of the Ku Klux Klan rally in Rapid City, South Dakota (courtesy South Dakota Historical Society)

As historian William Harwood put it, they were "the comfortable middle class . . . Protestants who had nothing to fear."[8]

Although perhaps more limited geographically, the connection in North Dakota between the Protestant middle class and the Klan could not have been clearer. The first organizer, or "kleagle"—and eventually the "Grand Dragon" of the North Dakota Klan—was F. Hadley Ambrose, the senior minister of the prestigious First Presbyterian Church of Grand Forks, who masqueraded for more than three decades as a trained and ordained minister. Throughout the 1920s, Ambrose drew huge Sunday night crowds as he railed against Catholics and an assortment of other "agitators." After studying membership rolls and voting records, William Harwood has concluded that Ambrose's closest followers were, once again, not the urban poor but the area's leading businessmen, professionals, and farmers, who feared the growing political power of local Catholics.[9] In the years between 1921 and 1928, Ambrose and the Grand Forks Klan succeeded in getting two Catholic school-board members fired and in returning several other municipal committees to a Protestant majority.[10]

A second and sometimes related way in which the Dakota elite distinguished between and among members of their class and community was by ethnicity. Settlers to the Dakotas came from a wide variety of northern and eastern European countries, particularly Norway, Sweden, Germany, and German-Russia, in patterns that closely resembled those of "old" and "new" immigrants to the United States at large.[11] In fact, in 1910 (the year when immigration peaked and began to subside due to increasing restrictions), more than 70 percent of all North Dakotans were foreign-born or the children of at least one foreign-born parent.[12] Generally speaking, the immigrants came from rural regions in the hope of acquiring land on the plains. As a result, the foreign-born often made up a larger proportion of the Dakota farm population than the town population. To those influential Yankees in town, the immigrants were accepted, individually and as a group, according to their success in becoming "Americanized." For Scandinavians living east of the Missouri River, this was a relatively easy task. By the 1920s, many had prospered on farms and some had moved into town and succeeded in business. A highly literate people, nearly all learned to read and write English.[13] In fact, as Fred Peterson has observed, Scandinavians quickly "came to personify the American image of substance."[14] Nordic in appearance, Protestant in religious ways, and ambitious in the marketplace, most Scandinavians blended in quickly to the "prairie mosaic." Even so, they remained the targets for local ethnic humor and advertising copy well into the 1930s.

Not so eager to act or sound like Americans were immigrants from eastern Europe and, particularly, those from German-Russia. These newcomers were in fact two-time immigrants, Germans who in the early nineteenth century had settled the steppes of Russia on the promise of religious freedom, exemption from military service, and the right to self-government. When Tsar Alexander II revoked the Codex of Colonists on 4 June 1871, however, German-Russians began to emigrate once again. More than 300,000 left the steppes for countries in North and South America, many of them finding new homes on the Great Plains. More German-Russians settled in North and South Dakota than anywhere else in the United States except Kansas.[15]

The experiences they brought with them from Russia influenced the ways in which German-Russians settled in the Dakotas. Rural German-Russians had lived in religiously homogeneous "closed colonies" that were culturally and geographically isolated from Russian society. These

Advertising cartoon poking fun at Scandinavian dialect and behavior
(Dakota Farmer, *courtesy Intertec Publishing Corporation*)

were the kinds of communities—and the kinds of cultural relations—they tried to recreate on the northern plains. As late as 1930, the vast majority of the residents of towns like Eureka, South Dakota, and Wishek, North Dakota, for example, were of German-Russian descent. Similarly, because they prized their unique heritage so highly,

German-Russians were not particularly interested in becoming "Americanized." Fearful of state authority, they disliked the public school system and often had their own schools, where the official language was German and the school year only a few months long. German-Russian churches (Lutheran, Catholic, or Hutterite) held German-language services at least until World War II. Finally, German-Russians stayed on the land longer than many other settlers. Resisting the urge to move into town or onto a new frontier, they bought up the acres others abandoned and acquired more and more property for themselves and their children.[16]

Because they actively resisted assimilation in these ways, German-Russians quickly became the targets of prejudice and stereotype. Gordon Isenmenger has written, for example, that "German-Russians were considered [by many] to be lazy, stupid, ignorant, and dirty."[17] Likewise, many state residents believed that German-Russian men drank too much and over-worked women and children. In Nebraska, the situation was much the same. There, Robert Welsch recalled, German-Russians were accused of being Bolsheviks despite their utter contempt for the new Soviet government. In truth, most other Dakotans did not know or care to find out very much about German-Russian culture. They just called the whole lot of them "Roosians"—a term that described people who dressed strangely and talked strangely, people who seemed to have no true "homeland" but did not choose to conform to the cultural precepts of their new home, either.[18]

Discrimination against the foreign-born, Germans and German-Russians in particular, came to a head during and just after World War I. At that time, the states joined the national drive to target and contain all "non-conformists" to the war effort. The first arrest in North Dakota came when a German-American farmer (and former German artillery man) from Marmarth, North Dakota, was sentenced to five days in prison for "joking" about and "threatening" the flag. After that, Germans were forced to ally themselves completely with the American cause.[19] In North Dakota, the anti-German "hysteria" culminated with the banning of all German-language instruction from the schools, the creation of new programs of "Americanization" for all "aliens," and the enforcement of morality legislation informed by the precepts of Anglo/Nordic Protestant culture.[20] Prohibition and women's suffrage, for example, were both passed in part to reform the traditional drinking habits and gender relations of the Germans and their Russian-born kin. In South Dakota, the Council of Defense ordered the "immediate cessation" of all activities using the German language. Churches were locked in Eureka; books were burned in Yankton and Faulkton.[21]

Religious and ethnic differences contributed to many of the notorious political divisions in Dakota society, especially between farm radicals and conservative Republicans. As we have seen, a lively, sociable, and patriotic commitment to politics was one of the most important bonds linking the diverse people of the plains. But the very real differences in their political views—views that may have been influenced by the differences between Protestant and Catholic theology—were among their most enduring divisions.[22] Beginning in the 1880s and 1890s and continuing until 1935, for example, many Scandinavian farmers organized to express through political action their grievances against the high cost of transportation, milling, and banking. In South Dakota, Alliancemen found more widespread support than anywhere else outside the South.[23] In 1894, they succeeded in electing a Populist governor and congressman as well as a Populist party majority in the statehouse.

In North Dakota, however, the farm radicals' finest hour came later, when in 1916 Arthur Townley, William Lemke, and Arthur LeSueur organized the Nonpartisan League (NPL). Supported and influenced by the regional Socialist party, the NPL was formed as an independent political group whose main goals were the state ownership of banks and grain elevators and the widespread use of consumer cooperatives.[24] Despite its calls for state socialism, an alliance with industrial workers, and concern about rising rates of tenancy, the NPL was not a movement of a Dakota "proletariat" or "peasantry" against big capital. In an important new study, Kathleen Moum has demonstrated that the "social origins of the Nonpartisan League" were decidedly middle-class: "men and women who came from small-farm immigrant roots." The typical "Leaguer" was a naturalized Norwegian-American who owned between a quarter- and a half-section of land and who employed seasonal labor on his farm. In two of the counties where the League was most popular, only one in ten farmers was a tenant.[25]

Pitted against the NPL was another middle-class political organiza-

Nonpartisan League rally near Steele, North Dakota
(courtesy State Historical Society of North Dakota)

tion: the Independent Voter's Association (IVA), composed largely of native-born Red River Valley businessmen and their small-town counterparts. In a series of heated and sometimes corrupt election battles, the IVA accused the NPL of making false promises to farmers and of misappropriating their funds. At the heart of the IVA campaign, however, was what they perceived to be the threatened socialization of the state's economy, the disruption of laissez-faire economics, and the promotion of trade unionism.[26] By 1922, the IVA had succeeded in ousting the NPL from power by playing on its prewar pacifism and Dakotans' growing fear of communism. In the meantime, however, the farmers had established a state-owned bank and grain elevator and had launched the political careers of several men who would retain power in the state for years to come.[27]

The competition between members of the NPL and the IVA was fierce, bitter, and sometimes dirty—so much so that, by the 1920s, the organizers of the NPL themselves called for a cease-fire.[28] As a child in Hope, North Dakota, Helen Parkman saw boys in fistfights in the schoolyard over their parents' politics nearly every day.[29] As the New Deal would fifteen years later, the NPL provoked such strong sentiment because it brought to the fore a conflict at the very heart of Dakota society: in this case, the conflict between the role of farmers and businessmen in a capitalist economy. With the exception of small colonies of Hutterites, all land-owning farmers on the northern plains operated their farms for a profit—that is, for capitalist gain. In the strictest sense, they were as much "in business" as their counterparts in town. Nevertheless, farmers in modern commercial agriculture, like workers in modern industry, were producers whose income was determined as much by others—middlemen, bankers, Wall Street commodities brokers—as by their own labors. It was easy enough for them to conclude that something was awry in an economic system that seemed to cheat farmers out of their "fair due." They believed that success ought to be based on individual merit, hard work, and character, but they saw that it did not always turn out that way. Often, they asked for the government's help in seeing that it did.

Businessmen, especially successful ones, had a different way of making money and often drew different conclusions about the health of the economic system. They were not so much the producers of goods as they were the distributors of them; they made money, in other words, by charging their customers (in many cases the farmers) more than what they themselves had paid for a given item. Small-town businessmen also had a stake in maintaining good relations with the big capitalists—Red River Valley and Twin City wholesalers and exchangers—who were the principal targets of the farmers' grievances. That the most influential of the small-town businessmen (like Tom Wangsness and Walter Burke, for example) actually had the ability to reward the "worthy" and punish the "unworthy," that is, both to make and to act upon character judgments, made the conflicts between farmer and townsman among the most enduring of all those that divided the petty producers of the northern plains.

The social divisions outlined above—between Catholics and Protestants, between Yankees, Scandinavians, and German-Russians, between "Leaguers" and "IVA'ers," and between farmers and businessmen—were, with some exceptions, divisions within the old middle class itself. All petty producers together, however, differentiated between themselves and those people who were not, for a variety of reasons, fully affiliated with their class. Chief among the people who did not fully share in all the ways of petty production were Dakota women.

Five generations of Dakota women
(Dakota Farmer, *courtesy Intertec Publishing Corporation*)

The old middle class can be seen as a family class in which "Mom and Pop" run the store and the family runs the farm. Yet, truth be told, many fewer Dakota women were independent producers than Dakota men. Moreover, even if a Dakota woman was married to a man who called himself boss, chances were that she called him that, too. However much they produced for sale in eggs, butter, or home-grown chickens, women rarely owned property in their own names or fully shared in decisions about the distribution of profits. Indeed, married women's working lives were more closely analogous to indentured servants than independent producers. At the same time, community traditions and rituals reinforced male dominance. Public posts were nearly always filled by men, of course, and some of the most important clubs, lodges, and community rituals specifically excluded women from participation.

Dakota society also was divided by class. However strong the values of petty production were to Dakota culture, not all Dakotans were petty producers. There were tenant farmers, wage-laborers, clerks, and other types of employees. Dakotans had nothing against these kinds of work per se; even Walter Burke had started out as a cashier. As the *Bismarck Tribune* said of presidential candidate Herbert Hoover's days as a waiter, however, wage work was—and ought to be—done "as one fighting step up the ladder," by young men and women starting out and making their own way.[30] Those older people still "employed" or renting must, Dakotans often assumed, be lazy, unambitious, unskilled, or somehow otherwise flawed. They might eventually "make good," but it was unlikely. In the meantime, as long as they worked and did not make trouble, they were treated kindly by employers, landlords, and—if need be—by the various county poor commissioners. Still, they were never fully included in the organizations and rituals of community life.

Lackluster tenant farmers and permanent wage-laborers were not at the very bottom of the social hierarchy in Dakota communities, however. Broadly speaking, in towns where "everybody worked" and good people "did their best," the truly disenfranchised were those who appeared not to work at all: Native Americans on nearby reservations, drunks, beggars, gypsies, tramps, prostitutes, drifters, "ne'er-do-wells," and other "riff-raff." When it came to charity for these unfortunates, they were not as lucky as the widowed, elderly, orphaned, or "working poor." The editor of South Dakota's *Woonsocket News* put it bluntly: "Any able-bodied man is able to make his own living without begging. Make him work for what he gets."[31] In a culture of small producers, those who chose not to produce did not belong.

The differentiations between the old middle class and the working and nonworking classes were much easier to recognize than those between religious, ethnic, and political groups. Almost every town, for example, was divided into good and bad sections by sides of the railroad track or quality of the land.[32] Similarly, there were differences in the prestige of different clubs and lodges, but membership in no club whatsoever was beyond the pale. And, in an age of rising consumerism, differences between "us" and "them" could also be recognized by the cars Dakotans drove or did not drive, the radios they were or were not able to buy, the credit they were or were not able to receive. Finally, class divisions were reinforced through traditional "patterns of deference," rules that dictated who deserved a "Sir" or a "Ma'am," who deserved a tip of the hat, and who deserved just a plain first name. From a very young age, people in Dakota towns learned who were the "better sort," who were not, and how they could tell the difference. Moreover, they knew to which group their families belonged and into which group they most likely would fall. In the end, barring a most extraordinary change of circumstance, Mike's children would also wonder how it felt to owe a banker ten dollars.

For all their good intentions, the people of the northern plains neither lived nor worked together as simply and cooperatively as they said they did. Instead, an elite group within the old middle class, and the old middle class as a whole, recognized, reinforced, and derived power from divisions that at the same time they ardently denied. And, yet, internal divisions were only part of what threatened the realization of Dakotans' most cherished ideals. Less apparent but no less important were the ways in which Dakotans' very bonds were untenable. Like countless others in the nineteenth century, Dakotans struggled to balance their loyalties to individuality, success, and progress with loyalties to community, cooperation, and tradition. Moreover, they did so in the face of the increasing professionalization, urbanization, and bureaucratization of American life. With each passing decade, the balancing act so fundamental to their culture became more and more precarious. At the onset of the Great Depression, balance was already almost impossible to sustain. In 1925, the modern world of progress had moved so far away from the sacred world of tradition that making a choice for individual success was both dangerous and profane—and still, Dakotans had not seen the worst.

The story of one man's life—his upbringing, education, success in business, and role in the Americanization of his community—sets forth these contradictions with particular clarity. Until his recent death, Theodore Friedrich Straub was among the wealthiest men from the north central section of South Dakota, one of many Dakota businessmen whose small businesses (having survived the depression) prospered in the postwar boom. In the early decades of the twentieth century, however, Straub was not so different from his friends and neighbors. As a young man starting out, he wanted both to run a successful business and to stick by his family, his community, and his ethnic heritage. In one sense, he achieved all of this. But, by the end of his life, he suspected that his successes had masked some utter failures.[33]

Theodore Straub was raised in a large German-Russian family in Eureka, South Dakota, in the days when Eureka was a prosperous but relatively "closed" and traditional German-Russian community. His father, Friedrich, and mother, Marie, had come to Eureka in 1890 from Odessa. Like others in town, they worked hard to protect German-Russian customs in their household. For example, they required that only German be spoken at home and maintained a strict division of labor, education, and opportunity between the boys and girls. When Friedrich started a business, however, he also chose to accommodate a handful of "American" ways. He learned to speak and write English for his business transactions with Yankees and, more importantly, insisted that his boys complete their education in public schools so they could do the same.

The elder Straub combined German-Russian and American ways in his home as well as in his business. Before emigrating to America, he had learned to build furniture, a craft that traditionally included the carving of coffins. When he started out in Eureka, it was primarily as a furniture dealer and carpenter and, somewhat coincidentally, as a coffin maker. Not long after he arrived, however, a salesman from Minneapolis who sold embalming chemicals convinced Straub to learn how to prepare bodies for burial. Thus Straub also worked as a "mortician" for more than forty years, even though he was never formally trained, never carried a state license, and only practiced in the Eureka area. He was, in the strictest sense, a petty proprietor, and yet, in the transitional world of the immigrant community, he continued to care more about providing an important service to other German-Russians than he did about making a profit.[34]

The training of Theodore, Straub's oldest son, in the furniture and funeral business began in much the same way as his own but soon became something entirely different. Theodore attended the State College at Brookings, but he only lasted a year at his desk before beginning an apprenticeship with W. H. "Tug" Wilson at the Wilson Undertaking Parlor in Aberdeen. There, he slept at the funeral parlor on a cot near the embalming room, was paid little if anything at all, and learned his craft mostly by watching and assisting Tug. At the same time, he kept books for the business and read up on accounting and business law.

It was during the next year, however, when he was assisting at Coleman and Sons Funeral Parlor in Redfield, South Dakota, that Straub became convinced that a traditional hands-on education would not ensure his future success. He had waited a long time for his first chance to embalm a body on his own but, when it finally came, he was not as well prepared as he had expected. As it happened, a local farm woman, Mrs. Martha Heer, had died "when the tine of a pitchfork punctured her jugular vein as she slid down a haystack."[35] Young Theodore thus found himself trying to repair damage to Mrs. Heer's neck (a very visible part of a corpse), and he simply could not do it. Less than a calendar year later, he was back at a desk, determined to become a "qualified mortician" by taking a six-month course in "Mortuary Science" at the University of Minnesota.

The University of Minnesota's program was one of several around the nation that, as Burton Bledstein has noted, "professionalized" the traditional crafts of coffin-building and corpse preparation by making them more scientific and thus accessible only to trained "experts."[36] Among the courses offered in Minneapolis, for example, were embalming, chemistry, anatomy, and "funeral business management." As we shall see in detail later, white-collar experts, when they arrive under the auspices of the New Deal—and whether they were social workers, agricultural agents, advertisers, or journalists—often met with considerable suspicion from their Dakota "clients." That professional school might make him different from his friends and neighbors in Eureka never occurred to Theodore, however. That schooling might make him somehow detached from the people he served could not have been farther from his mind. Straub simply saw his education as a means for staying "up-to-date" in business and ensuring continued success. As he returned by train to Eureka from his stay in the big city, Theodore's goals were unchanged. He wanted most of all to succeed in business and to stick by his native Eureka, a place he still held closest to his heart.

What had changed for Theodore, however, were the ways in which he believed he should go about achieving his goals. As he put it, he was determined "to apply" what he had learned in Minneapolis by "advancing my father's method of handling the funeral portion of the business."[37] The list of deficiencies was long. "Straub's" had no morgue, no embalming facilities, no hearse, no automatic lowering devices for the graveside, no facilities for review, no floral services, no "memory" souvenirs, not even temporary markers for the graveside. To his father, these additions seemed completely unnecessary; German-Russian families customarily handled most of the details of the service and he simply prepared the body. To Theodore, on the other hand, they were the essence of progress and good business, the "innovations" he was "expected to carry on."

For all of Theodore's ambitions, change in the funeral business came slowly—at least while his father was still in charge. Old man Straub, it seems, wanted to risk neither a large amount of capital, the loyalty of his old friends, nor the timeworn customs of the community.[38] Nevertheless, when Theodore and his brother Werner took over in 1928, change took place at a rapid pace. Although they continued to sell furniture, the two brothers immediately assisted the county hospital in installing a morgue and redesigned their own old building into a fully equipped "funeral parlor." Soon, their services included all that they had lacked before, from fresh flowers from Minneapolis to courtesy checks of the gravesite to be sure the pall-bearers would not trip and fall. German-Russian customs changed more slowly but just as surely, by a combination of "the power of suggestion" with the authority of a local churchman who had also tired of conducting home services. When all was said and done, the Straub brothers succeeded in increasing both the profit and the prestige of their business. In 1947, theirs was the only funeral parlor in a sixty-mile radius of Eureka, and they reaped in profits what they had generated in total sales twenty years before.

After he retired to Sun City, Arizona, in the late 1970s, Straub wrote an autobiography, in part simply to describe but also, it seems, to explain his remarkable success. There, he revealed just how closely he had come to resemble C. R. Peters's "ideal" Dakota businessman described in chapter 2. Like Peters, Straub felt that his success primarily resulted from his hard work, good character, and modern business skills. He boasted, for example, that he and Werner had never traveled to places where they could not be reached and had never gone away when the other one could not "man the store." Moreover, they were thrifty and careful, doing all their own "janitor work," reusing cord and wrapping paper that came on their orders from Minneapolis, and limiting their advertising budget to local papers. Most of all, they continued to stay up-to-date with changes in their field, even adding carpet and linoleum to their furniture line in the 1950s.

But work and success were not all that Straub cared about. Most important of all to him, he reflected, was his commitment to his community and to the people who lived there. Early in his career, Straub vowed never to try to sell any product to a family for whom it would prove to be a "financial hardship." At the same time, he was a dedicated member of the Eureka Civic Club and active in his church and fraternal organization. To him, Eureka was one of the finest spots in all of South Dakota; he never tired of calling it "my town."

It was because Straub remained so deeply committed both to success and to community that, even in the rosy glow of his later years, some of the events of his life troubled him deeply. He recorded them in his autobiography not because he wanted to remember them but because he could not forget them. In either case, however, they provide access to the ways in which the culture of twentieth-century petty producerism was untenable even for its favorite sons.

The first troubling event that Straub recounted involved a competitor who opened a funeral parlor in Eureka in the early 1930s. This competition was "costly" to the Straubs, but, worse, the new people did not compete "honestly." He described the situation this way:

> Mr. Blair was ruthless as a competitor and exploited every means possible to degrade our reputation which we had considered beyond reproach. Wishing to remove our safety deposit box from the vault of the bank, I prevailed upon those in charge of the defunct bank to permit me to do so. Permission was granted with the stipulation that I would depart from the bank through the back basement exit to avoid anyone seeing the action. But somehow this leaked to [Blair, and he spread the word] that Straub had taken a bushel basket of currency from the bank vault. "How else

could they have made that kind of money if they had not over-charged their customers in the past years?" was the propaganda they spread around Eureka.[39]

To Straub's surprise and dismay, the Blair's tactics were quite effective: it was "with tears" that he learned that some of the family's "old time friends" had taken their business elsewhere.

What brought Straub to tears after the Blairs' success was not the money he lost to them. It was instead the lesson he learned about his society and culture. Rather than try to win business by offering a better service or a lower price, the Blairs won business by attacking the Straubs' character and reputation. When they succeeded, despite these "dirty" tactics, Straub was forced to see, at least momentarily, that "honest competition" was little more than a convenient fiction, an agreement among competitors not to break a certain moral code. There were no actual legal guarantees that everyone would compete fairly, nor were there sanctions against those who did not. In fact, the only pressure applied against the "dishonest competitor" was brought by the consumer who might choose not to buy from a business whose reputation was tarnished.

But the people of Eureka did "buy" from the Blairs, and that evoked an even more crushing truth for Straub. They believed that the Straubs had overcharged customers, that they had put their own self-interest above the welfare of the community by taking their money from the bank, and that they owned a "bushel basket of cash." In short, the people of Eureka had turned against Straub for being, as the German-Russians put it, "too big for his britches." When "old friends" took their business elsewhere, Straub saw that they were not really his friends at all.

Straub had a similar but more complex problem with a competitor in the late 1940s. Since the early 1930s, Theodore and Werner had employed a man named Philip Spitzer as a general assistant in all aspects of the furniture and funeral businesses. For most of those years, Spitzer had seemed to be the perfect employee, "conscientious," "loyal," trustworthy, and capable but not, Straub must have assumed, particularly ambitious.[40] He was, after fifteen years of employment, probably considered to be a permanent wage-worker, treated kindly by his employers but never fully included in the organizations or the structures of the community. But Philip surprised his community by radically changing his position. Not long after the Straubs trained him to do specialized floor installations and financed the purchase of his new home, Philip went out on his own. He competed directly with the Straubs in the linoleum and carpet trade. To add insult to injury, he prospered.

Straub described Spitzer's defection as if it had been one of the greatest personal and professional blows of his career. Once again, his feelings were not for the money he lost on the "considerable investment in Spitzer's training" as much as for the truths Spitzer's departure revealed. Just as the Blairs had, Spitzer showed Straub that there were no guarantees in a capitalist economy. Anyone who had the means could go into business—and the money he or she made, dirty or clean, had the same value in the marketplace. But Spitzer's sins went beyond the Blairs'. Spitzer broke not only the unwritten rules of business but also those of class, community, and family. Like a good son, a good employee should listen, obey, and imitate his father but never compete with him. Strictly speaking—in the world of tradition, respect, and community—patricide is unthinkable.

Yet Theodore Straub may have felt he had committed a form of patricide. Although he discussed at length the problems he faced from competitors, he was a great deal more reserved about something that worried him even more—the way that the innovations he had made in the business, ostensibly to help his father, ultimately had displaced him. By the end of Friedrich's life, there seemed to be no important place left for him in the business. He sat in the workshop, opening packages and making small repairs, telling stories of old times and entertaining customers, but that was all. He never spoke of current business affairs or attempted to offer his advice but confined himself to family matters and caring for his grandchildren—work that in his youth he would have left to the "womenfolk."

As troubling as it was, Friedrich's inactivity was not nearly as tortuous as his silence. "He never complimented me openly about the changes I made," his son wrote sadly. In fact, to the contrary, Friedrich just before his death had criticized Theodore, saying that Theodore was "traveling at too fast a pace, going too much . . . was in danger of becoming involved in a company that might mislead me."[41] The elder Straub, it seemed, no longer recognized the business he had begun that, in the name of progress, his son had utterly transformed. When the end came for Friedrich, suddenly and quickly, many of the elements of German-Russian craftsmanship and community tradition died with him. That this "left a void" in his son's life was underscored by his attempt forty years later to make amends: the subtitle of his autobiography made no mention of the funeral business that he initiated in the 1920s but merely read, *The Life of a Furniture Dealer in South Dakota, 1908–1980.*

The bittersweet story of Theodore Straub's "success" in Eureka makes one thing clear: many of the imperatives of old-middle-class culture were difficult, if not impossible, to reconcile. Like others much less prosperous than he, Theodore Straub discovered that the price of progress, of being up-to-date, of pursuing profit above all else, was a loss of the traditional ways and friendships of community life. Nevertheless, his story also suggests that membership in the old middle class, defined partly by adherence to these conflicting ideals, required men and women to go on bringing together two seemingly separate worlds in one place, one family, even one person. This was an impossible task, a game that had neither a winner nor a satisfactory conclusion. Nevertheless, it was how most Dakotans lived every day of their lives.

No matter how golden they seem to some today, the early years of the twentieth century on the northern plains were not the "best of times." Bound by ideals of autonomy and productivity in the workplace and equality and service in the community, Dakotans sought to create a world where everyone could both succeed as independent proprietors and get along as neighbors. In reality, however, they lived in communities wracked by social conflict and ideological contradiction. Even so, the troubles of the 1910s and 1920s would pale in comparison to the 1930s. Dakotans had known hardship, discord, and internal strife before. They had known the frustration of dependence on outside capital and the feelings of exploitation it engendered. They had even known the pain of achieving a level of progress that did not seem to live up to expectations. But the greatest challenge to the strength of their culture was yet to come.

A final vignette from Theodore Straub's autobiography paves the way for our return to the experiences of the people of North and South Dakota in the Great Depression. As part of his attempt to be an honorable member of his community, in 1936 Straub was elected chairman of the Eureka Civic Club. This was a particularly significant honor because Eureka's fiftieth anniversary was only months away and Straub would be in charge of all the festivities. Like other towns, Eureka planned a big celebration, complete with parade, dinner, pageant, contests, and even a live radio broadcast from the Twin Cities. Deep in his booster's heart, Straub hoped it would be "the best of its type in the state of South Dakota."[42]

Straub secretly contacted *Life* magazine, thinking that perhaps the editors might be interested in covering the story of Eureka's celebration. To Straub, this idea was not nearly as far-fetched as it might sound to us; as we know, he considered Eureka to be a very interesting and important place. Eureka was a town, he recalled later, where churches and business organizations cooperated, people didn't "feud, backbite or hold a grudge," and everything was "friendly and hospitable."[43] Most importantly, however, Straub thought that Eureka had a promising future. He included these words in *Eureka!*, the town's celebration book: "The spirit of the pioneers who have come and gone before us . . . that spirit [is one] which holds out to all the inspiration for present accomplishments and the promise of future achievement for Eureka."[44] It was this future, most of all, that he believed the photographers from *Life* would want to depict.

Straub was not particularly surprised that *Life* was interested in his town; he only wondered why they demonstrated their interest in such an ungentlemanly fashion. After he let them know about the celebration, *Life* wrote back for more information and Straub sent them *Eureka!*. Then he heard nothing. Suddenly, one day, a man adorned with cameras walked into his store and said "I'm here for your celebration." Straub was taken aback. Nevertheless, the show went on. Straub considered the celebration to be one of the best he'd ever seen—"no accidents, casualties, or brawls," great exhibits, even an Indian tent, "where they killed a critter and got a real kick out of it."[45] Even better, the town made some money for the community chest. Altogether, the celebration was a huge success and all that he had intended: a positive, optimistic, colorful celebration of a little town with a wonderful past and a bountiful future.

Although he never admitted it, Straub must have been shocked when he saw the text and photographs that appeared in *Life* in August 1937.[46] Its title alone, "Eureka, S.D., Was Once the World's Wheat Mart," suggested that the editors had missed the point of the celebration, or, more likely, that they had altogether another point to make. The article said that Eureka, rather than a successful, progressive, and lively place, was "shorn of its prestige," and the celebration was just an opportunity to "relive the grandeur of its past." Of the twelve photographs they printed, six showed pioneers "bedridden," "old," or "grizzled," one showed pioneers' children in traditional dress, and one showed the town in 1895. Clearly, to *Life*, and perhaps to many of their readers around the country, what was interesting about Eureka was hardly the here-and-now but a bygone time when people were quaint, life simple, and crops plentiful. While the people of Eureka had their eyes on the future, people at *Life* were looking backward.

The editors at *Life* were both responding to and promoting a renewed interest in American culture and folklife among urban Americans in the 1930s.[47] After having laughed at them or just ignored them in the 1920s, many Americans were now rediscovering the people of America's heartland. This particular example suggests, however, that urban America may never have truly seen eye-to-eye with rural America. The people of the village, it seems, were not so easy to understand. As the government planners and reformers of the New Deal would soon find out, neither were they so easy to help, not even in their hour of greatest need.

4   CRISIS

The New Deal and the

New Middle Class

Grace Martin Highley was a welfare inspector for the town of Edgemont, South Dakota, throughout the 1930s. There, she saw the hardships that Dust Bowl conditions could bring to a community and its people. Unlike others who recalled it later, however, Highley saw the depression as much more than an economic or environmental disaster. The real crisis of the Great Depression was not in people's wallets, she felt, but in their souls. Describing why many "independent people" accepted relief after desperately trying not to, she said, "I think men face up to reality and do what they can to survive. . . . And I think that people compromise. I think [they] attach to something that comes somewhere near ideal, but in reality [they] reach out and take what [they] can if [they] need it."[1] Even so, the decade had been "a struggle. It was an ideological struggle" against dependence.[2] In short, Highley recognized what only a few professional historians have seen as clearly in nearly fifty years of scholarship on the 1930s. The Great Depression was a time of intense cultural crisis for the people of America's heartland.[3]

The experience of Dakotan farmers and townspeople reveals this crisis in particularly sharp detail. As we have seen, the northern plains was home to one of the last bastions of old-middle-class hegemony, a region where the men and women often associated with the traditional ways of small production maintained authority through a combination of sheer numbers and shared beliefs. Nevertheless, theirs was hardly a simple or harmonious society; nor was it even entirely traditional. Dakota society was rife with internal conflicts that pitted its members against one another and replete with ideological contradictions that pitted its members against themselves. Dedicated as much to progress as to tradition, as much to competition as to cooperation, as much to profit as to the common good, old-middle-class culture was forged at once of steel and of quicksand.

Since the late nineteenth century, the urbanization, professionalization, and bureaucratization of American society had threatened the foundations of old-middle-class culture. The Great Depression, however, rocked them to their core. In those years, wholesale economic disaster made it impossible for Dakotans to achieve the ideals and goals that bound them together. Economic imperatives, likewise, laid bare the internal divisions that tore Dakotans apart. Most significantly, however, the Great Depression forced Dakotans to confront, as they previously had not, the essential contradictions of their culture. The political upheaval of the 1932 election empowered once and for all the people, policies, and ideals of postproducerist America. It gave real control over the fates of farmers and townspeople not to the familiar foes of weather, illness, or railroad rates, but to a new kind of middleman—the experts, advertisers, agents, and advisors of the new middle class. Like hard times themselves, the new middle class was not new to the northern plains, but its profound cultural authority—its power to decide matters of survival itself—certainly was.

Dakotans thus fought against hard times on three fronts at once. First and foremost, they struggled to put food in their mouths and clothes on their backs. But they also endeavored to keep intact the ideals, expectations, and structures of everyday life that formed the backbone of their society. Most of all, they sought to come to terms with the new middle class, the welfare state, and managerial capitalism as a whole—people and structures they often supported as much as feared. Together, their separate battles became one: a struggle to make their guests feel welcome without letting them take over the house.

The Dust Bowl disaster challenged first what I have called the common chords, the shared ideals and aspirations that held Dakota society together. Some of the ways in which this happened were easily apparent. Rising interest rates, increased costs, mortgage indebtedness, and croplessness, for example, made it nearly impossible for the majority of Dakotans to remain independent property owners. Similarly, it was hard for neighbors to treat each other cooperatively when the world had turned into a race for depleted resources. But, if the power of cultural hegemony is to be judged by the degree to which certain values are taken for granted by a society (even by some members of that society who have not achieved them), then the power of a cultural crisis may be judged by the degree to which those same values are called into question. In Dakota in the 1930s, men and women stood proudly in defense of their special way of life. Even so, beneath it all, there were often as many questions as there were answers.

Most importantly, Dakotans were tied together by a belief in the work they did, physically taxing and financially frustrating though it was. Further, they believed that a positive attitude about their work and a sustained faith in the future was an essential element of their success. In the 1930s, however, it was difficult to do work well, to be successful at it, or even to try to think cheerfully about it. Lorena Hickok reported simply that "the chief trouble with people in South Dakota . . . is sheer terror. They are afraid of the future."[4] In fact, their terror may not have been so simple at all, but a deeply felt response to a shattering of confidence in the ability of a good man to do good work no matter what the circumstances. Edward Dwight, a banker from Springfield, South Dakota, described his outlook this way: "[I] just lived from day to day, didn't look for tomorrow, I didn't look back. [I'd] just try to get through this day and the next day try to get through it."[5] From time to time, a few virtuous Dakotans betrayed their own anxieties by urging their neighbors to feel otherwise. "What we need in North Dakota is more guts," wrote a businessman to the *Bismarck Tribune* in 1936. "Cheer up! North Dakota is all right."[6]

It was not only the grown-ups in Dakota who began to question the future, however. Throughout the 1930s, Dakota youth turned away from agrarianism and small-town life at a rate even higher than their parents' generation had, suggesting that those who would carry the future did not choose to take on its burdens. North Dakota sociologist Donald Hay discovered some of the reasons why these young men and women were so discouraged. Like others around the country, Dakota youth were in a permanent holding pattern. With no money to get started even on a rented farm, no employment opportunities in the cities, and nothing but hard labor at home, they delayed marriage, dropped out of school, and sometimes gravitated to extralegal activities.[7] Moreover, those who were lucky enough to "get a start" did not encounter the same working conditions that their parents and grandparents had. Without a large inheritance, for example, it was nearly impossible to start a store or business or to buy a farm. Young people had always made up a disproportionate number of Dakota tenants, but, in the 1930s, they began to stay longer and longer in that position. As one researcher put it, "Farm tenancy is rapidly becoming a lifelong tenure status rather than a first step up the agricultural ladder toward farm ownership."[8]

As they had for more than a decade already, in the 1930s Dakota young people stopped wanting to get started in their parents' worlds in the first place. In 1927 more than 87 percent of farmers encouraged their children to go into farming, but by 1938 less than half of Dakota high schoolers wanted to take their advice.[9] Instead, when asked what occupations they planned to follow, they listed jobs that were more exciting, less isolating, more urban-oriented, financially more secure, and overwhelmingly more new-middle-class than farming: the boys listed aviation, engineering, and mechanics and the girls listed secretarial work, clerking, and cosmetology.[10] So baffled was sociologist Hay by these results that he wondered aloud "why [North Dakota youth] are dreaming of occupational pursuits . . . [so] much different from the work [they] will certainly be doing."[11] That Dakota's young people were dreaming of being different, however, was exactly the point.

Ann Marie Low's brother Bud was one Dakota boy who gave up his dream of farming in the 1930s and gravitated instead to labors far afield from small production. He made the decision shortly after a prize heifer he had raised since birth had died—by his hand—of a heat- and drought-related illness. "There were no words or tears," Low recalled later. "Bud just went into the house and got his gun. Somehow to me, the look on his face when he shot Isabelle stood for this whole tragedy of a land laid waste, a way of life destroyed, and a boy's long struggle ending in despair."[12] Bud Low chose to become a civil engineer, and he served his country as such in World War II. Except for short visits, he never returned to the Stony Brook country, and Low never again thought he was really happy. In 1947, he shot himself.[13]

The economic imperatives of the Great Depression also called into question the viability—indeed, even the righteousness—of community support. As we have seen, being a good neighbor was equally important to Dakotans as being a good worker. In the 1930s, when so many of their neighbors were in need, Dakotans tried harder than ever to stick together and to help each other. Even so, many times they discovered that the fruits of neighborliness were often simply too meager to make a lasting difference.[14] All the neighborliness in the world would not save a drought-ravaged crop, for example; and it mattered little how many church suppers were given if no one remained to attend them. Even Oscar Fosheim, whose Farmers' Holiday Association (FHA) came as close as any organization could to successfully institutionalizing these traditional habits of mutuality (see chapter 5), admitted later that depleted resources sometimes led to depleted neighborliness. He recalled that he had always liked to help people who needed it, "until my wife said, 'Now you'd better figure out, are you supporting . . . your family or everybody but your family. Look at the linoleum on the floor. It's patched and there are patches on the patches."[15] In such a world, neighbors began to resemble competitors more than comrades.[16]

But harder still to confront than these realizations were the private decisions—sometimes made in the blackest night—to shop in a different town because prices were lower there, to eliminate townships "because they served no purpose commensurate with their cost," or simply to pick up and move away. Not surprisingly, many Dakotans justified decisions like these in terms of dollars and cents. One local researcher, for example, explained the migration of many physicians from the smaller towns of Ward County, North Dakota, to Minot this way: "The physician must make a living [and so] he goes shopping where the shopping is good."[17] Others, perhaps more thoughtful, saw migration as a betrayal of the land and society they had struggled so hard to cultivate. After her husband decided to move west, Rachel Custer despaired. "What did one do when one no longer had a bed, a stove, or a table? . . . What did one do for an address? Without a mailing address, how did a person even know who she was? How did her children—Oh God!—how would her *children* know who *they* were?"[18] More than anything else, Rachel did not understand how she or her children could ever have identities if they forsook their roots. But forsaking ones roots was among the "choices" Dakotans made in a time when survival itself was at stake.

For those who stuck it out on the northern plains, doing good work and remaining loyal to the community were further complicated by the relief programs initiated by the federal government in 1933. Like most Americans—including Franklin Roosevelt—Dakotans believed that accepting emergency relief "went against the grain." In order to avoid it, Dakotans depleted their life insurance, their savings, their livestock herds, and finally the charity of friends and relations.[19] Eddy County, North Dakota, farmer Hugh O'Connor refused surplus commodities again and again in the 1930s. "I simply told them, 'Not as long as I can get by. . . . I wasn't brought up that way. I was brought up to make my own way."[20] According to Lorena Hickok, even the administrators of North Dakota's State Relief Committee felt that "there must be something wrong with a man who can't make his own living."[21]

Dakotans worried less about the long-term effects of work programs than they did about the "dole," but they worried nonetheless. In fact, even those men and women who benefited from work programs were concerned about the ways in which they were administered. Steve Hakl of Dante, South Dakota, for example, labored several months for the Work Projects Administration (WPA), but he never endorsed the way it operated. "You know," he recalled, "they tried to distribute those jobs and make [them] last. They didn't want the job to be done.

And they didn't want anybody to work real fast. They said, 'Slow down!'."[22]

The problem, for people who had worked night and day to produce a crop or a living, was that WPA jobs were not real jobs but made-up jobs, or "make-work." Hugh O'Connor had even less success with the WPA than he had with the Surplus Commodities Corporation (SCC). Shoveling a road by hand when he could have graded it easily with a team of horses made him feel so "foolish" that he finally quit trying.[23] Those who persisted were called "reliefers" and had to contend with charges from nonreliefers of laziness and "shovel-leaning." In February 1935, for example, the editor of North Dakota's *Litchville Bulletin* advised men on WPA jobs that, "if all men who obtain relief . . . would give an honest day's worth of labor for every dollar given them, the rest of us would accept the present situation with greater equanimity."[24] No matter what jobs they held, there were few ways for Dakotans to feel right about the work they did in the Dust Bowl years.

Relief programs affected community relations, too, in ways that were at once less subtle and more insidious than the ways in which they affected work. As we have seen, most Dakotans lived comfortably in a world of rhetorical equality and actual discord. They lived in a world where the ideals of community, fraternity, and service were maintained through the activities and rituals of social organizations, but where, at the same time, sharp distinctions were drawn between and among neighbors on the basis of religion, ethnicity, political persuasion, occupation, and class. The depression upset this ideological applecart two ways at once. It highlighted power relations within the community, amplifying the differences between and among people whom Dakotans liked to say were the same. Simultaneously, however, it annihilated their equally important, if unspoken, distinguishing characteristics, and made people who were meant to be different very much alike.

We have already suggested one of the ways in which the depression highlighted the differences among Dakotans: it set even the best-hearted neighbors against one another in the race for depleted resources. The administration of New Deal relief programs, however, often extended this individual phenomenon to the community as a whole. Many of the programs, which were overseen by government officials, were administered by local people. As the administrator of farm relief in Rugby, North Dakota, explained, "As far as the Farm Security Administration was concerned, 'Nobody knows your neighbor better than your other neighbor.'"[25] This combination of intimacy and power could be as dangerous as it was effective. Homer Ayres of Sturgis, South Dakota, recalled that the local men "kind of liked . . . to meet the public and to [get] to turn them down on things. They felt pretty big and tough."[26] In fact, it was the very thought of "taking a check from a guy who sat behind you in fifth grade" that compelled George Custer to leave South Dakota for good.[27]

The depression and the New Deal also highlighted divisions among community members by making them more visible. In many towns, people who were on relief could be identified by the clothes they wore and the food they ate.[28] In others, relief programs brought the needy into the public eye. Al J. Vohs was the city commissioner of Williston, North Dakota, from 1931 to 1934. As in other towns, Williston's poor had customarily been cared for either privately, by charity organizations, or separately, in county poor farms that literally took the poor away from the community.[29] In the early 1930s, however, Vohs established a community soup kitchen downtown and tried to require people on relief to come there and eat together in public. His clients disliked the new system so much that he eventually let them take food back home with them. Still, he encountered other forms of resistance— some people would return his milk bottles to their local store and pocket the refund money.[30]

As the depression wore on, the experience of public visibility and concomitant vulnerability encouraged some men and women on relief to organize as bodies separate from the rest of their communities. In March 1935, twenty relief workers and their families marched on the Cass County courthouse demanding better food and clothing.[31] One year later, full-fledged strikes by WPA workers were common in many Dakota towns and cities.[32] Dakota reliefers were, in effect, imitating the actions of employed workers in their communities and around the nation, who were also organizing more vigorously and successfully in the 1930s than they had before. Construction of the new North Dakota capitol ground to a halt in 1933; milk and coal deliveries ended in Fargo in 1935 while organizing truckers and local citizens and police battled in the streets;[33] strikers surrounded the Morrell plant in Sioux Falls from 9 March 1935 to 9 March 1937;[34] and local units of the Teamsters appeared in all large towns in South Dakota.[35]

Even when local commentators supported these kinds of organizational activities, in principle, they worried about their long-term effects on community life. As for the WPA strikes, *Bismarck Tribune* editor John Simon wrote, "Time was when almost anyone would be ashamed to admit he was on relief. Most persons are still reluctant to do so. But there is a growing class of persons who . . . thinks of relief in terms of where they can get the most. [This is not] the attitude of the traditional American."[36] Charles Anderson was similarly dismayed at the prospects of a long, violent truckers' strike:

> Fargo doesn't want a Minneapolis or a Toledo or a San Francisco uprising. We do not want one group of our people doing battle with guns and clubs against another group. Scars that would grow out of such developments could not be lived down in a generation. . . . Involved in the controversy are men of Fargo . . . who have lived peacefully, side by side, and worked with each other these many years. . . . We have demonstrated that we are a community where men can go about their vocations peacefully and with understanding.[37]

Later that year, Anderson underscored what he considered to be the ideal relationship between employers and employees by describing the fifty-five-year-old Typographical Union's negotiations with the *Fargo Forum* as "marked by friendliness, mutual helpfulness, [and] understanding . . . a proud record."[38]

The depression also made some members of Dakota society appear to be less different from the rest than they had appeared before. Although rarely explained or expressed, Dakotans had extremely important and intricate criteria by which they judged their neighbors' worth. Neither the drought nor the relief administrators took these criteria into account, however. When a hard-working family was wiped out through the vagaries of bank closings, price collapses, or nature's fury, they became, in other people's eyes, no different from the laziest and most "unworthy" members of society. The conflation of all the best and all the worst elements of society was exactly what Rachel Custer feared most in the 1930s. As her family rode west, she feared that the strangers who passed them would never know what they had been but would only judge them as they were at the moment, no different from any of the tramps, gypsies, beggars, and ne'er-do-wells that she had so often scorned. They would "think they were seeing another shiftless, roving family . . . a man and a woman who had never been willing to make commitments, never been willing to labor and sacrifice for roots."[39] Stripped of her material possessions and her ties to the soil, Rachel had lost everything that defined her status in the world.

But men and women lost status and self-respect even when they were "successful enough" to stay in their communities. With the benefit of relief, those in town who had always been the poorest were "rich"; their children had red apples in their lunch buckets and new shoes on their feet; they could decide whether or not to share with their "wealthier" neighbors.[40] For a time, moreover, some community members who previously had no power whatsoever now had just enough to make a difference. In the 1930s, a town drunk like Mike from Garretson, South Dakota, who never before had been given the time of day, might have been able to deposit his relief check in Tom Wangsness's bank and to see that the banker was truly grateful for it. For his part, Wangsness was left with little more than his sense that he was still somehow better than Mike. Lorena Hickok spoke again and again of those Dakotans who, either by refusing relief or by being unqualified for it, were left with nothing but their pride. These were the people, she said, who "were hidden" and "hungry" in their "handsome houses . . . suffering in lonely silence, locked in pride and centuries of ideas about their worth as individuals."[41] However socially powerful it was, pride bought little food to put on the dinner table.

In the 1930s, everything the people of North and South Dakota knew, everything they had always taken for granted, was turned upside down. They could not work, they could not help their neighbors, and they could not maintain the usual balance of power and authority in their communities. For all their resounding impact, however, these problems did not simply drop from the sky with the dust and grasshoppers. As we have seen, many problems were initiated and many others exacerbated by the very programs designed to help Dakotans. In other words, the struggle of the old middle class to maintain cultural relations within their communities was only one of the battles they fought in the Great Depression. The other was the struggle they waged for cultural authority between themselves and their benefactors—the men and women, the ideas and ideals of the New Deal. Warren Susman suggested that the depression was a liminal moment in the century-long match between a "Puritan-republican, producer-capitalist culture, and a newly emerging culture of abundance."[42] Even he did not recognize, however, how much that struggle was based upon the complicated relationship between, and the contradictory elements within, each worldview.

The most compelling expression of the complicated relationship between the people of the Dakotas and the people of the New Deal can be found on the pages of Ann Marie Low's diary. Like many other Americans, Low found it easier to bear her suffering if she could blame someone or something for it. So intensely fond of the land and landscape of North Dakota was she, however, that she never blamed nature for her troubles. Even in the first terrible years of the drought, she saw beauty in the hills surrounding her family's farm.[43] It was only later, when "government men," relief agents, and a "tribe" of Civilian Conservation Corps (CCC) boys from the city came to live nearby—to try to convert her father's land into a wildlife refuge and finally to condemn it—that she began to feel differently. One day, after visiting a new CCC headquarters, dam, and road system, she rode her pony up a high hill and looked down at the Stony Brook country. For once and for all, that night, she decided, "I will not miss [this land] very much. After all the changes the government is making, it isn't home to me anymore."[44]

Between 1932 and 1937, Low found countless reasons to criticize the government and its representatives, but the fundamental problem, in her eyes, was this: the government men did not understand her land or her people, but they wielded enormous power over the future nonetheless. She laughed, for example, at the CCC boys when they neglected to stock extra provisions before a blizzard and bitterly decried the "make-work" they had to do.[45] Worse than their ignorance and wastefulness, however, were their attitudes toward local people and the local way of life. "They made no secret of the fact [that] they considered us a bunch of yokels living in a mess of geology poorly begun and never finished," she maintained.[46] They were, plainly enough, a different kind of people with a different vision for her world and different ideals for its future. Stony Brook had once been filled with "good-hearted . . . helpful" people. Now it teemed with "lallygagging side-winders" and typical city folks.[47]

As clear-cut as Low made the difference between government men and Stony Brook people sound, a closer look at her text suggests that they may not have been diametrically opposed. Like Theodore Straub, Low had nothing against modern ways, new ideas, or any other mark of progress. She did not particularly enjoy the rigors of teaching in a one-room schoolhouse, for example, and looked forward to an appointment in a consolidated system. Likewise, her favorite spot on earth, after the Stony Brook country, was the Penney's five-and-dime store in Jamestown, where she could see a "fascinating stock of goods" and an enchanting basket on a wire that carried money and receipts between customers and an upstairs office.[48] Finally, even the government men must not have seemed terribly unappealing to her; after turning down two proposals from local farm boys, she married one of the managers of the wildlife refuge. He was hardly a neighbor; upon receiving his assignment at home in Massachusetts, he had to pick up a map to find North Dakota.

Like Low, many Dakotans located their impressions of the 1930s in their opinions of and relationships with the people and policies of the New Deal. Whether their opinions were more or less supportive of reform than hers, they were just as much the complicated products of the complex contradictions of old-middle-class culture. Low was not all wrong: generally speaking, the people of the New Deal came from a different culture and harbored different notions about Dakota land and its future. Not producers themselves, but members of a white-collar, professional-managerial, or "new" middle class, they brought reformist notions about production, land use, and community organization to people who, for the most part, wanted assistance but not "help." Although they resisted reform and outside authority, however, Dakotans also welcomed the New Deal's support and recognized its approach as the way of the future. Finally, Dakotans may have realized the ways in which New Deal policies, however radical they sometimes seemed, were themselves rooted in the traditional American moral code. The cultural crisis of the Great Depression was, in other words, based in the divergent visions of old- and new-middle-class Americans but was complicated by the many ways in which those visions were similar as well as different. In the end, such a complex interaction left Dakotans feeling two ways at once about the changes in their world and not knowing exactly how to resolve their mixed emotions.

Not all "New Dealers" were members of the new middle class. Franklin Roosevelt, Henry Morgenthau, and Francis Biddle, as well as most of the advisory members of the National Industrial Recovery Administration (NIRA) were wealthy upper-class gentlemen or industrial leaders.[49] In many agencies, however, especially in those that assumed authority in the Dakotas, men and women of the new middle class had a large measure of control over policy formation and administration.[50] Not surprisingly, then, many of the programs, and the ideals behind them, reflected the shared values and experiences of their creators. This connection between class, culture, and policy did not pass unnoticed by most Dakotans. Nearly every concern registered by the Dakota press or the general population began with the assumption that the policies of the New Deal were the products of outsiders, people who may have had good intentions but who needed to "learn a thing or two"—at least.

That the new middle class did not know or understand their "clients" as well as they could was a cutting criticism indeed for people whose culture, history, and authority were founded on an ability to analyze and communicate. Growing out of the violent divisions between industrial workers and owners in the late 1900s, the new white-collar class took its stand upon expertise and established institutional structures to defend and reproduce it. As Jean-Christophe Agnew has argued,

FSA inspector examines a pile of "barnyard lignite" (manure)
in North Dakota (FSA, courtesy National Archives)

this "cultural gate-keeping" included the establishment of "journals, associations, and foundations, of examinations and degrees."[51] Although they engaged in diverse occupations that ranged from company management to advertising and social services, the members of the new middle class had much in common: they owned not a piece of land or a store of goods but a body of knowledge and skill; they acted not to produce a product but to reproduce a set of relationships; they held nothing to pass on to their children but a passion for education and for certain intangible skills—"Speaking, listening, observing, measuring, and . . . [using] their minds to analyze and solve social problems."[52] They saw America not as a world of producers but as a society of consumers ready to receive their services, ready to judge others more often on the basis of personality than character.[53]

At the same time that members of the new middle class began to influence business and professional spheres, they also made their presence known in government. Between 1875 and 1920, the disruption of what Steven Skowronek has called the traditional American antistatist "world of courts and parties" was at once uneven and sure.[54] Beginning with the railroads and the army and culminating in the multifaceted governmental reforms of the Progressive Era, experts, managers, engineers, and bureaucrats rationalized and centralized government structures and government relations. In the decade following World War I, these changes picked up pace even more. Herbert Hoover, himself an engineer, reorganized parts of the federal government into "associative" sections and divisions, much as he had the Food Relief Service.[55] In the Department of Agriculture, for example, state-trained agricultural economists became the mainstays of research, policy development, and education in the 1920s.[56]

Despite all of this, it was not until Roosevelt's New Deal that the new middle class came together in such overwhelming numbers and with such overwhelming authority that they could influence the nature, style, and direction of an entire administration.[57] To some observers, it seemed as though these new men and women—sociologists, economists, social workers, professors, and lawyers—simply descended on Washington "in an endless stream," bringing with them "an alertness, an excitement, an appetite for power, an instinct for crisis, and a dedication to public service which became the essence of [the city]."[58] They shared more than a certain esprit de corps, however. They also shared the presumption that their special skills were essential to solving the present economic and social crisis. As Arthur Schlesinger put it, "They were all at home in the world of ideas . . . and they were prepared to use intelligence as an instrument of government. They considered themselves . . . generalists, capable of bringing logic to bear on any social problem. They delighted in the play of the free mind."[59]

More precisely, even when they disagreed about the details of certain policies, the new middle class brought to the Roosevelt administration several overarching ideas about how the New Deal ought to go about helping the American people. A number of New Dealers, for example, were dedicated to notions of centralized economic planning. Stuart Chase, the best known publicist for the development of a governmental "technocracy," described the need for planning this way: "Our businessmen and politicians have obviously failed us . . . the torch must be borne by another class . . . the men and women who have grasped the hand of science."[60] Although many of Chase's specific policy proposals were rejected by more moderate decision makers, the ideal of planning remained intact within the administration. Moreover, the concept of a "managerial revolution," wherein a new politically neutral "intelligentsia" would direct the course of government and industry, gained popular support in this period.[61]

The ideals of neutrality and objectivity were the second overarching concept that the new middle class brought to the New Deal. Just as they believed that systems, including social systems, could be effectively counted, weighed, measured, and analyzed, they believed that those measurements—and the people using them—could remain wholly "scientific" and objective. Moreover, they believed that measurements could be presented in a precise and unbiased way. Importantly, it was not just scientists who learned to "document" the depression this way. "Overnight journalists" like Lorena Hickok, photographers like Arthur Rothstein, social science caseworkers, and realist filmmakers all set out to record the "truth" of the depression crisis.[62] Behind all of their stark images, however, lay a single presumption: that a document could speak plainly and persuasively for itself and for its silent, objective author. In short, while the New Dealers themselves were rarely politically neutral, they believed that their programs, systems, methods, and "interests" were. As Arthur Holcombe argued, they believed they were simply "the servants of all classes [whose interests came] nearer to coinciding with the general interest than those of any class."[63]

Finally, with the special skills, "sanitized" knowledge, and innate understanding of the New Deal experts came the presumption of their authority to make decisions and act upon them. Again, Stuart Chase spoke most extremely here, contending that there was "a desire among large numbers of people to have their behavior controlled and their lives planned."[64] Others, who respected the ideals of a participatory democracy and the intelligence of the populace somewhat more than Chase did, believed nonetheless that they knew what was best for the people and, hence, that their most important task was to educate them. In nearly every bureau, policy-making was centralized within the Washington administrative complex. Officials often consulted local people, regional committees, senators, and congressmen at great length before developing a firm policy. But, as historian Gilbert Fite put it in regard to the Agricultural Adjustment Act (AAA), "Grass-roots opinion was more revered in theory than in practice by policy-makers."[65] After seeing none of his organization's suggestions put into practice at the federal level, one North Dakota farmer wondered whether their letters and opinion papers had not just been used for "starting fires."[66]

It was at the United States Department of Agriculture (USDA) that the installation of the new middle class had its greatest impact. In a department that before 1920 had been filled with "old-boy" agrarians, George Peek alone now championed the older style. All the rest, as Peek put it, were "boys with their hair ablaze"—professors, economists, lawyers, and more lawyers.[67] For a time, the department's most influential spokesman, Rexford Tugwell, was also its most controversial figure. Tugwell made no bones about the fact that he now preferred urban to rural life and that part of his job was to help farmers to see his point of view.[68] Even more moderate and sympathetic leaders, like Henry Wallace, adhered to Tugwellian notions of centralized planning and control.[69] Despite his respect for the small farmer and his "hick" image in Washington, Wallace too was a "service intellectual," a trained expert who sought to bring his special skills to bear on social problems of the agricultural Midwest.[70]

The AAA reflected the newfound authority of the USDA intellectuals. Beginning in the 1920s, Professor M. L. Wilson became a "nearfanatical advocate" of his plan for controlling the production of domestic agriculture.[71] By 1932, the leading USDA figures (John Black, Mordecai Ezekiel, Wallace, and Tugwell) had gathered around Wilson and brought his ideas "into the Roosevelt campaign."[72] After Roosevelt's inauguration, the agricultural economists asked farm groups (some of whom were supporting other schemes) for their endorsement of domestic allotment and their help in implementing it. The organization that represented most Dakotans, the Farmers' Union, refused to endorse the plan, but its rivals, the Farm Bureau Federation and the Grange, did endorse it. Nevertheless, even these groups were not involved in creating the farm policy but only in endorsing it, explaining it to their members, and implementing it after passage by Congress.[73] Without this support, the AAA would never have been born. As we will see in detail in chapter 5, however, the AAA was hardly the farmers' baby.[74]

As the drought worsened, USDA policies became intent on thoroughly reforming, rather than just controlling, the ways of American farming. While moderates worked on shelterbelt systems, water conservation programs, rural electrification, and refinancing ideas, more radical thinkers like Tugwell considered policies that would remove some farmers from the land and reform the customs and aspirations of those who remained. As they saw it, the crux of the problem lay in the culture of commercial farming itself, wherein farmers worked their land solely for profit and neglected both ecological and communal prerogatives. Thus they decided that not just habits of the hand but also habits of the mind needed reform. The Great Plains Committee, for example, listed eleven "attitudes of mind" that, they felt, had contributed to the Dust Bowl crisis, from the notion that "man conquers nature" to the idea that "a man can do with his property whatever he likes."[75] The reformers hoped that farmers, with education, could see the part they had played in bringing about the Dust Bowl disaster.

Some of the most famous artifacts of the Great Depression are products of the ideals and authority of the new middle class in the USDA. Beginning in 1936, Roy Stryker of the Resettlement Administration—later renamed the Farm Security Administration (FSA)—sent photographers throughout America's rural areas to document the plight of the rural poor. By doing so, he hoped to "show America to Americans"—that is, to urban Americans who might not otherwise grasp the importance of his former student Rexford Tugwell's expensive programs of reform.[76] In 1939, Edward Steichen called the products of this effort "the most remarkable human documents ever rendered in pictures."[77] The best known, especially Dorothea Lange's "Migrant Mother" and Arthur Rothstein's "Fleeing a Dust Storm," are from the southern plains. But a handful of photographs from the northern plains also caught the nation's attention. Arthur Rothstein's "The Skull," "Children of a Sub-Marginal Farmer in Pennington County," and "Migrants Heading West" tell a poignant tale of suffering and land

Arthur Rothstein, "The Skull"
(FSA, courtesy National Archives)

mismanagement. Looking at these pictures, few urbanites could have doubted the seriousness of the agricultural disaster on the plains: the camera, as we all know, never lies.

However much they seemed to capture the "truth" of the Dust Bowl, the FSA photographs were also deeply encoded with the "ways of seeing" specific to the new middle class. The documentary style itself, of course, reflects the experts' attempt to fashion a reality whose authorship would appear only incidental to the final product. In actual fact, this couldn't have been farther from the truth. To shoot "The Skull," for example, Arthur Rothstein first photographed the cow skull where he found it, then picked it up and carried it to a location that provided better light and shadow for the composition. When he was found out

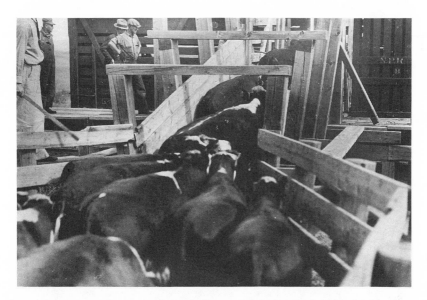

*Leo Harris, "Beef cattle being loaded for market at Killdeer, North Dakota,
one of the largest shipping points for beef cattle in the Northwest"
(courtesy State Historical Society of North Dakota)*

by the North Dakota press, he spent years justifying his work. Whatever his reasons for "faking" the picture, Rothstein's actions revealed
that authorship—and the author's point of view—were at least as important to the picture as the subject itself. Likewise, the notion that
the FSA photographers tried to stay outside politics was farcical,
given their explicit instructions to "include evidence of land misuse and
mismanagement."[78] Finally, that Rothstein and others believed they
could come to understand plains culture well enough to capture it on
film simply by driving through town for a week or two suggests nothing if not simple arrogance toward their subjects. Indeed, it suggests
that the photographers believed that old-middle-class culture was relatively simple, not particularly complex, and perfect for depicting on
the unidimensional plane of the still photograph.

All told, the New Deal era saw an unprecedented increase in the
absolute number and the cultural authority of the men and women of
the new middle class. In work, in residence, in values, in aspirations
for their own and their nation's future, and in their "ways of seeing,"
the members of the new middle class were notably different from many

Arthur Rothstein, "Farm Boy near Dickinson, North Dakota"
(FSA, courtesy National Archives)

of the people they sought to help. Nonetheless, they derived power from the assumption that they could disinterestedly and objectively see, understand, and document what was best for other Americans. The New Deal was, in short, a period of exhilaration for the experts of Roosevelt's administration—a feeling that differentiated them even further from their clients. Fed, clothed, housed, employed, feeling good about the work they did, they came alive amidst despair. Some even recalled the period as "one of the best of their lives."[79]

Very few of the differences between themselves and the people of the New Deal escaped the watchful eyes of the folks on the northern plains. From the beginning of the New Deal period, even those Dakotans who believed that the New Deal was "the most practical plan yet proposed" questioned its administration and administrators.[80] Some

Leo Harris, "Janet Morgan, age eight months" (Dakota Farmer, *courtesy Intertec Publishing Corporation)*

Dakotans—long-term Democrats, in particular—were quicker than others to accept the New Deal, and all Dakotans liked some policies, like Rural Electrification and Social Security, better than others. Only a few Dakotans were ever as unendingly negative in their assessment of the New Deal as was Ann Marie Low. Many felt instead that they owed their lives to the New Deal's timely intervention. Nevertheless, like her, Dakotans worried that New Deal programs were the products of outsiders who did not fully understand their land, communities, or culture, but who had the power to dictate the future even so.

Arthur Rothstein, "Vernon Evans [of Lemmon, South Dakota], Missoula vicinity, July 1936" (FSA, courtesy National Archives)

In her visit to North and South Dakota in 1932 and 1933, Lorena Hickok was introduced to the range of concerns that would dominate debate about the New Deal on the northern plains until 1938. She found two kinds of disgruntled Dakotans: those who did not support Roosevelt and who resisted any kind of government intervention, and those who welcomed his reforms but worried about their long-term effect and complained about their bureaucratic implementation.[81] What bound both supporters and opponents together, however, was a basic suspicion of and alienation from the "Brain Trust." On 27 October 1933, Hickok sent a telegram from Minneapolis that presaged her experiences in the Dakotas: "[Farmers] here still feel [FDR] is sincere and acting in good faith but listening too much to theorists."[82] Ralph Hansmeier, a farmer from Aberdeen, South Dakota, explained this antipathy when he told her why so many farmers supported the proposals generated at a five-state governor's conference but not those of the Hundred Days. "You see, those governors live out here. They know what we're up against. As I said, maybe their plan needed

Leo Harris, "Fence Love"
(courtesy State Historical Society of North Dakota)

changes . . . [but] the President it seemed would not listen to anybody but Wallace and the 'Brain Trust.' Well, Wallace and the Brain Trust haven't done much for us."[83]

As New Deal programs got under way and more and more Dakotans found their lives and communities improved by them, most men and women learned to support, or at least to find a way to live with, their reforms. Exactly how this came about will be reviewed in detail in the following chapters. Nonetheless, concern about the Brain Trust and its intellectual imperialism continued. A survey of editorials and letters to the editor in local newspapers between 1933 and 1938 reveals that at least three areas of dissatisfaction with the New Deal existed in this period, and that each was based in opposition to the Brain Trust and new-middle-class authority. As Charles Day put it in April 1933, "The world is leaning too heavily on college professors. They are well-meaning and have excellent book education but they draw overly much on the field of theory. They are removed from the practical aspects of life." [84] Well-meaning or not, by 1938 Joseph Score of Bottineau County, North Dakota, was inclined to call them "white-collared, supercilious nincompoops." [85]

The editors surveyed worried, first of all, about the contradictions embedded in some New Deal programs. Just as the farmers who spoke with Lorena Hickok could not understand why they had to pay a $10 inspection fee to certify that they had no money, the editors could not see how New Deal policy fit together as a whole. To Charles Day at the *Sioux Falls Argus-Leader*, for example, the agricultural proposals pitted farmers from one section of the country against those from another. "If it weren't so tragic, it would be funny," he concluded. [86] The editor of South Dakota's *Plankinton Herald* saw the same irony in "the government's move to create millions of new acres of farm lands by constructing irrigation projects and an official offer . . . to cut acreage." [87] A year later, a radical farm paper, North Dakota's *Williams County Farmers' Press*, decried the difference between the NIRA minimum wage and the much lower WPA maximum wage, saying that "the world seems to be getting more cockeyed every day." [88]

Dakotans who wrote to the editor of the *Dakota Farmer* mentioned similar contradictions and impracticalities. Relief programs rewarded those Dakotans who had been lazy all along, argued G. J. Merkel, and punished those "with a full corn crib." [89] Likewise, allotment programs encouraged farmers to lie about their past yields and surveyed land lines. [90] In an even broader recapitulation of these concerns, however, farmer/correspondents contended that the contradictions of the New Deal had brought a wholesale shift in the relationship between the government and common citizens. For example, a South Dakota farmer remarked that, when federal agencies accepted 100 percent mortgages on crops to cover seed loans, they were hardly helping farmers remain independent property owners. To the contrary, these kinds of "no-share croppers" simply had a new kind of landlord.[91] A farmer from North Dakota put the problem even more clearly. Whereas small-town bankers and other creditors had known farmers as individuals, federal credit agencies knew them only as numbers standing in line. Old friendly courthouses, too, had become just one more part of the "monster bureaucracy" that was tearing farmers' lives apart. Much of this trouble, he argued, came down to the paternalistic nature of the helper/client relationship: "The monster thinks the common man is too dumb to think for himself and that the monster must do his thinking for him."[92]

Secondly, many Dakotans complained that the policymakers could never understand the farmers' point of view because they were from urban backgrounds. As Day put it, "The trouble with so many leaders in Washington and New York is that they have a strictly urban and industrial viewpoint. . . . The producer is far in the distance. His problems are strange to them."[93] Farmers who wrote to their local papers also wondered why they should listen to the advice of men who had themselves never turned a single acre of sod. The image of "fat salaried men" trying their hand at farming was the source of many jokes. "Oh, they'd be crackerjack farmers," T. Johnson of Trail Country suggested dryly.[94]

Conservative editors supplemented complaints about urbanism with complaints about political radicalism. The *Fargo Forum*'s Charles Anderson reported in 1934, for example, that the people of North Dakota were "crying out" against Rexford Tugwell's ideal of a planned economy. Tugwell may sound like a conservative today, Anderson warned, but his heart really lies somewhere east of Leningrad, "where industry is government and government is industry."[95] That same year, Anderson published a cartoon entitled "Brain Trust Member on Vacation," depicting a professor trying to row a boat sideways to "experiment," playing golf by "collectivism," and trying to find his way home without "turning right."[96]

A third wave of criticism of the New Deal and New Dealers occurred during the submarginal land purchase and resettlement programs. Despite their fears that the drought was "breaking the optimism" of the people and that some kind of land-use reform was in order, Dakota editors trod a careful path when it came to resettlement and the underlying presumption that old-middle-class culture needed reforma-tion. For example, although John Simon encouraged limited readjust-ments, like changing western lands from cropping to grazing, he contended that quitting Dakota altogether was one adjustment Dako-tans would never make. "Giving up is not in our vocabulary," he con-tended.[97] Other editors rejected the notion that somehow their love for the land and their community was usurped by their desire to make money. T. E. Hayes, a frequent columnist for the *Dakota Farmer* in 1933, declared, "We have made our homes here. Our back is against the wall, and we've dug in."[98] Charles Day explained his support for west-river Dakotans (the especial beneficiaries of resettlement schemes) in no uncertain terms: "There is more of faith and loyalty to the square inch in western South Dakota than in any other place in the world," he boasted. "Residents resent the current implication of un-productivity and we are inclined to respect them."[99]

Editors and their correspondents made it clear that if anyone in Washington thought that Dakotans "wanted their lives planned and their behavior controlled," they had another think coming. They were well aware of the ways in which the New Deal was disrupting com-munity life already, and they did not welcome wholesale reforms of their culture. For all their criticism, however, their relationship with these urban visitors was not all that simple. Dakotans did not, after all, just put up with the New Dealers; they had asked them to come. Many Dakotans had demanded a new, federally sponsored solution to the crisis (and had been demanding one for forty years); others, more conservative initially, ultimately endorsed New Deal reforms in the name of progress. Finally, whether Dakotans would admit it or not, the New Dealers were not as completely different from their clients as they appeared to be. In the end, the New Deal, as unprecedented and disruptive as it sometimes was, rarely challenged traditional morality or the fundamental precepts of agrarian capitalism.

Dakotans' acceptance of the New Deal is most obvious in the political sphere. For decades a Republican fortress, both North and South Da-kota went solidly for Roosevelt in 1932. Moreover, they did so again in 1936, when the New Deal was not just a promise but a reality. There are two reasons why this happened. First, Dakotans liked Roosevelt personally. Like North Dakota governor William Langer, Franklin

Roosevelt had a charismatic personality and a commanding presence that, when augmented through a skillful use of the media, reassured Americans of the significance of individual action in a time of collective crisis.[100] In fact, some Dakotans must have been even more reassured of Roosevelt's power to change their lives than the president had intended them to be: between 1932 and 1938, more than forty Dakotans wrote letters to Eleanor Roosevelt asking her to send them things they needed—old clothes, musical instruments, cash, shoes, glasses, and dentures. Often, they did so as if the president's wife were a personal friend, ready to help out in their hour of need. When South Dakota farm woman M. Catalina, for example, was unable to pay rent or buy food for her baby, she first went for help to the community welfare agency. The cold stares of its agents, however, made her feel "like a beggar." As a last resort, but still insisting that she did not want "charity," she asked Eleanor Roosevelt to send her the money she needed.[101] For such people, the Roosevelts' accessibility stood in direct and ironic contrast with the impersonal styles of the new-middle-class agents they had sent to implement reform.

Dakotans also supported Roosevelt because they were literally desperate to have someone try something to change the course of the economy.[102] For all their grumbling, Dakotans hardly sat at home rigidly protecting the status quo or the "old order," as did upper-class voters in some eastern states. To the contrary, they ardently called for "bold, persistent, experimentation." Even Charles Day, who was more often than not a stalwart critic of New Deal programs, applauded Roosevelt's courage to change. "Surely Franklin Roosevelt can never be labeled a 'do-nothing' President," he wrote.[103] Day waxed almost eloquent in an effort to help readers accept changing times. "So long as this world is a living thing and the people are alive and breathing," he began, "there will be change. . . . Life itself is a flux, and to be frightened of change is the first admission of death."[104] Change, even in government relations, it seems, was a mark of progress.

It was not just during the depression but throughout their history that the people of North and South Dakota welcomed "practical innovation" in the name of progress, even as they also worried about its long-term effects.[105] As we have seen, Dakotans came to the northern plains to make their own way and to live as independent property owners. In the late nineteenth and early twentieth centuries, however, living off the land also meant living with the prerequisites of the market. For most, it meant trying to make a profit as well as trying to make a home. Rather than simply berate the new technology that increased yields and profitability, most Dakotans accommodated themselves to it, albeit with mixed feelings.[106] Between 1880 and 1890, for example, some Dakotans used grain seeders, threshers, and self-binders; by 1900, they had mowers, dump rakes, and power hay loaders; by 1930, North and South Dakota farms were ahead of the national average in mechanized farm equipment, including automobiles, trucks, and combines.[107] By 1935, there were as many tractors as horses at work in the state.[108]

The same trend toward modernization is evident in the purchase of consumer goods. Rather than hold out for horses and home-spun, farmers and their families bought cars, trucks, dry-goods, and "ready-to-wear" as soon as they became available.[109] Farm women, especially, welcomed the opportunity to "trade" for mass-marketed goods rather than to spend the time and energy necessary to produce them at home. Indeed, as we will see in chapter 6, traditional women's production seems a lot more fulfilling to historians with hindsight than it did to women with experience. That only 10 percent of farm households in South Dakota had running water in 1930, for example, did not indicate an ingrained fondness for pumps, buckets, and late-night journeys to the outhouse, but rather the priorities of families with limited incomes and male heads of household. When farm wives were asked in 1932 how they would spend $1,000, more than 80 percent put running water at the top of the list.[110]

Advertisers for farm equipment and consumer goods reflected and reinforced the desire most farm families felt to keep up with modern times. In an advertisement for Armour's new hog and cattle marketing service in 1930, for example, readers were asked, "Who would care to go back to the good old days?"[111] Similarly, a virile and productive-looking farmer representing the Republic Steel Corporation announced to his wife, "Farm life is changing, Mother, and we must change with it."[112] But a local firm, the Nash-Finch Company of Grand Forks, North Dakota, best displayed the tug-of-war most Dakotans felt over modernization. In an advertisement for their "toasted" coffee,

Several authorities speak for the quality of Nash's coffee
(Dakota Farmer, courtesy Intertec Publishing Corporation)

the company set its stock beside two different "proofs" of the product's superiority: a "scientific" test from food chemists at the Van Cleve Laboratories in Chicago, and secret ballots given to a group of "typical American small-town grocers." Science, in this instance, acted as a supplemental persuasion to ordinary common sense; Dakotans could pick the authority most persuasive to them.

In the real world, however, there were precious few times when Dakotans, like Nash-Finch's grocers, could vote on aspects of modernization. As a result, there were plenty of opportunities for them to worry about the long-term consequences of changes they had simply accommodated. In 1928, for example, Mrs. Lulu Thompson of Mitchell, South Dakota, wrote a poem in which she listed all the changes—from empty blacksmith shops to empty church choirs—that she believed had accompanied the introduction of the automobile.[113] It seems highly unlikely, however, that Mrs. Thompson herself did not own a car. Mrs. Enid Bern was a great deal more perceptive about change. Like Ann Marie Low, she had begun her teaching career in a cold and isolated one-room schoolhouse but had moved to a large consolidated high school. Thinking back on those two experiences, she admitted, "Progress brings about changes and, of course, progress is what we are striving for. But as with all changes, something fine . . . something intangible is lost."[114]

Dakotans' mixed feelings about progress and change were nowhere more evident than in their reaction to government expansion and bureaucratization. As we have seen, many Dakotans had supported active interventionist federal government from as early as the mid-1880s. By the early twentieth century, nearly every Dakotan supported federal programs of one kind or another, from the moderate McNary-Haugen Act to the much more radical Nonpartisan League (NPL) proposals for state-owned and regulated industry. At the same time, however, Dakotans also cried out against excessive taxation and a lack of "economy" within the state governments and, in the 1930s, initiated huge and sometimes devastating cutbacks in state budgets. Until now, historians have recognized this trend both to welcome and to disdain government spending as a manifestation of the mysterious "Western split personality."[115] For the old middle class, however, this ambivalence was not so much a mystery as a reasonable product of their desire both to progress and to hold fast to the control of their own communities.

Dakotans' mixed feelings were sometimes captured in lesser-known documents, too. Over the course of the 1930s, a photographer whose work never became world famous—in fact, his work never even left the states' borders—took pictures of his people in the midst of the depression crisis. Photographers were, of course, among the first old-middle-class businessmen to set up shop in Dakota Territory: nineteenth-century Americans had already learned to capture their life experiences on film for posterity.[116] Leo Harris, who called himself "the cowboy photographer of the northern plains," was among these small businessmen who took studio portraits in the 1920s and in the 1930s branched out into freelance photography for newspapers and magazines. Much as the FSA photographs did, Harris's photographs focused on west-river images. They did so, however, for an altogether different reason. Rather than look for the most pathetic, downtrodden, heart-wrenching images, Harris sought out those that captured the region's spirit of adventure, vitality, and conviviality. Rather than a skull, for example, Harris shot well-fed cattle on their way to market; rather than empty-eyed, hungry children, he found well-cared-for, bright, thriving ones; rather than isolated and beleaguered souls, he found two men and a woman courting on a west-river fence post. For all their obvious differences, however, Harris's photographs had much in common with photographs in the FSA collection. He, too, used the camera as a tool for the documentation of his life and times, in an effort to convince others of the "reality" of their circumstances. Although they tended to be considerably less subtle than FSA photographs, Harris's photographs were far from the portrait-type shots of his nineteenth-century predecessors. Further, Harris's "Fence Love," like Rothstein's "Migrants Heading West," played hard and fast upon western stereotypes—especially cowboys and ranchers—without explaining that these subjects were but "cowboys for a day," participants in Killdeer's twenty-fifth anniversary celebration. In short, Harris, too, was "showing America to Americans," even though it was a different America he wanted to portray (see photographs above).

If Dakotans were more like New Dealers than they liked to admit, the reverse was also true. In the early twentieth century, and even as late as World War II, members of the new middle class—with their pens, pads, yardsticks, and cameras—were not so much the foreign visitors of their clients as they were their distant friends and relations. As C. Wright Mills pointed out in 1951, new-middle-class Americans (and sociologists in particular) have historically come from the ranks of the small-town middle class.[117] They have been, in other words, men and women pushed or pulled from their homes to a more secure and prestigious way of life, and who have gained a certain nostalgic fondness for the world they left behind; thus they have returned to use their new skills in service to those "back home." This was certainly the case at the USDA. Whatever farmers thought of the "nincompoops," county agents sent by the AAA to educate farmers were very often the sons of farmers themselves.[118] Even the leaders in Washington, from Henry Wallace to Rexford Tugwell to Roy Stryker, had a rural world somewhere in their pasts.[119] Despite having learned to love urban life-styles and to differentiate themselves from their rural relatives, they had not traveled as far as they thought they had. Every one of them, after all, had chosen to work for the Department of Agriculture.

It is not surprising, then, that many of the ideals and most of the long-term consequences of New Deal reform on the northern plains were not as radical as they appeared, either.[120] Many were, instead, rooted in the presumptions of traditional American agrarian capitalism. William Bremer has argued persuasively that beneath liberal ideals of work relief were traditional notions about the relationship between production, hard work, and self-respect.[121] No New Dealer advocated a system of long-term handouts; to the contrary, they admired Americans' productivity and drive as much as anyone else did. At the USDA, respect for traditional values was similarly in force. With only a few exceptions, New Dealers did not want to destroy the way of life of the small family farmer but only wanted to improve it in the ways they saw fit. Moreover, even those "fitter" ways were not completely foreign to the rural world. When Tugwell and the members of the Great Plains Committee spoke of encouraging cooperation, subsistence, and community and discouraging the profit motive among small farmers, for example, they wanted to change the *proportionate*

President Roosevelt visiting near Mandan, North Dakota (courtesy State Historical Society of North Dakota)

balance of two sets of values that, as we have seen, were already present in old-middle-class culture. They wanted, in short, a little more neighborliness and a little less acquisitiveness, a lot more concern for the common good and a lot less concern for individual success. After a year or two of photographing the "lower third of the country," even the FSA photographers began to document the traditional small-town virtues of America's heartland.[122]

Thus on some level the New Dealers did in fact understand the people they served. Moreover, when they wanted to, the "fat salaried men" knew just what to tell their clients in order to acquire their loyalty and support. Speaking in Bismarck in 1936 to advocate water conservation and submarginal land purchase programs, a well-advised President Roosevelt did not lecture his audience to change their foolish ways. Instead, he told them, "I [have] a hunch that you people [have] your chins up, that you are not looking forward to the day when the country would be depopulated, but that you and your children expect to stay here. And that is what we all want to see. . . . I say you are not licked."[123] Dakotans lined the streets for miles to see him, cheering the man that some called "Savior."[124]

It was an extraordinarily complex and complicated relationship between two sets of values, backgrounds, and ideals that marked the struggle between the old and new middle classes on the northern plains in the Great Depression. Their cultures were different, that was clear. Even so, the two cultures were not diametric opposites but were related and equally contradictory worldviews that were competing for power and control on the local level. Understandably, Dakotans reacted to the depression and New Deal with mixed feelings. It was not that they did not know what to think; people like Ann Marie Low always knew their own minds. It was, instead, that they thought (and acted) two ways at once: they were both thankful for and fearful of outside assistance and progress. Ill-fed, ill-housed, and ill-clothed, the people of the Dakotas were also ill-at-ease, struggling for cultural confidence amidst the most severe cultural crisis they had ever known.

Not all the turmoil of the New Deal period stayed bottled up in the hearts and minds of North and South Dakotans, or even within the borders of North and South Dakota. Upon one occasion, at least, Franklin Roosevelt himself was privy to the full weight of their irresolution. In fact, it is within a collection of two hundred letters to Roosevelt, written by North and South Dakota clergy in the fall and winter of 1934–35, that the cultural crisis detailed above is best encapsulated.[125] Whether or not the president ever understood the complexity of their responses, or whether he even read them at all, they nonetheless captured the inner meaning of the Great Depression for many Americans.[126]

In late September 1935, more than 100,000 clergymen across the nation were surprised to find a letter from the president in their mailboxes. What he wanted from them seemed, on the surface at least, to be simple enough. In brief, Roosevelt asked them for a progress report on the New Deal. He asked them for their "accurate and unbiased views" on conditions in their communities. "Tell me," he wrote, "where you think our government can better serve our people. . . . We shall have to work together for the common end of better spiritual and material conditions for the American people."[127]

Letters from well over two hundred Dakota clergy joined the flood of responses to the president. All were carefully written, some were typed, and a handful were quite long and detailed. Still, when they were assessed, it was difficult to say exactly where the Dakota clergy stood on New Deal policy. The clergy, like the newspaper editors, cautiously endorsed some programs, particularly Social Security and the AAA. But they also worried about long-term effects on local communities. They were concerned that the dole "destroys honor, self-respect, and self-pride," and that work projects, although somewhat better, "tempted cheaters and idlers."[128] All in all, the clergy were happy the New Deal was helping in the present crisis but were nonetheless worried about the future.

Even more ambivalent than the specifics, however, were the styles, tones, and other messages of the letters. The letter from Reverend Holzhausen of Garrison, North Dakota, portrayed the problem pointedly. Holzhausen responded rapidly and vigorously to Roosevelt's request; his four-page letter arrived within two weeks of the president's and went into great detail about local conditions. Then, suddenly, at the end of the letter, Holzhausen included a disclaimer: "I am only a humble minister of the American Lutheran Church," he closed, "and do not desire to mix up in government affairs."[129]

Reverend Holzhausen and the rest of the Dakota clergy were already mixed up, however. The confusion for them lay in what Roosevelt had asked them to do. No matter how it appeared, his request was not simple at all. When Roosevelt asked the clergymen for their "help" in assessing the New Deal, he asked them to step outside their communities and take on the role of a government official, an "unbiased and accurate" expert, a documenter in black and white. But Dakota churches were the sacred headquarters of tradition, charity, and neighborliness, and clergymen were powerful leaders in every community. Despite their own desires to be successful and up-to-date, the clergy had an enormous stake in maintaining the traditional ways of community life. As much as they welcomed reform, knew their towns needed help, and liked the idea of assisting the president, they did not want to be reformers. They were independent professionals, mediating between God and humankind. Still, they knew well that their position, like old-middle-class culture itself, was sorely threatened by the Dust Bowl crisis.

The clergy already had some experience with this kind of request. For years, rural sociologists had tried to enlist rural clergy in the Middle West to help them in their effort to "modernize" the church.[130] They wanted the rural church to stop focusing on faith and the particulars of denominationalism, to become "community conscious," and to sponsor clubs, meetings, and lectures not necessarily related to the church. The sociologists encountered a mixed response from the clergy. Some liberal, mostly urban, Protestant congregations took up these "community" missions from their national offices and promoted them locally. But researchers also reported that many rural clergymen were resistant to these new ideas, particularly to the implication that they should act less like ministers and more like experts or managers. One clergyman in South Dakota responded to a questionnaire on the role of his church in the community this way: "Ours is not one of the much publicized Social Gospel churches; we face the tremendous task of proclaiming adequately the Gospel message. . . . Whether the community has a baseball team . . . we believe, is not within the concern of the Christian church."[131]

As familiar as Roosevelt's subtextual request to the clergy was, it was no easier for them to address than it had ever been. In fact, the increasingly harsh circumstances of their lives made the letter even more difficult to answer clearly. Nineteen thirty-five had been a horrible year on the northern plains and 1936 promised to be even worse. Because they were employed—but dependent upon incredibly small salaries and the generosity of their parishioners—rural clergy were among the poorest members of their communities. Some churches were also in jeopardy. Frederick Errington, for example, was the last minister his Congregational church would ever hire.[132] In Napoleon, North Dakota, O. E. Kinzler was preaching in the basement of a new church the congregation could not afford to complete.[133] These kinds of experiences informed the clergy's judgment that their communities needed federal intervention. The more they recognized this need, however, the more they feared the consequences of it for their own positions.

Dorothea Lange, "Church on the Great Plains, South Dakota, 1938"
(courtesy Dorothea Lange Collection, The Oakland Museum, Oakland,
California)

The clergy's internal struggle was reflected most clearly not in their impressions of the New Deal per se, but in the subtexts of their letters. On one level, it appeared that they could hardly wait to respond to the president's questionnaire. They did exactly what he asked them to—and more. With only a few exceptions, the clergy were deferential, enthusiastic, and cooperative. Many wrote letters over three pages long; others enclosed newspaper clippings or reprints of sermons they had given. One man even sent along his résumé and offered to campaign for Roosevelt locally. The clergy were flattered by Roosevelt's request; it appealed to their own need for prestige and importance.[134]

A second look at the clergy letters, however, reveals that they remained troubled by Roosevelt's request. Specifically, they were disturbed by the conception of themselves as experts and used the letters to locate a place for themselves as moral reformers outside the formal structure of the bureaucracy. The first and most obvious way they did this was by relying on the word of God for their authority, thereby rejecting the language of science. Hactor Moe, for example, relied on passages in Jeremiah to explain why hard times had fallen on the promised land.[135] Believing that drought had been sent to earth as a punishment for sinfulness, John Drewelow of Mott, North Dakota, also feared God's retribution for the AAA's program of crop reduction and wrote, "Like in days of old we should rather produce what can be produced under prevailing conditions, and when there is a special abundance, lay by the surplus for a time of dearth."[136]

Not only did the clergy rely on the Bible, but also they strongly advised Roosevelt to do the same, saying in essence that the country's problems could not be studied by experts but only "apprehended by faith." So, instead of putting the New Deal into religion, as Roosevelt might have liked, they asked him to put religion into the New Deal. For example, W. W. Gunter of Rock Lake, North Dakota, asked Roosevelt to compare the country to the woman in Luke, who had "seen many physicians but never been cured."[137] N. W. Stoa from Parshall, North Dakota, was a great deal less cordial when he suggested, "It seems our beloved country would actually see prosperity if all our officers would guide our nation according to the will of the Lord as revealed in the Holy Prophets. Surely that means more than to merely have the right hand on I. Cor[inthians] Chapter 13 at the time of inauguration."[138]

Roosevelt probably expected to be told to rely on lessons from the Bible, but he may not have expected to be told how to reform his personal life. Ministering to him directly, however, was one more way the clergy cemented a place for themselves outside—or perhaps above—the new-middle-class bureaucracy. For example, some clergy chastised the president for his alleged drinking habits; one from North Dakota also criticized Roosevelt's lavish birthday party.[139] V. H. Dissen dug even deeper than this: Roosevelt's weekend fishing trips, family divorces, and "disregard for traffic laws" were reasons why Dissen had "lost confidence" in the New Deal.[140]

The clergy demonstrated what they believed was their most important contribution to the government by bestowing their blessing on its work. Nearly every letter ended with a prayer or benediction. "Your 'Social Security Program' will be like a balm in Gilead to the aged and the helpless poor," wrote C. E. Peters and H. M. Andersen of Viborg, South Dakota. "May God help you and spare you and bless you that you may be able to carry on."[141] A blessing like this was obviously a gift that no new-middle-class intellectual ever could (or would) give to the president. In this way, the clergy agreed to help the president, but only on their own terms and according to their own ideals. Their "counsel and help" was freely given, and yet it was not the product of scientific objectivity but of traditional old-middle-class values.

What the clergy thought of the role of "social science" in their communities was revealed in their descriptions of the New Dealers they had encountered there. All too often, it seemed, these were men associated with corruption and immorality. The new middle class "functionaries" who came to administer relief were "selfish and greedy" and were "chiselers and unworthy people," wrote Felix Hummer and Lorenz Weber.[142] In Milbank, South Dakota, Monseigneur Grabig complained that the administrator of relief there had been arrested for drinking and driving and performing other unmentionable acts of "filth" on the town's main thoroughfare.[143]

The problem was not that every individual bureaucrat in every town was immoral. The way the clergy saw it, the problem was that the operation of the bureaucracy threatened community stability—not to mention their own authority. The clergy complained, for example, that the system did not understand the unstated differences between community members, did not distinguish between "good" and "bad" people or between the "worthy" and "unworthy" poor. As Harold Mercier from Gann Valley, South Dakota, put it, in his town the relief system treated equally "honest, thrifty and dependable citizens" and "indifferent and shiftless" citizens. According to Reverend Egan of Madison, South Dakota, the relief system made these groups indistinguishable as it forced "good, substantial citizens," who "because of no fault of their [own] now find themselves without funds or property," to become just as dependent on the government as the "unemployed set."

The clergy found the New Deal programs most objectionable, then, when they seemed to usurp the authority of the clergy—and the old middle class in general—to define and prescribe cultural values in their own communities. In a world of independent producers, the clergy held a role, in the manufacture of morality and the production of character, equal to or greater than that of local businessmen. Suddenly, it seemed that the government, with its overwhelming power and privilege, was competing with them for both the moral education and the moral evaluation of local citizenry. From O. E. Kinzler's perspective in the basement of an unfinished church, the consequences of this kind of dishonest competition were disastrous. "As a whole," he contended, "the relief has lowered the moral standards. Three fourths of the reliefers spend nearly all their spare time in the saloon. Their families have nothing for the Sunday School or church. The churches of this town are just about to close for the lack of personal and financial support. One church has closed. But there are Four Saloons and I heard Seventeen Bootleggers. You say this is a dark picture. It cannot be made too dark."[144]

For Kinzler, like many other clergy, the darkest picture of all was one in which people could live their lives outside the guiding hand of the church and the strong arm of old-middle-class social control. The way he saw it, this grim picture of moral and cultural chaos was exactly the one the New Deal threatened to paint.

Although the clergy undoubtedly spoke for the most conservative members of their communities, the problem they articulated was common to all. First, the depression had placed the imperatives of need and power over those of equality, community, and traditional morality. At the same time, New Deal relief had offered to them a Faustian choice: if Dakotans accepted the government's help, as they so desperately needed and wanted to, they also had to accept the ideas and the power of the outsiders who controlled it. Complicating the choice further was that the "devil" in this case did not seem altogether unfamiliar to them but was, instead, a slightly altered version of themselves. As Enid Bern understood, change was good, but it came at a price.

This was the dilemma that the depression and the New Deal presented to all the people in North and South Dakota. How could the old middle class cooperate with and benefit from the New Deal, the new middle class, and modernity in general without being disembowelled by them? For rural people living in a "modern" world for half a century, this was a familiar enough problem. Nevertheless, Dakotans still had no ready solution. Over the course of the decade, they would employ several different strategies in their attempt to persist in the midst of change. Ultimately, they would succeed by making cultural compromises on a grand scale. Where they began, however, was not with compromise but with anger and frustration. Most Dakotans began trying to resolve the crisis on Main Street by resisting it.

5   RESISTANCE

Agrarian Insurgency and the

Farmers' Holiday Association

By the spring of 1932, many Dakota farmers were troubled—and angry. Drought and dust, together with low prices, high costs, and insurmountable interest rates, had made it impossible for them to make a living. But financial conditions alone did not account for the anger. Dakotans also believed that they were witnessing the wholesale destruction of the values and social structures upon which they had built their lives. These were times, the editor of North Dakota's *Dickinson Farmers' Press* contended, when "the good farmer [was] in equally bad straights [*sic*] as . . . the shiftless, improvident neighbor who never did . . . show any signs of honest industry and conscientiousness. A worthy farmer cannot be expected to sit back and watch his work of a lifetime taken away from him without raising his hand in protest."[1]

Protest they did. Between 1932 and 1935, thousands of Dakotans joined the Farmers' Holiday Association (FHA), a new farm organization championed by Milo Reno of the Iowa Farmers' Union. Founded to raise prices for farm commodities and to stop foreclosures on farm property, the FHA brought the farmers' concerns into the national spotlight. During the early New Deal period, the governors of five states, in addition to Henry Wallace and Franklin Roosevelt, listened to FHA leaders' proposals; few of these politicians, however, heard what they were actually saying. Farmers—from Dakota, at least—feared not just for their land, their families, and their communities, they feared for the survival of an entire way of life.[2]

Rescuing old-middle-class culture in the midst of the Great Depression was not a simple task. Nor have its complexities been fully appreciated since. Although most historians of the FHA have understood that farmers were fighting for more than economic remuneration, even its premier student, John Shover, underestimated the full breadth of the cultural issues at stake. Further, Shover misrepresented the supposed demise of farm radicalism at the hands of the New Deal. Rather than staging what he called a "revolt of tradition against modernism," the FHA was demanding a solution to the farm crisis that would perpetuate the mixture of old *and* new ways that gave meaning to their lives.[3] Thus when radical farmers signed on for the Agricultural Adjustment Act (AAA) in 1933, they were not surrendering to modernism but forging a compromise between themselves and their reformers. And, although joining forces with the government spelled the end of active protest for most Dakota farmers, some continued to look for alternatives to the New Deal's reforms. In short, the ideals, the actions, and even the "demise" of the FHA provide important windows on the cultural crisis of the Great Depression and on the way men and women on the northern plains first sought to resolve it.

When Dakota farmers joined the Farmers' Holiday Association, they had two important historical precedents upon which to base their actions. The first, of course, was the unique legacy of farm radicalism on the northern plains discussed in chapter 3. From the time of statehood until the 1930s, farmers in the Dakotas formed or joined at least five different farm organizations. The most important of these was the Nonpartisan League (NPL). Like the others, the NPL advocated the rights of small property owners and other "dirt farmers," emphasized their economic and moral importance to the nation, and implemented a host of reforms to protect them. In North Dakota, where the NPL had particular success, it established state-owned grain elevators, terminals, a bank, and a creamery. By doing so, the League suggested that the survival of petty entrepreneurship in modern American society depended both upon cooperation among property-owners and structural support from the state. Importantly, however, the NPL never advocated government control over production but only wanted regulation and state ownership of the traditionally exploitative industries of "middle men." The NPL demanded government help on its own terms (as the FHA would fifteen years later), without the interference of government experts who thought they knew what was best for farmers.[4]

It was the 1931 "Cow War" in southeastern Iowa that provided the immediate impetus for angry farmers to organize in protest.[5] The struggle of members of the Iowa Farmers' Union against a state-imposed tuberculosis test for livestock prepared the ground for the larger farm revolt. From a practical standpoint, it mobilized the disgruntled membership of the Union and thus facilitated Milo Reno's subsequent organizational campaign. But, from an ideological standpoint, the Cow War was even more prophetic: the ideas behind the initial struggle, the actions taken during it, and even the agreement that ended it paralleled closely the ideals, actions, and accommodations of the FHA. The Cow War was in fact a microcosm of later events that would involve thousands more farmers and last considerably longer.

Cedar County, Iowa, the hotbed of the Cow War, was both similar to and different from neighboring counties in the Dakotas. Land was more fertile in Iowa than in the Dakotas and the drought somewhat less severe. But, in some areas of western Iowa, the rates of bank failure, farm mortgage indebtedness, and foreclosure were just as high. Under these conditions, the compulsory tuberculin test was, as John Shover put it, "salt that stung the wound of economic discontent."[6] According to a 1929 state statute, all Iowa cattle had to be tested for tuberculosis in any county where more than 50 percent of farm owners approved of the program. Any livestock that tested positive were sold to slaughterhouses, with partial compensation from the state and federal government to the farmer. The testing was to be done by agents from the Agricultural College in Ames, veterinarians who often traveled great distances to the testing sites, were strangers to the farmers, and represented not only the government and its creed of scientific agriculture but also a rival farm organization, the Farm Bureau Federation (FBF).[7]

Iowa farmers had three complaints about the testing program: they distrusted the veterinarians; they felt frustrated by the inaccuracy of the testing and the meager compensation it brought; and, most importantly, they believed that their rights as independent property owners were being infringed. To most farmers, these three ideas were closely intertwined. When government authorities they had never liked forced them to comply with a law that, in their view, rarely worked, they felt a significant loss of autonomy. Milo Reno, future president of the FHA, voiced these conclusions in a characteristically vituperative fashion. The problem in Iowa, he contended, "lies in the fact that [the farmers'] property is no longer their own. Any little shyster who has come out of a certain college in this state can go to a farmers' property and conduct a test which is more apt to be wrong than right."[8]

The actions taken by angry farmers followed logically from the grievances they shared. Desiring local control over their property, they organized into small, community-based units of the Farmers' Protective Association (FPA) and took direct action to obstruct the testing. Similarly, drawing on a long history of cooperation, they made use of their "neighbors" to turn away the outsiders. In Tipton, West Liberty, and Wilton Junction, mobs of 200 to 500 farmers first met the veterinarians with stubborn determination and then with eggs, mud, and clubs. After several incidents like this, Governor Daniel Turner dispatched three regiments of the Iowa National Guard to Cedar County and arrested the leadership of the FPA. The soldiers remained in southeastern Iowa for more than two months, guaranteeing that all the cattle there would be tested.

According to most accounts, the Cow Warriors were defeated plainly and simply by the brute strength of the state police. But agricultural historian Theodore Saloutos has suggested another reason why farmers were willing to lay down their arms. Critical to the peacemaking in Iowa, Saloutos believes, was the state's agreement to allow farmers to choose their own veterinarians and, potentially, to receive more complete compensation for their livestock.[9] In this scenario, the farmers "gave in" not so much to brute force as to a compromise that preserved their ideal of local control. State leaders had rather cunningly, it now seems, held out to farmers a promise of ideological and cultural persistence in exchange for a significant increase in their own authority over farmers' property decisions.

As cunning as it may have been, this compromise only pacified farmers for a short time. Continuing concerns about declining income, decreased independence, and the increasing role of the government in agriculture erupted into the organization of the national Farmers' Holiday Association at the Iowa State Fair on 3 May 1932. By 1932, farmers from eight other midwestern states shared Iowans' fears, and together they were prepared to take even more radical action against the government. When the protests of this new organization were finally lain to rest, however, they would be stilled by a deal strikingly similar to the one made in Cedar County.

True to their heritage, North and South Dakotans lost no time spreading the word of the new farm protest organization.[10] Excited by Reno's powerful rhetoric and by the idea that farmers (like bankers) should have a "holiday" until the business climate improved, farm leaders hit the campaign trail with vigor unmatched since the heady days of 1915. Emil Loriks, a Farmers' Union official from Oldham, South Dakota, for example, logged more than 10,000 miles for the FHA in his Ford in the summer of 1932.[11] To the north, Usher Burdick and Charley Talbott worked through Farmers' Union locals to recruit as many as 50,000 state residents. "I brought a little baby back from Iowa," Talbott would boast later, "and Burdick made it into the largest farm organization in North Dakota."[12] Whether or not they were as large as their leaders claimed, the North and South Dakota Farmers' Holiday Associations undoubtedly had enthusiastic and broad-based support. In South Dakota, Loriks's steering committee included representatives from the Bankers' Association and the South Dakota Chamber of Commerce.[13] As for North Dakota, the editor of the *McKenzie County Farmer* contended that "practically without exception every citizen in North Dakota is behind the proposed 'Holiday' or strike."[14]

The ideas that interested farmers (and small businessmen) in the FHA were encapsulated in resolutions written soon after the initial

THEN, HE WOULD START SOMETHING!

John M. Baer cartoon advocating farmers' adoption of a cost-of-production scheme, 1932 (courtesy State Historical Society of North Dakota)

recruiting campaigns. The South Dakota organization, for example, gave voice to a variety of plans, including tax relief for farmers and tax increases for corporations. But their most important goal was to raise prices for farm products. In a radio address in September 1932, Loriks pleaded, "We ask you farmers to STOP bankrupting yourselves and the business institutions of your towns by throwing your farm commodities on the market below the cost of production. Everybody realizes that cost of production for the farmers means prosperity for all."[15] In North Dakota, the resolutions passed in a Jamestown meeting in August were similar: along with NPL-inspired proposals for railroad regulation and an increase in available currency was the bottom line—farmers should not and would not sell their products until they received at least the cost of production for them.[16]

If there was a single rallying-call that united the various state associations, it was the notion they called "cost of production." For ordinary farmers, cost of production acted like a campaign slogan indicating their opposition to the federal government's domestic allotment plan, but for Reno and other leaders it was an intricate formula for establishing just compensation based on farmers' expenses.[17] In either case, however, it captured many of the complicated conservative and progressive, traditional and modern ideals of old-middle-class culture. Ultimately, the cost-of-production program would not be the be-all and end-all for farmers; it was rather easily replaced by the AAA. But the ideals and aspirations represented by cost of production did not disappear so easily. They had to be addressed by the advocates of the new system before it could generate any support at all.

Perhaps the most traditional ideal of the FHA was captured in the phrase "cost of production." As national Farmers' Union secretary John Simpson explained in detail at Senate hearings on the domestic allotment plan (which he ardently opposed), it was the farmers' ability to *produce*, and to make independent decisions about *production*, that needed the government's assistance and support.[18] Thus the cost-of-production scheme would pay a fixed price for whatever the farmer sold on the domestic market through licensed processors and leave it up to him to decide how much extra to market at world prices. "Never try to regulate the farmer," Simpson told senators. "Turn him loose. If he is fond of work, he will have a big excess that he does not get much for; but what the homefolks use he will surely get paid for it."[19] Simpson compared farmers not to industrial workers in a "worldwide agricultural plant," as his opponent Henry Wallace did, but to owners of public utilities.[20] In short, the FHA farmers wanted a program that would define them first and foremost as producers and businessmen and that would leave them in full control of property and production decisions.

And yet, these farmer/businessmen did not want merely to be producers and had no intention whatsoever of returning to the strictly self-sufficient world of their distant forefathers. The FHA farmers wanted to get a "fixed price" for producing what they chose to produce so that they in turn could consume what they chose to consume. Like the editor of the *Minot Daily News*, farm leaders generally agreed that it was the farmers' "lack of buying power" that hindered their overall well-being.[21] In fact, the cost-of-production formula itself included a standard budgetary allocation for consumption. As Simpson saw it, the average American family was actually *entitled* to consume a wide range of goods and services, from household wares to higher education, hospitalization during childbirth, dental care, and even "some recreation."[22] So important to farmers was consumption that Simpson contended that the higher prices they received for their crops would ensure lowered outputs. Given the choice, he argued, even a farmer would rather consume—shop, take vacations, and buy cars—than produce. Pretty soon, he warned, "you [senators] will be complaining about the old fellow being shiftless and not working enough."[23]

This strange image of the government encouraging farmers to drive around in their Fords while their fields lay fallow was founded on a second idea that similarly mixed new and old ideals of farm politics—the notion of agrarian economic essentialism. As Clifford Anderson has argued, the tenets of American agrarianism underwent a significant metamorphosis in the 1920s and 1930s, with the "emphasis shifting from moral to economic terms."[24] The new agrarianism, based on the economic essentialism instead of the moral exceptionalism of farm life, was central to the thinking of FHA leaders. "We are essentially producers and we are also the chief consumer," contended Loriks. "[Those of us] who think in terms of building a new economic interest are possessed of a vision. [We] are the ones who will ultimately change society."[25] At bottom, then, the cost-of-production ideal rested on the notion that "the farmer [was] the man on whom depended the prosperity of everyone";[26] hence, his work deserved guaranteed support.

Finally, the underlying mixed ideal that welded all the others together in the cost-of-production scheme was the importance of local and individual control and state support. As we have already seen, the FHA plan allowed farmers to make decisions about production. The farmer was "let loose" (if completely insured) in his own small business. Faced with Roosevelt's proposed domestic allotment plan, this scheme also counterposed the need for state or federal control. The domestic allotment plan, Simpson averred, would require "an army of workers"—200,000, by his calculations.[27] The cost-of-production plan, on the other hand, would require far fewer workers and, moreover, would shift the burden of supervision from the farmer to the processor.[28] In this world, no new-middle-class bureaucrats would find their way onto farmers' land or into their record-books. In short, the FHA farmers did not envision a world without an active state. Rather, they envisioned a world with a supportive, interventionist state that, despite its activity on behalf of the farm industry, still recognized that the changes it sought were best left "up to you and me"[29]—the individual farmer and his community.

Like the Cow Warriors, the FHA farmers took actions that logically followed, in form and in content, from the grievances and objectives stated in their resolutions. The most widely publicized action was the farm strike of October 1932, but in North and South Dakota farmers employed two other strategies: antiforeclosure strategies and farm legislation. In fact, although North and South Dakota's strikes were generally less successful than those in Iowa and Minnesota, their organizations were more effective in stopping farm foreclosures and in enacting strong farm legislation.

The first concerted action of the national organization was the farm strike called on 21 October 1932, less than three months after the initial organizational campaign.[30] The idea behind the strike was simple enough: since farmers were not getting back what it cost them to produce their crops, they were determined to withhold them from the market until prices rose to that level. Again, the strike underscored the farmers' desire to control their own property, in this case their crops, and to demonstrate to the nation the profound economic importance of their industry. As they had for many years, the farmers drew on their common desire to overcome middlemen and speculators and on their common notion of agrarian essentialism to justify their actions.

But they depended on a third and somewhat more precarious shared ideal when they planned the strike. As we have seen, the ideal of cooperation and mutual assistance was a critical component of old-middle-class ideology, and this was as true for the striking farmers as for any other Dakotan. To the editors of the *Dunn County Journal*, for example, the ability to show cooperative strength was especially important, since "the farmer has always been secretly regarded as a 'dub' by men of affairs. . . . Get ten farmers together and you will have a scrap, they say."[31] But like the others in their class, farmers wanted to cooperate not only to show what good neighbors they could be but also to derive the individual benefits it promised. Emil Loriks, for example, defined the ideal of cooperation as "neighbor helping neighbor in business . . . [toward] the welfare of each member of society."[32] Similarly, the farm strike depended upon neighborly cooperation, each farmer supporting the next, so that in the end all could receive higher prices.

Not surprisingly, the tension inherent in the notion of cooperation for individual gain was both the doing and the undoing of the farm strike. Not long after it began, farmers discovered that prices were not rising as quickly as they had hoped, in part because some farmers were not cooperating and others were only cooperating long enough to see a slight rise before they cashed in for themselves. In light of such difficulties, most state leaders were left to decide whether or not farmers should picket local roads and forcibly stop all produce shipments. While Loriks and Burdick vacillated, tempers flared (especially in southeastern South Dakota and northwestern North Dakota), and the widespread support the organizations had enjoyed began to slip away.[33] Finally, Reno called off the strike from Des Moines and local leaders followed suit.

Although the farm strike did not succeed in raising prices by more than a few cents, the actions taken by Dakota FHA members against foreclosures and evictions were much more successful, largely because they made more successful use of the traditional habits of neighborly cooperation. Beginning in the fall of 1932 and continuing into 1935 and 1936, farmers organized on the local level to protect farm and household properties from the auction block. In general, most antiforeclosure actions had two stages. First, when farmers heard that a neighbor was close to losing his property, an FHA-established "Council of Defense" mediated between the farmer and his creditors, seeking an extension or a refinancing of his debts.[34] Next, if these conciliatory

Members of the Farmers' Holiday Association stopping a foreclosure sale in Casselton, North Dakota (photograph by George Tice, courtesy State Historical Society of North Dakota)

attempts failed and a foreclosure proceeded as planned, farmers would gather for a "penny," "barnyard," or "Sears and Roebuck" sale. At these, huge numbers of farmers gathered to intimidate other bidders and bid ludicrously low prices on the items for sale. At the end of the auction, all the property went back to the original owner.

Colorful stories of antiforeclosure actions abound in the written and remembered histories of the Dakotas, which illustrates the strength of the farmers' desire to protect their property and work cooperatively. An early penny sale in Milbank, South Dakota, netted only $6.30 to the auctioneer but earned twice that amount to pay for lunch for out-of-town guests.[35] North of the border, however, sales sometimes took on a less sociable tone. In one situation, a sheriff tried to outsmart farmers by arriving at a farmstead at dawn and finishing the eviction proceedings before protesting farmers could arrive. When they came, however, the sheriff was told "in no uncertain words, that if everything was not put back in its proper place he would have to suffer the consequences."[36] In another, the Steele County FHA executive board paid a personal call on a banker preparing to foreclose on a woman whose husband had recently killed himself. FHA chairman Ed Cooper pointed at the banker and reportedly said, "If you foreclose on that woman, we'll hang you." He did not and neither did they.[37] Most common, however, were the many times North Dakota farmers called upon the authority of the state to halt an eviction proceeding. In Casselton in 1934, for example, several hundred farmers had gathered to prevent the eviction of a tenant farmer when a telegram arrived to do their work for them: "You are hereby directed not to evict Axel Hanson of Casselton," it read, "Signed, Governor William Langer."[38]

"Wild Bill" Langer's direct support of penny sales reflected farm legislation strategies. State leaders, in addition to supporting strikes and antiforeclosure actions, worked hard to achieve state political and legislative support for their broad programs of reform. In South Dakota, for example, the 1932 Democratic sweep of the state legislature carried several members of the FHA to Pierre, where they worked diligently to enact farm relief proposals. Chief among these was the Ore Tax bill, sponsored by Emil Loriks and Oscar Fosheim, the "Gold Dust Twins."[39] Basically, the Ore Tax bill sought to increase the burden of taxation on William Randolph Hearst's Homestake Mine in the Black Hills and to relieve farmers' tax burden accordingly. The measure was controversial and evoked classic neo-Populist, anticorporate, NPL rhetoric from its sponsors. "South Dakota is helping to nourish these beasts [the Hearst interests] whose tentacles reach into every corner of our land," Loriks contended. "Do you know that they are sucking eighteen to nineteen million dollars out of one gold mine in South Dakota annually? . . . You members of the Farmers' Union . . . [are not fighting] just a local enemy—you [are fighting] the biggest menace to democracy in America today."[40] After sponsors agreed to decrease the amount of new taxation somewhat, the Gold Severance Act was passed in the 1935 legislative session.

The North Dakota state government (again staying true to its heritage) supported the FHA initiatives even more directly than the South

Governor William Langer
(courtesy State Historical Society of North Dakota)

Dakota government did. In fact, two actions taken by Governor Langer were unmatched by any other politician nationwide.[41] The first was Langer's foreclosure moratorium, which granted the National Guard authority to prevent foreclosure on any farm or small business property. Langer had never minced words on evictions. "Shoot the banker if he comes on your farm," he proclaimed during the 1932 gubernatorial campaign. "Treat him like a chicken thief."[42] Usher Burdick wrote later that Langer's moratorium was based on an 1862 territorial law that disallowed all foreclosures when farmers "could not get a fair price due to circumstances beyond their control."[43] Nevertheless, bankers and other businessmen fought against the moratorium, and the state justices fought over it. In the meantime, however, the authority of the proclamation and the confidence it gave farmers helped to stop innumerable foreclosure proceedings and kept many farm families at home in North Dakota, at least for a time. In rural counties, nearly 100 percent of the electorate voted for Langer, even when he came under indictment by a federal court. Rumor has it that some North Dakota farmers continued to vote for him as a write-in candidate long after he had died.[44]

The second action Langer took in support of the FHA and farmers was the Wheat Embargo.[45] Like the farm strike, the Wheat Embargo, begun in the fall of 1933, was intended to halt all sales of wheat until the price rose to cost-of-production levels. All shipments of Number One Dark North Spring Wheat and Number Two Amber Durum were terminated within the borders of the state. With the exception of a six-day lift, Langer's embargo remained in force until 15 January 1934, when it was ruled unconstitutional. During the three-month period, prices rose somewhat but not to cost-of-production levels, in part because no other state governors would join in Langer's actions. The embargo did succeed, however, in bringing Langer to national attention and into a war of words with Secretary of Agriculture Henry Wallace. To Langer, the farmer was "the forgotten man of the New Deal" and Wallace was just one more "professor."[46] To Wallace, Langer was another "hell-raising boy" in open alliance with a "misery-ridden, desperate farm group" with whom he had "never seen eye-to-eye."[47]

Taken together, FHA actions in North and South Dakota—the strike, antiforeclosure actions, and political motions—demonstrated the strength of the farmers' conviction that they deserved state-sponsored assistance in receiving a fair price for their products and in protecting their property. "We have the right to ask the federal government for aid and assistance in times of great emergencies," cried Loriks. "It is the duty of government to come to [our] aid."[48] Nevertheless, these actions also showed what kind of state aid the farmers wanted—overarching government protections and guarantees that would leave the major business decisions to individual farmers and local communities. Even the Wheat Embargo, the most authoritarian of all the farm actions, did not tell farmers what to grow, or where or when to grow it; nor did it keep them from being paid for their product. Instead, it hindered the actions of perennial foes of the farm radicals—grain dealers, middlemen, and speculators. In other words, FHA ideals and actions seemed to derive directly from the complicated culture its members shared. Traditional in its desire for autonomy, independence, local control, and cooperation, but modern in its emphasis on state aid, consumption, and individual gain, the FHA was a clear expression of the paradox deep in the heart of old-middle-class culture in the Great Depression.

Detailing the supposed demise of the FHA is at once a complicated and a simple business: while the leaders of various state organizations went their separate ways in the mid-1930s, the farmers generally went in only one direction—toward support for the New Deal and the AAA. Together with Milo Reno, William Lemke, and E. E. Kennedy, some farmers supported the blatantly anti-Semitic, perhaps even antidemocratic, Union party in 1936 because, as Alan Brinkley suggests, it continued to nurture their communal and antibureaucratic ideals.[49] Others found solace in Bill Langer's continuing radicalism, the alternative proposals of the Townsend Plan, and the Frazier/Lemke Refinancing Act.[50] But few farmers in the Dakotas pursued these alternatives as vigorously as they had supported the FHA. To the contrary, after the government's program of domestic allotment had been explained to them in the winter of 1933–34, as many as 95 percent of Dakota farmers in some counties signed up for it and dropped their plea for cost of production. On one level, then, farmers' allegiances were bought out by the New Deal's offer of cash-in-hand today rather than a thoroughly reformed agricultural system tomorrow. As we shall see, however, some aspects of the program that paid them immediately were like the program they were fighting for. Hence, it was easy enough to accept.

Although we can never know what farmers thought or said about the AAA in their private moments, we can know what they were told about the program and, to some extent, how they responded to that information.[51] Like all good new-middle-class workers, the county agents who were sent to "educate" and enroll North Dakota farmers in the AAA wrote careful reports to their supervisors that were, in turn, carefully filed at the Agricultural College in Fargo.[52] Although they originated from quite diverse counties, the reports held a great deal in common and, in fact, outlined a similar chain of events. After voicing their initial objections and (in some cases) trying to fudge their applications, farmers responded positively to the agents' pleas for cooperation. Finally, with administrative authority delegated to men in the community, the AAA got under way.

Understandably enough, the AAA agents were not particularly forthcoming in their descriptions of the problems they encountered when they first arrived in their counties. Nevertheless, a few of the farmers' initial reservations about the AAA can be discerned between the lines of the agents' reports. For starters, very few farmers had affection for county agents. A vast majority of Dakota farmers were members of the Farmers' Union, the most politically radical and small-farm-oriented of the three farm organizations in the twentieth century, and, like their fellows in Iowa, they often associated county agents with the FBF, with its large-farm politics and big-business connections.[53] Moreover, Dakota farmers had always had mixed feelings, at best, about county agents' attempts to "help."[54] In North Dakota, county agents came to work in most counties between 1915 and 1925, but by 1928 more than two-thirds of them had been sent home, the first victims of county government economizing. Even those who managed to keep their jobs, like Ben Barrett of Emmons County, had to fight for them with body and soul. Barrett stayed put only by taking a steep cut in salary, agreeing to put Farmers' Union members on his steering committee, and risking his life in a breakneck attempt to talk to each of his major opponents just before a countywide meeting was held to fire him.[55]

Thus when the time came to take the AAA to the farmers, and the USDA turned to the local county agents to do it, they had to assign "emergency agents" to cover many of the counties in North Dakota. Some of these new men were surprised just to see farmers show up at their offices. Charles Eastgate of Stark County remarked, for example, that farmers were beginning to follow his advice in matters of record- and book-keeping. "Many of them have had to come to the county agent for the first time," he remarked, "and some are finding out that he does not have hoof and horns and that he does have some valuable suggestions in the handling of farm business."[56] In Ransom County, farmers began to come in more and more, but the agent had to depend upon local businessmen and prominent farmers to do the explaining for them and to set "right misconceptions prevalent before the establishment of the emergency agent's office as a medium of disseminating authoritative information."[57]

Emergency agents, however, ran into problems that went beyond the farmers' distrust. They had to try to counter certain "misconcep-tions" that farmers harbored about the program. No agent went into great detail here, but most suggested that the problem centered—as we might expect—on a "false prejudice" against the idea of acreage control.[58] New settlers in Sioux County, for example, could not under-stand how they could ever produce less than what they had produced on newly broken and drought-stricken land.[59] Similarly, the German-Russians of Sheridan County "were afraid that the government was giving them a Russian Five-year Plan . . . [and telling] them how to run their farms."[60] Even more common, however, were the farmers' complaints about the program's red tape. Almost to a man, the agents reported that the program was confusing to the farmers, especially to "slow-minded German-Russian and Indian" farmers.[61] In Renville County, the agent said that one particular form that demanded a care-ful mapping of farm boundaries was "a little too much" for most of the applicants.[62]

For all the ways in which the AAA application was probably quite confusing, one of the most common "errors" the farmers made seemed to be not so much a product of their "slow-mindedness" as of their continued resistance to the idea of production control and domestic allotment. Again, in almost every case, agents reported that farmers overestimated the past production levels of their farms in order to en-sure a higher allotment under the plan. When added together, all of the farmers "mistakes" equaled huge "overruns" for the county as a whole. In Renville County, for example, the agent was left with 45,000 acres above what the home office had assigned him. His explanation of the source of the overrun was simple enough: some of the initial census figures had been inaccurate, many property boundaries had been "mixed up" since homesteading days, most production figures were "just estimates," and in every township some of the farmers were "liars."[63]

This suggestion of continued resistance to the AAA, even among its applicants, begins to unravel the complicated web of reasons why Da-kota farmers agreed to sign up for the AAA at all. One reason was as obvious to observers at the time as it has been to historians ever since: Dakota farmers wanted and desperately needed money—and as much of it as they could get. Moreover, as we have seen, they believed they deserved to receive support from the federal government. In Ransom County, the agent feared that farmers did not understand the plan's "full significance" but "rather were interested in it solely as to the amount of money possible for them to receive from the government."[64] In beleaguered Renville County, the situation was much the same. Nearly all the farmers' questions "concerned only the amount of money they were going to get." Agent J. A. Bartruff even suspected that his clients did not have faith in the AAA for its own sake but in "absolute despair . . . were willing . . . to try anything."[65] In Benson County, the farmers' economic considerations had perhaps the most ironic consequences of all. Thrilled that they were finally coming to him to learn more about planting, seeding, and harvesting efficiently, the agent nevertheless knew all too well what had accounted for their change of heart: their desire to reap as much as possible from their limited acreage and thus to make more money from it than the government had planned.[66]

As important as these economic considerations were, there was also a more subtle reason why farmers agreed to go along with the domestic allotment program. Like the Cow War compromise, the AAA seemed to allow for a high degree of ideological and cultural persistence even as it required farmers to relinquish some individual authority to the government. Whether or not the New Deal administrators conceived of it this way, they were savvy in their approach. Although some of them wanted to reform the culture of the old middle class, they did not underestimate its strength and armed themselves accordingly. In the end, they won the farmers over not so much with weapons of force as with gentle persuasion.

The way that AAA agents appealed to farmers on a cultural rather than a strictly economic level is often acknowledged as one of the reasons for the program's success. M. L. Wilson and Henry Wallace insisted that the programs, once under way, be supervised by local citizens. The North Dakota agents reported enthusiastically about this approach and the reasons why it seemed to work. Like the agent in Ransom County, they set up local committees to help process paperwork, to answer questions, and even to "adjust" the overruns on final figures. They hoped that using local men this way would help "in forming a favorable opinion of the program as a whole."[67] The agent in

Sioux County was the most forthcoming here. He explained that "people [must] feel that it [the AAA] was their association and not some association forced on them by outsiders." For this reason, he wrote a weekly column in a local newspaper and always gave it "a local touch . . . so that people reading it would feel that it was their county's program that was being organized."[68]

Related to this was the way in which the AAA allowed farmers to retain limited control over production decisions while it nevertheless defined their roles chiefly as consumers. The cost-of-production plan emphasized consumption, but it was in subordination to its image of the farmer as a producer/businessman. As farmers figured out quickly enough, the AAA only told them how many acres they could plant on; it did not say what they had to plant there or how much they could reap from those acres. In its loopholes, then—including that which could allow for some "overestimation" of previous yields—the AAA allowed farmers to retain a measure of individual control over production, no matter how limited (or even ineffective) that control eventually might be. At the same time, it gave tacit support to the notion that agriculture was such an important industry that it deserved the government's wholehearted assistance.

Finally, the AAA and its representatives borrowed heavily (and heavy-handedly) from the farmers' familiar language of cooperation for individual gain. In official parlance, all participants in the AAA were called "cooperators" and all nonparticipants were called "non-cooperators." But the gentle rhetorical persuasion went further than labels. In his letter to farmers at the beginning of the AAA campaign, agent C. W. Wolla of Nelson County fit in the words "co-operate" or "co-operation" at every moment he could. In one place, he was even more culturally correct: he asked them to "co-operate in a hearty and neighborly way."[69] Importantly, the term could also be used as a not-so-gentle rebuke against the farmers' acquisitiveness. In Ransom County, the agent told his clients that, whatever they thought about it, "the allotment payment was not to be a gift or even a subsidy, but was rather a payment to be well-earned by co-operating."[70] We can imagine that the moralistic harshness of his words may have fallen on deaf ears in the meeting hall. As the farmers saw it, they for generations had "well-earned" their payment from the government, whatever it was called; cooperating together to receive benefits as individuals came naturally enough to them to make the whole program sound easy and, indeed, even familiar.

So it was, through a combination of economic inducements and ideological persuasions, that most of the farmers on the northern plains came to accept the AAA and to set aside the most potent weapons of farm protest. For each farmer individually, this compromise did not seem so great, even though the domestic allotment plan differed substantially from the cost-of-production plan he probably preferred. Even after agreeing that the government could decide how many acres they would plant, farmers were left with much of what they had demanded initially: protection for their roles both as producers and consumers, local control in administrative matters, an unwritten understanding of agrarian essentialism, and the ideal of farmer cooperation. As John Shover has remarked, Milo Reno and the radical standouts of the FHA could offer little more to members than continued sacrifice in exchange for the hope of an unchanged world. The New Deal, on the other hand, asked for only a little bit of sacrifice in exchange for cultural persistence and a lot of cash. For farmers in the AAA, the future seemed theirs to control—bright, prosperous, and, for the most part, still unchanged. What radical farmers could not anticipate, however, was that their cooperation with the government would become one of the most important developments of the New Deal period, and that it would have perplexing consequences for generations to come.

6   TRADING

Dakota Farm Women and the

New Structures of Patriarchy

When Dakota farmers struggled to save their land, maintain their way of life, and come to terms with the New Deal, they did not work alone. In the barnyards, gardens, kitchens, and bedrooms of Dakota farms, women confronted the same multifaceted devastation that men did. And yet, Dakota farm women's experience in the Great Depression was also unique. At once members of and outsiders from the old middle class, women brought a different perspective to the struggle with modernity. Further, they developed relationships with different kinds of new-middle-class representatives. Ultimately, they took a much more positive outlook on the changes that were wrought, at least in the domestic sphere. As Dakota women began to think of themselves more as consumers than producers, more as farm housewives than farm wives, more as helpers than partners, they believed their difficult, dangerous, and often-belittled lives could only improve.[1] Even so, they rarely suspected what was at stake in the trade.

Dakota women shared the burden of farm production throughout the early twentieth century. In fact, these "invisible farmers" were the producers of goods for home use as well as goods for cash sale.[2] According to a government report issued in 1920, for example, 89 percent of women in the central United States cared for flocks of poultry; they raised chicks, collected eggs, and slaughtered mature birds. The average flock of 102 birds indicated that as many as half were raised for sale, not home consumption.[3] Additionally, 93 percent of midwestern women participated in dairy production and 33 percent sold the butter they made for cash. Sixty-seven percent had sole responsibility for the farm's garden.[4] Farm women also contributed to the family's income by producing as much as 70 percent of what it consumed, from preserves to pies, quilts to coats, diapers to dolls.[5] And, of course, they bore, raised, and taught children, thereby increasing the farm's labor force. In every Dakota community, women prided themselves on the contributions of their kitchens, gardens, cows, flocks, and broods; they knew that they were crucial to the farm's survival.[6]

The way most women spoke of it, productive work was not just an important way of helping their husbands, it was an indication of their shared class status. Whatever the realities of male supremacy in the household, Dakota farm women believed that their work made them partners with men on the farm. One South Dakota woman saw farming this way: "What team work this farming takes! . . . [I see] the farm family as a team hooked to a piece of machinery. . . . The Husband and Wife as the lead team, while the children followed behind pulling their shares of the load, when they are old enough to have been broken to the harness."[7] In fact, not to produce was not to be a farm wife at all. Writing in 1938 about a young wife's frustrations on the newly broken prairie, Rose Wilder Lane associated idleness with prostitution. "What's killing me is being no use. I can't even trade-in my eggs and butter to help on the groceries. I'm nothing but an expense. It's not right. It's against nature. It makes me feel like we're not married."[8]

Scholars consider the old middle class to be something like a "family class"—one in which the independence of a family farm or a "Mom and Pop" grocery store depends on the voluntary exploitation of all family members and in which all members share the status that productive labors afford.[9] And yet, as real women have always known, Mom and Pop are rarely equal partners at the store. However much they pro-

Mrs. Karl Maag tends her family's garden in Gregory County, South Dakota (Dakota Farmer, *courtesy Intertec Publishing Corporation*)

duced for the farm, Dakota farm women did not participate fully in financial decisions, nor did they share in the distribution of the farm's profits.[10] In fact, in the 1920s and 1930s, it was still widely understood that a married woman's labor and its products actually *belonged* to her husband to do with what he pleased. In 1920, for example, only 16 percent of midwestern women retained the money they made trading eggs and butter.[11] Also, at a time when the frequency of sexual relations remained "the man's say-so," few women had access to reliable birth control.[12] More often than not, a woman's "marriage contract resembled an indenture between master and servant" more than a partnership between petty proprietors, and the work she did resembled a duty more than a business opportunity.[13]

But women's work did not just support the structures of old-middle-class patriarchy; it also provided the foundations of women's culture, where some women found the very kind of status and intimacy missing in their marriages. As Glenda Riley has pointed out, women on the plains had a great deal more in common with each other than they did with their husbands.[14] Indeed, one of the most difficult things for women about coming west was leaving behind female relatives and friends.[15] As a result, they tried to reproduce the intimacies of women's relationships in their new communities. For some, like Laura Ingalls Wilder's mother, Caroline, this meant organizing a sewing circle with a Swedish neighbor who spoke no English and whose husband Caroline believed "would never become more than an hired man."[16] In settled communities, women gathered regularly (and perhaps more selectively) to quilt, exchange recipes, and help one another during confinements, illnesses, and threshing times. Home production lessons, home remedies, and even midwifery skills were shared among women, passing from mother to daughter in a web of knowledge and skill menfolk had little or nothing to do with—despite their overall authority within society.[17]

Women's production in the early twentieth century must be seen as a crucial part of the farm economy. At the same time, however, it must be remembered for what it was—hard, exhausting, sometimes debilitating labor that was not always as fulfilling as we might like to recall. As a woman from Towner County put it, "I think—yes, not only think but know that man's life is easier than woman's. . . . I often think of that old saying, 'Man works from sun to sun but woman's work is never done.'"[18] Women's work, however, did not just tie them to menfolk who "owned" their labor. It also provided a central bond in their relationships with other women. In the 1930s, Dakota women's work would become even more crucial and even harder than before. As a result, many women would begin to consider ways in which their working lives could be made less taxing. But, when they did so, they found that maintaining bonds with other women based on shared expertise and skill would become the most challenging task of all.

Beginning in the late 1920s, drought and dust severely diminished the chores traditionally associated with men's farm production. There was little farm work to do in a region "blown out" by dust storms. At the same time, however, those conditions increased the importance of women's production. As Dorothy Schwieder has demonstrated in detail, Dakota women produced "half or even more" of a farm family's total cash income in the 1930s by increasing the size of gardens and poultry flocks and the amount of eggs, butter, and cream for sale.[19] Equally important were the ways in which farm women saved their families' money. All over America, women practiced "small economies," like making "last-year's dresses into this year's styles."[20] And, in North and South Dakota, these economies were hardly small. There, farm women made "Pillsbury's Best" flour sacks into underwear, men's suits into boy's pants and coats, worn-out shoes into wearable shoes, corn cobs and Russian thistle into fuel, ashes into cleanser, and any scraps of fabric into "something for the children" at Christmas. Altogether, women's farm production in the 1930s "often became the main stream that provided life and sustenance to all concerned."[21]

However sustaining it was, women's work in the 1930s was as physically taxing as it had ever been, and perhaps even more so. Ann Marie Low's descriptions of cleaning up from a dust storm and hauling water in a drought suggest that the peculiar labors of the 1930s could damage a woman's health beyond repair. In 1936, "North Dakota Homemaker," a contributor to the *Dakota Farmer*'s "Home Page," asked readers how many had thought, "Oh dear, there are so many things to do and every one of them must be done by me. I don't know where to begin."[22] Along with the stress of "making do or doing without,"[23] developed new reasons for an ancient fear—isolated childbirth. With many fewer midwives, less gas for the car, fewer telephones, and no money to pay, what if a doctor couldn't be reached—or wouldn't come—when a baby was due?[24]

It was also a strangely dissonant moment in American history for Dakota women's labors to become more, not less, important to the economy. On the northern plains, as elsewhere, women had entered the paid work force in record numbers in the early twentieth century. In 1925, 44,000 South Dakota women were gainfully employed in over thirty occupations.[25] In the 1930s, however, public opinion against the employment of married women reached a feverish pitch, and both states banned their employment by the government. Many married women continued to work outside the home, and women's home productions increased; yet the value of all kinds of women's work was under siege. In 1936, one reader of the *Dakota Farmer* even wondered about the work women did on their own farms: "Is it fair for a farmer's wife to cheat a young man out of a job [as a hired hand]?"[26]

Americans worried about the effects of women's work for three reasons. First, most Americans, including the administrators of New Deal relief, believed that support given to a woman was support taken away from a man.[27] Secondly, industries and corporations worried that if women were busy producing in the 1930s they would not have enough time or interest in consuming manufactured products and therefore would delay economic recovery.[28] Finally, many social workers and "family relations professionals" feared the effect of gender-role reversal on the self-esteem of unemployed husbands and warned against the possibility of abandonment and family breakdown.[29]

Although they were never studied by sociologists, Dakota homes in which farmers were "blown out" and farm wives were busier than ever were probably not the most tranquil milieus. Two Dakota women told Jeanne Westin in the 1970s that the poorer their families became, the crankier and more abusive their menfolk became. When Ella Wesner called her husband for dinner, for example, he often just ignored her. When it came time for bed, however, he was attentive enough; she "had to give in to keep the peace." "He wanted to be the head of everything," she recalled, "including me."[30] Young Edna Anderson couldn't remember "how many times [she] got whipped for hardly batting an eye."[31] In such trying circumstances, it was best, many women concluded, to be both productive and submissive. "Don't forget that when you married your husband," suggested Mrs. L. H. of Meade

County to a young woman who told the "Home Page" that she wanted to help more often with farm work, "he automatically became the bread-winner—the head of house. Why take the responsibilities from him? Let him shoulder the duties and he will think more of you for it. . . . Many women are the managing factors of the farm and house, but do it with tact . . . not muscle."[32]

Given these difficult circumstances, it should not surprise us at all to discover that most Dakota farm women hoped for an easier, safer, and more "tactful" way of life in the 1930s; nor is it surprising that they listened attentively to the myriad representatives of urban mass society who claimed they could provide it. In a region where only one home in ten had electricity or running water (compared with nine in ten in Cleveland), the working lives of women more closely resembled those of seventeenth- than twentieth-century women. And, to make matters worse, Dakota women knew their lives did not have to be so hard. In 1935, one utterly exhausted woman wrote to the *Dakota Farmer*'s "Home Page" and explained how difficult life was without the kinds of conveniences other women enjoyed. "When one has not modern conveniences, one can't keep the house bright; especially when one has no rugs, no paint on the floor, nor anything else of that sort to make things look nice. . . . It is very different in beautiful houses where everything runs with power and everything is up-to-date. . . . How nice it would be for . . . hard-working women to enjoy pushing a dust mop along waxed floors, instead of scrubbing slivery unpainted floors. I would gladly trade."[33]

It was long before the Great Depression, however, that Dakota farm women had begun hoping to trade old labors for new conveniences. So much had changed by 1930, in fact, that an advertisement for the Dakota Home Service boasted, "We do not see many home-made [goods] now and we are glad of it. Yes we are glad because farm folks in the Dakatas [*sic*] can use their time to better advantage. If we expect others to buy our products we must be prepared to buy their goods."[34] An advertisement like this both mirrored and reinforced changes taking place in women's home production. There were, undoubtedly, plenty of homemade socks worn on the northern plains that year. Even so, purchasing "ready-made" and other manufactured goods had become an accepted part of the farm economy by that time and was unquestionably considered to be women's work.

Only very few Dakota pioneers settled the plains before the advent of industrial capitalism, and thus only those few faced complete self-sufficiency. For most pioneers, following the train across the plains meant guaranteed access to a market for wheat and the availability of at least a few manufactured goods: salt, flour, sugar, nails, fabrics.[35] Still, when trips to town were as infrequent as once or twice a year, women were not always brought along. "Trading"—which often included bartering or negotiating over price—was up to menfolk armed with their family's wish list. In the 1910s and 1920s, better roads into town, rural free delivery to the countryside, and the ubiquitous Sears and Roebuck catalogue made "shopping" a much more regular part of Dakota life.[36] At the same time, a new cast of experts and advisors began to support the notion that buying things was as natural a part of women's domestic responsibilities as making them.

Susan Strasser has been instrumental in increasing our understanding of the development of a mass market and its impact on women's lives. Beginning with the introduction of brand names and extending into the creation of new products, sales, advertising, and distributing and retailing techniques, Strasser describes a virtual revolution in American marketing that coincided with—indeed, helped to create—modern, corporate, organizational capitalism.[37] Critical to the success of this revolution, however, was the participation of the mythic person advertisers called "Mrs. Consumer." By 1930, when two-thirds of all manufactured products were bought by women, advertisers knew whom to target in their campaigns and whose roles as consumers to reinforce. Corporations saw women as their families' "purchasing agents," familiar with brand names, competitive prices, and product information.[38]

In the Dakotas, there were three main ways in which Mrs. Consumer was sold on her new role and provided with new information. Dakota women most immediately encountered the realities of shopping in their local stores. Although every town still boasted traditional one-proprietor stores, a surprisingly large number of chain stores appeared in the late 1920s. By 1930, the largest of the grocery chains,

Red Owl Stores of Minneapolis, claimed to have stores in forty-four North Dakota towns and thirty-three South Dakota towns.[39] In response, many locally owned stores organized a buying association called the Independent Grocer's Association (IGA). By organizing their collective wholesale buying power, IGA stores hoped to offer comparable prices and variety. In 1931, the chain store industry reported at least some activity on the northern plains in twelve more retail areas, including shoe stores, department stores, hardware, lumber, and drug stores.[40]

The new emphasis on price and availability in Dakota stores reflected a shift in the relationships among shopkeepers, customers, and manufacturers. The traditional old-middle-class storekeeper was an expert on all products and gave credit to worthy customers and first-person service in all sales. In stores where the price and availability of name-brand goods were of foremost importance, however, the store owner served more as a facilitator between customers and corporations and advertisers.[41] Indeed, in chain stores, the storekeeper was not even the owner but just a manager paid a salary and relocated from town to town. The chains did not seek to diminish but to accent the differences between themselves and their locally owned competitors. One 1930 Red Owl advertisement quoted a customer who claimed that even the task of picking her own groceries off the shelves was a "privilege."[42]

Women first gained information about products, prices, and the job of shopping itself through the media. In the 1910s and 1920s, many Dakota women had access to national forums like the *Ladies' Home Journal*, *The Farmer's Wife*, and syndicated radio programs, each of which lent considerable space to advertising directly to women.[43] But local publications like the *Dakota Farmer* reinforced women's roles as consumers as well. Along with product descriptions, advertisements showed women in the process of making consumer decisions or profiting at home from having made those decisions. Likewise, articles from the Home Economics divisions of the State Agricultural Colleges reinforced consumer behavior through discussing the nutritional values of purchased foods and the pros and cons of abandoning home production for store-bought goods.[44]

Ironically for farm women on the northern plains, the Home Econom-

One modern homemaker, having made the right consumer decision
(Dakota Farmer, courtesy Intertec Publishing Corporation)

ics movement began in order to find worthwhile tasks for urban women "who had nothing to do" because home production had waned.[45] In order to make housework more meaningful and enjoyable, home economists aspired to elevate its status to that of a "profession." As Barbara Ehrenreich and Deirdre English have remarked, however, in the early twentieth century, "making home-making into a profession . . . meant, of course, making it into a science."[46] Thus, under the influence of Christine Fredericks's work in scientific management, home economists moved quickly from their initial goal of "teaching women to be good consumers" to teaching them entirely new kinds of work to do at home with consumer products, including bookkeeping, infant care, menu planning, household sanitation, and beautification.[47]

With the enactment of the Smith-Lever Act in 1914 and the establishment of the Agricultural Extension Service in Brookings and Fargo, "home management" came to the Dakotas. In 1920 and 1921, the federal government spent $11,000 on home economics programs in South Dakota and $24,000 on them in North Dakota.[48] In both states, the message was clear: "The modern home had technological and scientific content."[49] In the 1924 circular, "That Kitchen!," for example, agent Ruth Willard encouraged women to redesign their kitchens based on "efficiency principles."[50] The kitchen should no longer be considered an "old-fashioned" spot for all kinds of family activities but should be a "workshop . . . for business."[51] Agents gave 4-H Club girls "Scorecards for Health and Good Looks" to ensure proper sanitation and personal hygiene in the home. Along with nutritional information, girls were reminded of the importance of yearly visits to the dentist, "attractive and dainty" underwear, frequent bathing in clean water, proper "elimination of body poisons," and well-fitting shoes.[52]

Such appeals to nutrition, sanitation, scientific management, and even consumerism itself must have seemed cruelly absurd to women living in the Dust Bowl years. What possible chance did a farm girl then have of rinsing her hair in "five separate waters," and what chance did a farm wife have of convincing her husband not to shave in the kitchen? A series of letters to the *Dakota Farmer* suggests, however, that even though Dakota women's working lives seemed to have gone back a generation, their sights remained set on ideals instilled in better times. Indeed, it would be a great error to portray the depres-

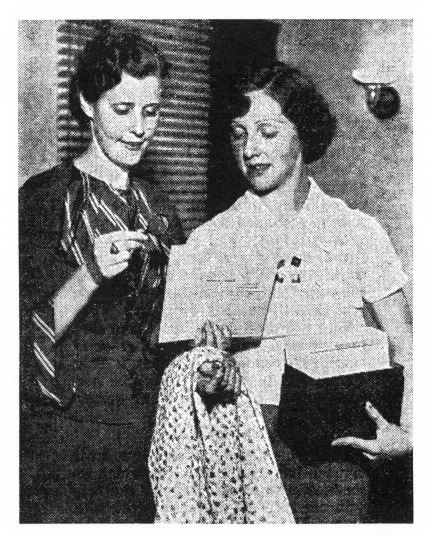

*Agents from the Home Extension Service who taught women about buying fabrics (*Dakota Farmer, *courtesy Intertec Publishing Corporation)*

sion years as ones in which home production was the sum total of rural women's consciousness. In many ways, what Dakota women were doing and what they were thinking had very little in common.

What Dakota women were doing was apparent enough; many began producing items, such as soap, wheat flour, toothpaste, thread, and coarse fabrics, that they had not made for forty years.[53] But the simple fact that women were making things did not mean that they were glad not to be buying them. In fact, the opposite may be true. Most women, for example, were not thrilled to be doing more outdoor work like milking or helping in the fields. As we will see in detail below, they believed that hard outdoor work—and productive labor in general—was unbecoming to the "modern homemaker." Other (often older) women, however, encouraged their sisters to see that working outside and becoming a modern homemaker were not entirely incompatible goals. "I'd rather work [outdoors] and help my Hubby when I'm needed and get a few modern conveniences and then enjoy the evenings together," wrote a woman from Renville County.[54] Eva Clair of Kingsbury County suggested that women simply sing this song while milking, to remind them of what their work was really for: "Swish, Swish, Swish/ Dresses, Dresses, Dresses/Shoes, Shoes, Shoes/Shirley Temple, Shirley Temple, Shirley Temple."[55]

Likewise, what farm women said they wanted to do when they were inside required the home management skills of the farm housewife more than the production skills of the farmer's wife. In a long set of responses to two provocative letters in 1934 and 1936, Dakota farm women debated what they believed to be the most important aspects of their work. Even though the issues discussed were highly contentious, respondents had more in common than they would acknowledge. Between the most mud-slinging and most supportive letters emerged a quorum of women who wanted healthier, happier children; cleaner, more modern homes; and a way of life that more nearly resembled those of their urban counterparts. Moreover, with some reservations, they continued to respect and follow the advice of the experts who claimed they could provide what women wanted.[56]

When she reprinted a letter from Mr. H. Shakleton on 26 May 1934, the *Dakota Farmer*'s "Home Page" editor Mabel Sensor must have known it would raise a ruckus. Certainly, Mr. Shakleton's child-rearing philosophy was extreme, even for her most conservative readers. Complaining about all the ill-behaved children he saw in church and around town, Shakleton offered some of the techniques he used raising his own seven offspring. "Obedience can only be obtained through spanking," he wrote, "and spanking at an early age. I would not think twice about spanking a two-week-old baby if it were not behaving as I expected. All my children know that I mean business."[57]

Almost immediately, and for six months afterwards, letters poured in to the paper from readers lambasting Shakleton's philosophy. Mrs. Emma Schaeffer told of the cruelty she suffered at the hands of one such strict father and how he had nearly ruined the lives of her siblings.[58] Others were equally outraged. "Meanness in children can be traced back one or two generations, as a rule, and it can be a mark," wrote one mother of eight. She needed to use "very little punishing of any kind. . . . It is love, faith and trust, that make strong, kindly children."[59] "Kindness is best," agreed one grandmother.[60]

On the other hand, although no reader would admit to punishing a newborn baby, many agreed that there were parents who neither tended nor disciplined their children closely enough. "A mother who cannot tend her children is one who should not have them," wrote a woman from Campbell County.[61] Several stories of egregious misbehavior were contributed, including one from a woman who described a visit from two toddlers whose rambunctiousness nearly "wrecked my nerves," but whose mother only "laughed and said 'All children are alike.'"[62] More often than not, readers agreed that a well-timed spanking or paddling sometimes taught important lessons. "I raised my children with a barrel stave," wrote another woman, "and I raised them up quite often."[63]

But, whether their authors believed in corporal punishment or not, the letters written in response to Mr. Shakleton shared a common belief. As one "grandmother from the Badlands" put it, "Child training is our most important work."[64] For centuries, women busy producing in the home had reared their children while they worked, giving little thought to tending a child's individual psychology, schedule, or ability.[65] On a farm in particular, it was work enough just keeping children fed and clothed, much less "trained." Yet, by the 1930s, farm women had clearly received the message expounded by child experts, social workers, and home economists since the turn of the century: that "just being a mother is a mighty big job."[66] Suddenly, taking care of a baby required more time, space, and knowledge than ever before. Even though Dakota farm women could not possibly have spent the five hours daily on baby chores that Washington, D.C., housewives did in 1925, they were beginning to believe that the work of raising children should come before home production.[67] According to one reader, the best reason to learn to "manage time" in the home was to have enough left over from work to be a "real mother."[68] "If more women would spend more time bringing up their children instead of running their legs off after dust mops, brooms, and chickens, we would have more 'angels' and fewer 'devils' in our homes."[69]

As Dakota women came to believe in scientific motherhood, they came to wonder whether they, or their mothers and grandmothers, knew everything about the job.[70] "A more challenging, all-engulfing occupation than ever before," child-rearing also had its newest set of experts, whom Dakota women were eager to consult. When, on 23 May 1934, a county agent suggested that Dakota women write the government's Bureau of Women and Children for its free pamphlet on child care, she was so overwhelmed by requests for more information that she simply printed the address in the paper.[71] Similarly, Dakota women, like others around the world, followed with interest and admiration the care of the famous Dionne quintuplets, whose farming parents were deemed unfit to raise them, and whose training was taken over by a host of government bureaucrats, doctors, psychologists, nurses, and corporate sponsors.[72]

Dakota women revealed how complex their aspirations and motivations were in the 1930s when they responded to a letter from "Dere Teacher" of Bern, North Dakota. As it happened, "Dere Teacher" had a bone to chew with farm mothers, especially those who sent their children to school in clothes so old and smelly "that one can barely stand next to them in the schoolroom." Moreover, she complained that farm women did not do enough to keep themselves up-to-date and suggested they begin to use cosmetics so as not to be an "embarrassment" to their children.[73]

Because "Dere Teacher" presented a multipronged attack, responses to her letter were likewise quite varied. Several farm women apologized for their peers who were either too poor, too lazy, too ill, or too ignorant to keep their children clean.[74] Others took the opposite tack and asked the teacher why children who are sent off to school clean come home "dirty as a pig."[75] A third group suggested that clean-

Experts select
Quaker Oats for
Dionne Quintuplets

WITH the whole world of food science to guide them, experts in charge of these bouncing little wards of the King put them on Quaker Oats. Its Vitamin B for keeping fit does children such a world of good. Doctors say this vitamin combats nervousness, loss of appetite and constipation, for those who lack Vitamin B in the diet. Play safe. Serve your family Quaker Oats daily.

Raise your children on the same oatmeal
they give the Dionne 'Quints'!

● Mothers! On the Dionne Quints the world has showered its model methods of raising children. QUAKER OATS was selected as the cereal for these precious babies even before their first birthday! Consider that recommendation for *your* children and serve Quaker Oats daily. It is rich in Vitamin B, the vitamin Doctors say combats *constipation, poor appetite,* and *nervousness*—for both children and grown-ups, who lack that vitamin in the diet. QUAKER is flaked from the cream of the oat crop. Flavory. Surpassingly good. For about ⅓c per dish, it supplies amazing material for growth, muscle and food-energy. The *only* oatmeal with Sunshine Vitamin D also. Order from your grocer. Either 2½ minute quick-cooking, or regular. Quaker and Mother's Oats are the same.

One of many local advertisements linking the Dionne quintuplets and scientific motherhood to the purchase of consumer products (Dakota Farmer, courtesy Intertec Publishing Corporation) liness and hygiene be added to the school curriculum and that the schools themselves be provided with access to clean water.[76]

But not a single farm woman suggested that it was acceptable for farm children to go to school smelling like the farm. "Smelly" was associated not with productivity but with being "shiftless, dirty, and disgraceful."[77] Ruth Schwartz Cowan reminds us that standards of cleanliness, like housekeeping and child-raising, are culturally determined. In a time with fewer clothes, no power washers, and no running water, people and their houses were dirty as a matter of course: the Saturday night bath before Sunday morning church service was a matter of habit.[78] In North and South Dakota in the 1930s, farm women still did not have these conveniences, but sanitation standards were clearly elevated nonetheless. "I have no quarrel with our pioneer grandmothers," wrote a South Dakota mother. "Their (hygiene habits) were habits of necessity. Is there any reason we, under entirely different circumstances, should live the same way?"[79] Similarly, a North Dakota woman asked, "I think it is time we mothers should practice a little sanitation and stop yelling that times are too hard. After all, water isn't so scarce and soap is cheap. . . . It isn't necessary to smell like stock because you work around it."[80]

But what of farm women using cosmetics? "Dere Teacher" couldn't really have meant that women without toilets or sinks, women who might preserve as many as 1,500 quarts of food a year, should try powder and rouge? Yes, she did, and many—though far from all—of her correspondents agreed. In fact, it is striking how much appearance, personality, self-improvement, and a cheerful attitude—cornerstones of what has been called "the farm feminine mystique"—had become part of women's consciousness by the late 1930s.[81] Whereas, in 1930, a farm woman who was troubled by excess facial hair was advised to get her mind back on her work, in 1936, a mother feeling worn-out was advised to "go to a beauty parlor and get a finger wave."[82] By the middle of that year, even the *Dakota Farmer* was running a weekly column called "Style Chat," which included make-up ideas, dieting techniques (to "whittle away bulges"), and tips on the latest fashions from Paris.[83] In 1938, readers began to share ideas on new "self-improving hobbies" and a ten-step attitude-improving program.[84]

Since some readers adamantly opposed the emerging "beauty culture," its advocates were explicit in their justifications. One reason, for example, that they claimed to use cosmetics was "to be pleasing to one's husband."[85] No matter the heat or the workload, another woman added, "hubby likes you to look pretty."[86] Indeed, a man had a right to expect an attractive wife waiting for him after his day in the fields. The new self-improving hobbies and decidedly selfless and cheerful attitudes further guarded against the possibility of abandonment. Reading psychology, learning about the opera, starting a collection, or simply "going 15 minutes without using the words 'I' or 'me'," would keep "a husband or children" from "beginning to climb away intellectually."[87] "If you are experiencing the daily torture of seeing your husband drift away from you," suggested a writer in late 1937, "try a daily perfumed bath."[88]

In using cosmetics and beginning new hobbies, in attempting to look "neat and trim" instead of overwrought and overweight, farm women were consciously trying not to look like farm women. "I don't know any reason why a farm woman shouldn't look as nice as a town woman," argued one reader in January 1937.[89] Truth be told, Dakota women knew that hard-working farm women—however productive they were—were as often the butt of jokes as the object of praise. Even advertisements in the *Dakota Farmer* (which one might think would be sympathetic to them) portrayed farm women who helped with outdoor work as somewhat pathetic. Many women hoped, then, that by shifting the emphasis of their work away from productive activities "the days of the hick farmer [would be] gone forever."[90] In other words, farm women knew that home management and the feminine mystique "were the trend of modern times" and that their traditional labors were not.[91] In support—however ambivalent—of cosmetics, one reader wrote a poem that might well have stood as a motto for the old middle class: "Be not the first when the new is tried, nor the last to lay the old aside."[92]

As they shifted allegiances from production to consumption and from farm work to housework, Dakota women undoubtedly secured much of what they had hoped for in their hardest times. From the 1920s on, infant mortality decreased, maternal and child health in-

Two advertisements linking women's farm labor with humor or pathos
(Dakota Farmer, *courtesy Intertec Publishing Corporation*)

creased, the availability of birth control widened, and fewer women were broken by sheer physical labor. Moreover, for whatever reason, farm women stopped being familiar sources of American humor. Even the bonds of patriarchy have loosened for farm women; today, the products of their labor do not legally belong to their husbands. According to one study, farm families have a more equitable division of labor than urban families.[93]

And yet, this turn to domestic labor and the farm feminine mystique can also be seen as another chapter in the centuries-old pattern of the "masculinization of agriculture," whereby Dakota farm women became that much more "invisible" in the farming enterprise. Today, nearly all of farm women's independent productive labor has been replaced by consumer goods or superseded by technology. But women are hardly idle. In fact, as Christine Kleinegger puts it, today's farm woman does not do less work, only less important work.[94] According to recent studies, 75 percent of farm women's time is spent shopping, bookkeeping, chauffeuring, "go-fering," or in paid, off-farm clerical employment.[95] Meanwhile, the increasingly technological aspects of farm-work are left to the men.[96] It could be said that today's farm marriage no longer seems like an indenture but resembles a contract between a high-tech businessman and a pink-collar employee. And, on a larger scale, it represents the continuing dependence of the old middle class, in its effort to avoid proletarianization, on the structures and beneficence of the new middle class.[97]

Moreover, if the overwhelming presence of patriarchy has receded somewhat from the farm family, the overwhelming fact of male dominance in American society has not. It has merely "taken a different historical form."[98] Along with women's production, women's expertise—the realm of knowledge and skill that transcended economic status in the exhausting days before home economics, scientific motherhood, and the farm feminine mystique—was lost. Although individual women's friendships are likely as important as ever, women's expertise is surely not. Today, experts are rarely other women but are those professionals who were in ascendance sixty years ago—extension agents, advertisers, manufacturers, child psychologists, doctors, and scientists.[99] Indeed, some farm women are reluctant to even see women as a group with separate political interests, much less a separate culture.[100] Moreover, if their relationships with their husbands are more equitable today, farm women have new bosses and new providers in the offices of small towns and the paychecks of government programs and federal loan policies. However generous, these new father figures have taken considerably fewer vows.

For many Dakota women—and, undoubtedly, not a few men—the lesson of the 1930s was not to "make yours" or "fix yours" but to "get yours and to get it for your children. Nothing else matters. Not having that stark terror come to you again."[101] To get what they needed, farm women looked to the new products, roles, ideals, and work habits expounded by new experts across the land. In choosing to find security through the farm feminine mystique, however, farm women were "trading" more than they knew.

7 COMPROMISE AND ITS LIMITS

The Reconsecration of the

North Dakota Freemasons

Of all Dakotans who struggled against hard times in the 1930s, those of the Farmers' Holiday Association (FHA) were the most visible and most vocal—and their wives were the most invisible but perhaps most significantly transformed. Still, the men and women who made their living from the soil were not the only Dakotans who felt the pinch of hard times. Nor were they the only Dakotans who made important changes and compromises in order to survive. Men and women who had never dreamed of joining a radical farm organization also discovered that staying loyal to their families, communities, and traditional roles meant working out new relationships with the New Deal, its agents, and other representatives of the new middle class.[1] No one escaped the harsh realities of the depression decade, just as no one escaped its dirt and grime.

Yet if any group of people could have avoided the suffering, it would have been the Masons. From the earliest days of settlement, the Grand Lodge A.F. and A.M. of North Dakota had been "the archetypical . . . as well as the most popular and prestigious"[2] secret fraternal order on the plains. Because its membership was limited to leading businessmen, professionals, and farmers, being a Mason in North Dakota was nearly equivalent to being successful.[3] Masons were not tenants, small farmers, or businessmen mortgaged to the hilt. Also, since one of their functions was to "validate and facilitate the exercise of masculine power," Masons did not include women.[4] They were, instead, members of the unacknowledged but omnipresent Yankee, Scandinavian, Protestant, Republican male elite within their class. As they liked to boast, the North Dakota Masons were "the best men" in every community.[5]

For all their wealth and worth, however, the Masons also had to struggle in the 1930s. And, for all the ways in which their concerns may seem frivolous or even self-indulgent in light of the life-and-death needs of those around them, their struggle was in fact more revealing than most. The Masons suffered dearly when dues, fees, and other expenses became difficult or impossible for members to afford. But, more importantly, they suffered from the decreasing interest in and authority of their order. Once the central actors in community affairs, the Masons had to learn to share that place with other clubs, outside experts, and government reformers. Still, they wondered: after making the changes they needed to keep members interested and involved and after accepting shared authority, would anything significant remain? In the 1930s, the Masons sought to reestablish their identity and to find a new role for the future, in part by looking for validation in the past. As members of a club whose overarching purpose—and overwhelming burden—was the protection and celebration of old-middle-class culture, their response mirrored the strategies adopted by their class as a whole.

Freemasonry had come to the Dakotas with the very first white men who ventured there.[6] Following the Civil War, the secret society founded in Great Britain and again in the American northeast recovered from the political campaigns against it and experienced an important rejuvenation. Thus soldiers at territorial forts and community builders along the Red River carried the goals, ideals, and secret rituals of their "craft" with them as they traveled. As Lynn Dumenil has written, the organization provided its members with entertainment, sociability, prestige, single-sex camaraderie in a literally "separate" sphere, and (most important of all) a middle-class "badge of respectability"—the declaration that the Masonic code of "temperance, sobriety, honesty, industry, and self-restraint" was also one's own.[7] Finally, the Masonic "temple" was a place where those ideals and morals were celebrated through religious ritual and with a religious kind of seriousness.[8] On the frontier, as elsewhere, Masonry was a "sacred asylum" where men joined together both to promote and to protect middle-class morality and culture.[9]

When the population in the Dakotas boomed, so did the craft.[10] In 1889, when the North and South Dakota Grand Lodges were established, there were already 1,300 Masons in the north. Two years later, the number had almost doubled, and by 1909, when growth slowed somewhat, there were nearly five times as many Masons. During and after World War I, membership surged again, profiting from expansion west of the Missouri River and a national craze for "joining."[11] In 1922, North Dakota Grand Master Edwin Ripley made this enthusiastic, if ill-fated, prediction: "The gain during the last three years has been 2,763 [new members] or 25 percent. It is safe to assume that we shall have at least 50 percent growth every ten years. That means in 1932 we shall have 22,000 members, in 1942, 33,000, in 1947 . . . no less than 40,000 Master Masons in North Dakota."[12]

It was just as the Masons reached the peak of their popularity, however, that their troubles began. The first problems they faced were due to the rapid growth itself.[13] Leaders worried, for example, about their ability to provide old-age assistance for so many new members and to preserve a feeling of intimacy in large urban lodges.[14] Similarly, they were concerned that the leaders of small rural lodges had been so overwhelmed by the business of initiating new members that they were unable to do anything else.[15] Nevertheless, these were but the embarrassments of riches and were easily resolved through refinancing, reorganization, and assistance from the Grand Lodge.

Not so easy to handle were the problems associated with the changing character of the members and the different expectations they brought to the craft. It seemed to some leaders in the 1920s as if the craft were undergoing moral decay: reports of attendance, courtesy,

and decorum problems, arrests, and suspensions for "unmasonly conduct" filled the record each year.[16] Other leaders, however, surmised
that the new members were not actually less good men but simply less
serious ones, men who were interested in the social rather than the
business, the recreational rather than the ritualistic aspects of the
craft.[17] In fact, Grand Master Theodore Elton suspected that some
men had joined for no other purpose than to gain access to the Masons'
higher orders, especially the prestigious Scottish Rite and fun-loving
Shriners.[18]

That some Masons wanted a larger share of sociability and a smaller
share of religiosity revealed the most critical challenge the Masons faced
in the 1920s: developing a role for a "sacred" craft in an increasingly
secular society.[19] Sociologists from Edmund Brunner's Office on Town
and Country Affairs visited four North Dakota "agricultural villages"
in the 1920s and 1930s and reported important trends.[20] Although most
Dakota towns remained "fraternally crazy" until 1930 (significantly
longer than in other parts of the country), the nature of club activities
was nonetheless changing.[21] In Grafton, North Dakota, for example,
the Masons were the most "highly respected" club in town, but they
were now vying for new members with a recently organized Civic
Club. This group held twice-monthly luncheon meetings, sponsored
market days and other entertaining and profitable activities, and generally traded on the "personality . . . energy, and public-mindedness
of those in charge."[22] At the same time, the fastest-growing clubs in
Grafton were those that did no "business" whatsoever and also included women from time to time: the golf, baseball, and bridge clubs.[23]
All in all, it seemed, Dakotans wanted to join clubs that did more than
share secrets.

The Masons recognized the competition they faced from other clubs
in the 1920s and initiated two related procedural and ideological changes
to counteract it. The first was the "opening up" of the lodge through a
dedication to "Service" and community affairs. As William Hutcheson
explained in 1922, "Masonry is taking on an entirely new meaning . . .
transforming the attitudes of Masons of this jurisdiction toward Masonry itself and toward their duties as men and citizens."[24] Broadly
put, the transformation was from "speculative" (or intellectual) to
"operative" Masonry—"the putting into practice the lessons learned

in the lodge."[25] Walter Stockwell explained the reason behind the change in his typically candid fashion. "Masonry has work to do if it is to hold its present position."[26]

The "work" Masons chose to do varied widely according to the size and inclination of individual lodges. Lodges in Grand Forks and Fargo, for example, sponsored generous university scholarships, but those in LaMoure and Hebron sponsored Boy Scout troops.[27] In every lodge, however, the increased involvement in the community also prompted an increased desire to "transform . . . social and governmental institutions according to Masonic values."[28] Masons in Edgely and Mayville thus conducted "continuous school supervision"; the lodge in New England made sure "that the laws of the land are enforced in the community."[29] A fear of Catholics, Communists, and eastern European immigrants prompted some members to join another group that was devoted to 100 percent Americanism. In 1922, Grand Master Ripley demanded that any Mason who joined the Ku Klux Klan be expelled from the lodge.[30] In 1925, however, Grand Master Theodore Elton denied only any official affiliation of the two organizations. "Any Mason who desires to do so has every right to join the Klan," he determined.[31]

Part and parcel of the Masons' increased involvement in social and political affairs was their de-emphasis on ritualism. Prior to the 1920s, the Ritual of Freemasonry was all-important: it defined and reinforced the craft's sacredness, bonded members together with its secrets, and provided much of the lodge's allure to outsiders.[32] Moreover, its changelessness was evidence of the immutability of Masonry as a whole.[33] Over the course of the decade in North Dakota, however, nearly every leader stated the case against "ritualism for its own sake." "If Masonry is to devote itself mainly to Ritualism," said Stockwell, for example, "we confess to a feeling that we are spending our time and money in vain."[34] "Masonry means more than the wearing of a pin," agreed Ralph Miller.[35] In fact, some leaders argued that the ritual, critical as it once was, now could be changed or even deleted from certain activities. Master Charles Starke put the case against religiosity most sharply of all, saying, "There is nothing sacred about our ritual."[36]

Throughout the 1920s, the North Dakota Masons tried to retain their prestige by secularizing themselves, or, as they described it later, "by guessing the way people [were] going and getting in front."[37] Rather than protect their secret allure as they had in the past, they traded openly upon it in the community. And, for the greater part of the decade, the strategy seemed to work. In Grafton, for example, the Masons continued to be "very strong and well-supported" and to sponsor "very successful" projects.[38] Nevertheless, all was not well. Between 1927 and 1929, membership increases slowed to a trickle, funds for projects grew scarcer and scarcer, and leaders worried that the move away from ritual might have gone too far. Now that the prestige of the Masons depended upon their ability to display it, it also depended upon opportunities for that display. Masonic leaders had more work to do than ever in the 1930s, precisely because they had so little "work" to do.

By 18 June 1930, Grand Secretary Walter Stockwell had been a Mason for so long that he thought he'd seen it all. Speaking to the annual "communication" in Fargo, Stockwell admitted that "there [had been] differences of opinion and one or two incidents that [had been] unpleasant" in the Grand Lodge's forty-year history. Overall, however, "peace and serenity" had reigned.[39] So it was that the particularly unpleasant events of the coming decade would deal Stockwell a particularly hard blow. "I have never put in a busier year," he wrote John Robinson in 1934, "or one that has tried one's soul as this one has."[40] With membership plunging, the future seemed dim indeed for his beloved brotherhood.

As they had in the 1920s, the Masons of the depression decade wrestled with two different but related sets of problems: declining membership and the future role of the craft as it lost its central place in the community. The Masons, like other members of their class, continued to make significant compromises to changing times in order to persist. But they also decided what things they could not change without ceasing to exist. For the Masons, then, the real work of the depression lay in identifying those aspects of the craft that were sacred after all; it lay in finding a way to adjust but not to change.

When in 1930 Grand Secretary Stockwell reported the first decline in membership in the history of North Dakota Freemasonry, he admit-

ted that he had seen it coming.[41] Still, neither he nor anyone else fore-
saw the utter devastation that soon was visited upon their ranks. Between 1930 and 1944, the Grand Lodge of North Dakota lost nearly
5,000 members, or almost one-third of its total membership. Not since
1915 had there been so few Masons in North Dakota as there were in
1943. The smallest lodges suffered most. In 1934 the Berthold Lodge
surrendered its charter altogether; between 1935 and 1943, nine others would do the same. Others merged or consolidated, admitting in
effect that they "could not live up to their duties as Masons" on their
own. As the Special Committee on Consolidating Lodges reported in
1937, "one cannot but admire the love that a brother has for his own
lodge, and yet practicalities must be taken into account."[42]

The most important "practicality" to be taken into account was in
fact each lodge's "account"—its financial standing. Every lodge had
two sources of income and many lost the greater portion of them both.
First, they lost their capital investments (savings, stocks, and real estate—usually the temple) to bank closings and foreclosures. At the
same time, they lost income through unpaid dues and fees. In the
1920s, the number of Masons suspended for "non-payment of dues"
fluctuated between 200 and 300. Beginning in 1930, however, this number more than doubled—to 459 in 1932, 623 in 1933, and 650 in 1935.
The aging organization also lost large numbers of Masons (and their
dues) to death or demission (the voluntary dismissal of a member in
good standing.) All in all, the decrease in revenue was nearly cata-
strophic: in 1936 the Grand Lodge itself required a "special emergency
assessment" to avoid bankruptcy.[43]

As important as it was, the Masons' financial crisis was nevertheless
only part of the problem they faced. A larger and more interesting
problem was their continuing loss of authority and prestige within the
community. By devoting themselves to service as they had in the
1920s, the Masons had banked on their ability to serve their communities as well or better than any other group or individual and thus had
continued to attract well-qualified members. In the 1930s, however,
they had very few opportunities to cash in on their investment. They
had no buildings to dedicate and scarce funds for charitable activities.[44]
Moreover, much of the work they had done in the past—caring for the
aged and poor, for example—was taken over by the government.[45]

Then, the government sponsored new, well-financed and extremely active organizations of its own, such as the 4-H Club, homemakers' clubs, and local farmers' clubs.[46] Finally, the Masons could not compete with the attractions of radios and movie houses. In 1938, the Masonic Lodge in Antler reported candidly what must have been true in many places: they had "not much doing" in their community.[47]

To keep those members they had, attract others, and keep them all interested and involved, the Masons continued to make the kind of secularizing compromises they had initiated in the 1920s. Between 1930 and 1934, for example, they agreed on a significant alteration of their traditional prohibition of Sabbath Day activities: several lodges had had the opportunity to increase revenues by renting temple space to other groups who met on Sundays. Others had increased the interest of their own members by sponsoring "picnics on Sundays, at which time parades, drills, band concerts, baseball games and other athletic sports were the chief features of the program."[48] At first, some leaders were strictly against such a change, but eventually desire and necessity won out.[49] In 1933 new by-laws allowed for rental arrangements and, moreover, for Masonic outings with "musical, religious, or educational" programs.[50]

After even more heated debate, the Masons also changed their policies regarding "the liquor question." In the 1920s, leaders were outraged at numerous reports of Masonic intemperance and compared drinking to "open rebellion."[51] After the repeal of the Eighteenth Amendment, however, the issue became more complicated. Didn't the traditional Masonic prohibition against the membership of any person directly or indirectly engaged in the trafficking of alcoholic beverages pose "a great injustice" to an organization already in trouble?[52] To some, even a consideration of this issue was unthinkable. "We cannot compromise with evil," John Robinson argued in 1933. "Our history and tradition mark us out as an institution anchored to certain fundamental principles which remain the same at all times, regardless of [sudden changes in] public opinion."[53] Nevertheless, by 1939 a new policy had been suggested so that a wide variety of men who worked in and around the liquor trade could be Masons after all.[54]

Perhaps the most significant of all the compromises the Masons made in the 1930s regarded qualifications for membership. The issue took two distinct forms: financial qualifications and qualifications of class or status. First, the Masons had to decide what to do about the huge number of men who were already members but who could no longer afford to belong. It was a tricky question: as Lynn Dumenil has pointed out, the elitist nature of the supposedly egalitarian craft was protected by large initiation fees and annual dues.[55] Similarly, it had traditionally been understood that the craft could not "afford" to retain those members who could no longer afford it.[56] In the 1930s, however, this connection became problematic: if no one in North Dakota could pay Masonic dues, did that really mean that no one deserved to be a Mason?

Beginning in the early 1930s, leaders of local lodges and the Grand Lodge alike worked out strategies for saving their memberships. For leaders of small lodges threatened with complete collapse, nothing mattered as much as saving those members who were currently enrolled. Year after year they lowered fees, remitted dues, and conferred the honorary "life-time Mason" degree on as many men as possible. Leaders in Fargo, however, worried that such stopgap measures might threaten the long-term "reputation of this Great Order."[57] They suggested instead that a minimum set of fees and dues be set for future members and that remittance be employed as rarely as possible.[58] Nevertheless, they also demanded that current members be saved whenever possible. "Go out and see these members [who are behind in fees], learn their circumstances . . . and above all, if the brother is worthy and is in distress financially, or by reason of sickness or other misfortune, protect his membership," advised Robinson in 1934.[59] Such a seemingly simple suggestion betrayed an important shift in Masonic thinking. On the one hand, the Masons had no intention of making Masonry "cheap."[60] Even so, they were admitting that a good man could experience financial hardship and still be good enough to be a Mason.

Some evidence suggests that the Masons also adjusted their notions of what qualified men for Masonic membership in the first place. Once a wholly middle-class, Anglo/Nordic, Protestant organization, the new liquor by-laws of 1939 named waiters, truck drivers, warehouse men, and clerks as possible initiates.[61] Similarly, by the end of the decade, members began to remark (not always happily) upon the ethnic diversity of the membership.[62] In another instance, Robinson was convinced to accept for membership a young man who could hardly have been called a good man, much less one of the best of his community, as he had been named in a notorious paternity suit.[63] Most intriguingly, however, the Masons began to include some Dakotans who were not men at all. Participating in the nationwide trend away from single-sex leisure, the North Dakota Masons oversaw the expansion of their women's auxiliary, the Eastern Star, and the participation of wives and girlfriends at banquets, festivals, and other out-of-temple activities.[64]

For all the adjustments they did make, there was one seemingly much less significant issue on which the Masons never budged—gambling. From time to time throughout the decade, entertainment- and income-starved lodges sponsored lotteries to raise money for activities in the community.[65] Lotteries varied widely in their type and appeal, but the leaders' reaction to them was always the same: gambling was the ultimate expression of "unmasonly conduct." Any activity that "appealed to the gambling instinct," they proclaimed, even a game of "count-the-beans," was strictly forbidden.[66] As Charles Milloy explained, gambling represented schemes "for making easy money [for those] who desire to live by their wits rather than by hard work . . . [and] to get something for little or nothing."[67]

For the Masons, the trouble with gambling was much the same as it had been for antigambling reformers since the early nineteenth century. First and foremost, gambling detracted from the importance of work and production to the creation of wealth; it said in essence that a man did not actually have to make or do something to reap financial reward and, further, that capitalism was not a fair and rational system but was irrational, unfair, and could be played and manipulated. Perhaps most importantly to the men on the northern plains, gambling—and lotteries in particular (because one individual literally profited at the expense of others)—betrayed the cooperative ideal of work for a common good.[68] It was one thing for a Mason to have made money through "good work, true work, and square work" and to have lost it in a momentary irregularity of the market; it was quite another for him to try and "steal" it back from his neighbors.[69]

When they forbade gambling, the Masons employed a strategy altogether different from compromise. They worked instead to demarcate those aspects of Masonry that they would *not* compromise, those things that *were* sacred and immutable after all. As we shall see, this search took the Masons in many different directions, but, most significantly, it led to a recovery of the past and a reconsecration of ritual. What they discovered in both was not what they had already deemed "old-fashioned"—not Sabbath Day prohibitions, temperance, or a promulgation of secrecy—but the secular ideals of work and community that lay at the heart of old-middle-class culture. With their other bonds becoming more and more tenuous, these ideals would provide the "cement" Masons needed for now and the days to come. Moreover, however closely they tied it to their craft, the Masons were hardly the only Dakotans returning to past triumphs in search of validation for the future.

There were a number of different reasons why the Masons found a retreat into the past to be a propitious task for the depression decade. Digging up old stories, collecting photographs, and dedicating landmarks was, for one thing, inexpensive work that kept otherwise idle Masons interested and busy. Similarly, consecrating Masonic history honored the elderly Masons who were now passing. And the lessons of the past had a purpose, too: to inspire or admonish present-day Masons whose spirits might be flagging. Masonic forefathers had faced their share of trials, leaders reminded their flocks, and had survived them—without the "uncounted comforts and conveniences" members now enjoyed.[70] If they had not failed, why should their progeny, Stockwell liked to ask. "Are we any less resourceful than they? Are we any less devoted?"[71]

Most importantly, uncovering the pioneer past helped Masons identify the "starting point" of Masonry: those ideals and standards that had always been and would always be peculiar to their craft.[72] As early as 1930, one leader explained, "It is proper sometimes to look backward so that we may better look forward."[73] In 1935 Mark Forkner elaborated on this beginning: "The great sacrifices of our pioneer Masons . . . should constitute an incentive to us of the present generation . . . to emulate the noble qualities in our . . . present day."[74] Lewis Thompson was more didactic: "The ideals of our forefathers . . . who carried Masonry's banner to the far reaches of the Dakota prairies must be, can be, and will be perpetuated."[75] What mattered most about the pioneers, then, was not so much what they had believed and professed as what they had achieved—in other words, the "noble qualities" that had bonded them together would bond Masons together forevermore.

Orin G. Libby, professor at the University of North Dakota and Grand Lodge Historian from 1929 until his death, took on the job of determining exactly who the pioneer Masons had been and what they had believed and valued.[76] To do so, he began at the beginning, trying to discover, lodge by lodge, exactly who the original founders had been. In his first report, he stressed the elite nature of the club: the pioneer Masons were "the finest men that eastern communities could send us," he reported in 1930.[77] Along the way, Libby documented the productive activities of bankers, doctors, merchants, and lawyers— always mentioning their line of work, their struggles, and their ultimate success. Of those Masons who had come down from Canada, another speaker stressed the same kinds of "qualities," saying they were "truly among the finest people on earth."[78]

It was not just the elite nature of the early Masons that Libby and others documented, however. They also went over and over the ideals and values that were associated with Masonic pioneers, recreating in effect the bond between wealth and worth, capital and character that in the 1930s had been so sorely challenged. First, they looked at early Masons as workers and, not surprisingly, found that they had been hard workers, self-reliant and resourceful men who through good character and honest labor had enjoyed considerable success.[79] Moreover, they were good, generous, and "hospitable" neighbors—people from whom "you could get a meal anytime and they were all happy to have you."[80] Last but not least, they were fiercely loyal—to their God, nation, state, community, and, yes, local lodge. As many leaders recalled, the early Masons traveled by foot along unmarked paths and roads to "improvised" lodge rooms because, at bottom, "the brethren of that day were strong men who took their Masonry seriously."[81]

Two events marked the apex of Libby's attempt to invent an immutable Masonic character by recreating the Masonic past. The first, on 21 May 1935, was the dedication of a memorial to Lewis and Clark (both of whom had been Masons) at the site of their winter campgrounds along the Missouri River near Washburn.[82] Although Libby spoke at length about the significance of their exploration,[83] it was not that accomplishment that interested his committee but the ideals they carried with them. As committee chair John Robinson put it, they hoped that the marker would stand "to the courage, the heroism, the fidelity to trust, and the enduring service to country of these distinguished Masons."[84]

The second celebration of the Masonic past took on a more local flavor, as delegations from all over the state participated in a historical display and pageant at the Golden Jubilee Anniversary celebration. Again, what was included in the celebration revealed what had become so important about Masonic history. For example, Libby had arranged displays of three historical periods of Masonry, but the pioneer display attracted the most attention and enthusiasm. There, Masons saw photographs and documents of community builders they may have known personally, as well as pictures of their own lodges in earlier times.[85] In his opening welcome, Master Everest Fowler of Grand Forks reminded "the older members of the craft" why such a display was so important. "You can with pride," he said, "pass on to the younger generation . . . the past, with the positive injunction that they carry on from where you leave off." And, to the younger men, he concluded, "[You] have been handed a heritage by your forefathers which [you] must not fail to preserve."[86] Finally, in the hymn that followed, the heritage was revealed: "labor," "duty," "faith," "trust," and, finally, work accomplished "together."[87]

It was not enough, however, for the Masons simply to dig up the lessons and examples of the past, they also had to give them life in the here and now. To do this, they returned to the ritual that they so completely, if only briefly, had forsaken. As early as 1927, William Hutcheson worried that the ritual had become "a lost art . . . in some lodges" and recommended that "the study of the Ritual [be] made one of the subjects of [next] year's program."[88] In the 1930s, the Masons would do more than study the ritual, they would perform it again and again. In fact, they were told to perform some ceremonies at least twice a month, whether there was actually any reason to do so or not.[89] Then, once every year for three years, they held "reconsecration nights" when every lodge throughout the state met at the same time on the same night, performed the same rituals, heard the same lectures, and learned the same lessons.[90]

Over and again throughout the decade, Masonic leaders repeated why they believed this return to ritual was so important. For the most part, they emphasized the lessons that ritual taught. "[Ritual] may well be compared to the lens through which Masonry projects the sublime teachings," Forkner explained at the 1935 "Sit-in-lodge Night." "If there are any flaws in the lens the candidate for light will be compelled to look upon a faulty picture."[91] Not surprisingly, the lessons they revealed in the ritual were the same ones they discovered in the past—the importance of work, faith, loyalty, neighborliness, courage, service, independence—the foundation, in other words, of their culture. For Forkner, just three words summed up what Masonry had brought and would always bring to the world. "Faith, hope, and charity," he said, are the "cement that turns ceremony and symbol into a living reality."[92]

In short, the ritual of the 1930s was far from a return to earlier religiosity or ritualism "for its own sake." It was instead a way for the ideals presented in Masonic history to be sanctified in everyday life and used as a force for the future. Ritual was no longer important in the way that it bonded men together in secrecy and sacredness, but in the way that it gave them a renewed purpose and an initiation into Masonic history and values. Even if Masons could no longer be men of action, Forkner argued, they could nevertheless be men of "vision," taking the "spiritual" lessons of Masonry "into every walk of life."[93] Simply put, Masons believed that expressing their ideals through ritual was something they could *do*. Ritual was work as important as any work Masons had ever done before.

In 1937 Stockwell looked back on the previous decade and did not mince his words. "No Grand Jurisdiction has had a larger share of misfortune . . . than has North Dakota." Since the boom years, he recalled, internal and external pressures had brought Freemasonry in North Dakota to the brink of ruin. Even so, he could find reason enough to be proud and optimistic: "Everywhere there has been a determination to adjust [ourselves] to reality, to adopt new methods and procedures suited to new conditions." Now, he believed, Masonic influence was more important than ever—so long as it did not keep on adjusting. "In a world of unrest and social change," he concluded, "it is essential that there remain some things that are stable and unchanging. These days therefore constitute Freemasonry's greatest opportunity."[94]

As utterly contradictory as it sounded, Stockwell's description of the Masons' survival strategy actually made perfect sense. For the Masons, the trick to surviving the Great Depression had been to change some things completely and other things not at all. Religiosity and secrecy for their own sakes were gone. An exclusive position of power and authority was gone. But the ideals of work and community, retrieved from the past and revived through the ritual, remained. These ideals, sanctified now as projects in themselves, were the Masons' ticket to the future. When at long last membership increases began to show on the books again, the Masons were certain of their role. What was important about the Masons in 1945 was not what they could do—rather little in the complex postwar world—but what they could say and think and believe. Their purpose was, in short, to represent a way of life and a way of living to everyone else in the world who, presumably, could no longer achieve it. "Love thy neighbor as thyself," proclaimed Grand Orator Alexander Burr in 1945, the year that would mark the end of the Dakotans' "hard times" and the beginning of an era with frustrations all its own, "this is Masonic philosophy reduced to its fundamentals."[95]

8 RECONSTRUCTION

The North Dakota Capitol

and the World of Tomorrow

Despite their obvious differences, radical farmers of the Farmers' Holiday Association (FHA), their hardworking wives, and the well-to-do brothers of the Grand Lodge of Freemasons shared a great deal in the 1930s. All were sorely tested by economic and environmental disaster. They all lost independence and authority to internal and external forces of social change. Most important, however, they often employed similar strategies in their battles to survive the hard times. Cooperating with and encouraging change in many instances but standing fast in others, they outlined what they felt were "the permanent values" of life.[1] Finally, their overriding purpose—to preserve the precarious balance of ideals at the heart of their culture—was one and the same. As often as Dakotans professed that "the world of tomorrow is not going to be the world of yesterday," they nonetheless sought to face the future with the past firmly in mind.[2]

In these years, the people of North Dakota had an extraordinary opportunity to display what they believed their role in modern society would be.[3] It arose on Christmas Eve, 1930, with a portentous fire that destroyed the old red brick territorial capitol at Bismarck. Thus, just when the future was becoming dif-

The Bismarck territorial capitol in flames (courtesy State Historical Society of North Dakota)

The new "tower" capitol of North Dakota (courtesy State Historical Society of North Dakota)

ficult to imagine, North Dakotans set out to design and construct an edifice that would represent them and their culture for years to come. The stories behind the choice they made—how they made it and how they understood it later—told again of their ability to accept social change on their own terms. At the same time, however, they also revealed how tenuous that accomplishment could be. In the end, the North Dakota capitol stood as a monument to the three most significant, albeit contradictory, aspects of old-middle-class culture in the Great Depression: its malleability, its resiliency, and its vulnerability. In the Great Depression, the people of the northern plains built a skyscraper capitol and called it their own.[4]

No one forced the people of North Dakota to build a tower capitol. In its barest outlines, the seventeen-story North Dakota capitol—a colorless and stark example of the "machine aesthetic" of modernistic architecture—was exactly what the North Dakota Board of Capitol Commissioners set out to design.[5] Appointed by the legislature to construct "a capitol . . . of the highest efficiency, durability, taste, and beauty," the commissioners intended from the outset to choose a tower-type building.[6] The traditional dome-and-rotunda style was both expensive and impractical. Moreover, neighboring Nebraskans had just completed a widely acclaimed tower by Bertrum Goodhue.[7] Nevertheless, the commissioners did not intend to build a capitol, however "up-to-date," that thoroughly repudiated their traditional values. Instead, three times during the planning process they tried to infuse their own ideals into the modernistic design. Each time they failed. Ultimately, their intentions for and interpretation of the skyscraper capitol would be available only through the most careful and detailed translation.

The commissioners first tried to combine progress and tradition when they chose the architects for the capitol. In section 3d of the Capitol Commissioner's Act of 1931, the legislature mandated that the commission give preference to a North Dakota architect. Nevertheless, they recognized that "the construction of the Capitol for North Dakota is not merely a local enterprise [but has] a national character."[8] If absolutely necessary, then, the commissioners could select a "national firm" to associate with the North Dakota concern. This statute constrained the commission's selection in only one way: it dictated that the commission could not leave a North Dakota architect out of the design process. In the end, however, that was just what the commissioners would do.

Most North Dakotans supported the employment of a local architect both because they wanted to keep their tax money at home and because they believed that a local architect would design a building that represented their "spirit."[9] But the local architects themselves offered a rather different reason why the commissioners should choose one of them to do the work—loyalty to the old middle class and to its traditional ways of doing business. Professionalization had changed the business of architecture dramatically since the late nineteenth century.[10] Urban firms had grown larger and larger, hiring "an army of employees" to do much of the drafting work and allowing partners to concentrate on client relations and preparatory work for national competitions. In the meantime, architects at small firms in rural states hung onto the values associated with an older style of business.[11] Most still controlled the means of production, valued their skills as independent proprietors, and stood on their characters as well as their accomplishments.[12] "The architect's practice is upon the same basis as that of the physician and the attorney," explained one Dakota architect. "The selection of the best qualified man should be made upon a record for character, integrity, ability, and fitness for service."[13]

In a speech given to the commissioners in July 1931, Grand Forks architect Joseph Bell DeRemer reminded the board members that a vote for a North Dakota architect (and particularly a vote for him) was in effect a vote for craftsmanship and character, not bureaucracy and technology. "I am a descendant from a family of Builders," he began, "apprenticed at the age of fourteen to a master carpenter . . . before going to Columbia for an education. . . . I was not blessed with millionaire friends or relatives," he continued, "but was rather forced to make my own way in the world." At the time, his office was small but filled with "men of caliber" who were prepared to do "a man's job." If the commissioners doubted his skill, more than twenty buildings in Grand Forks provided a living exhibit. If they doubted his character, his application contained an equal number of references from his Masonic lodge.[14]

For all its bravado, DeRemer's address also contained a full measure of desperation, and, in fact, he had good reason to feel like a man "pleading for his life."[15] As we have seen, North Dakotans had no history of establishing cooperative efforts based on explicit invocations of class consciousness; DeRemer himself had appealed only to class-based self-definitions. Even the radical FHA had avoided overt rhetoric of class and class difference. To make matters worse, many of the values that bonded petty proprietors together—a loyalty to laissez-faire capitalism, for example—just as easily set them at each others' throats. In this instance, one group of architects led by T. R. Wells of Grand Forks sponsored a petition in support of hiring a local architect. At the same time, however, a second, anonymous group spread the rumor that "no architect in North Dakota is big enough to handle the job."[16]

It should come as no surprise, then, to learn that the commissioners employed criteria informed by old-middle-class values in their selection process but chose an outside candidate nevertheless. They handled the decision this way: rather than sponsor a design competition, the commissioners asked applicants to reply to a questionnaire and to send in exhibits, plans, and specifications of earlier projects. These they judged on the basis of business skill and personal character. As they told the governor, "The ability to conceive a beautiful design does not necessarily carry with it the ability and organization to perform . . . additionally equal or more important architectural functions."[17] The commissioners were not looking for men with artistic genius, but for those who "knew their business" and were "modern and up-to-date"— much like the men they fancied themselves to be.

Despite these criteria, or perhaps because of them, the small North Dakota firms never had a chance. The slick dog-and-pony shows given by the representatives of big firms were irresistible, and local firms inevitably suffered by comparison.[18] Thus the commissioners' decision was a simple one: they would hire the best national firm to associate with two of the best North Dakota men. By far the most impressive outside application came from Holabird and Root, a young Chicago firm whose accomplishments already included the Chicago Daily News and Board of Trade buildings.[19] Altogether, they fit every qualification for the job. Modern, up-to-date, practical, and even reasonably nearby, Holabird and Root was the perfect firm to associate with two lucky locals—William Kurke and Joseph Bell DeRemer.

As simple as this decision was to make, it was nearly impossible to implement successfully. DeRemer himself had anticipated that "the local associate would be of no more use than the fifth wheel on a wagon."[20] Before long, Holabird and Root made it plain that they, too, found the association cumbersome. Holabird simply told George Bangs, the commission's president, "Your state is penalized because . . . you have more [architects] than you need."[21] In the end, the association became little more than an inconvenient fiction. All the important design work was done in Chicago, and the North Dakota men handled nothing but local supervision. There is even reason to suspect that DeRemer stepped out of the project altogether in its final stages.[22] As a result, what the commissioners had endorsed was a capitol for, but not a capitol by or of, the people of their state. Today, it remains an interesting example of early work in the modernist style, strikingly out of place in its rural landscape.[23]

The commissioners worked to attach localism to modernism a second time when they tried to convince the architects to face the capitol in North Dakota brick instead of Indiana limestone. The reasons they failed this time, though, were at once simpler and more complex than they had been before. In the end, the North Dakota capitol could not be faced in brick because local firms could not produce the necessary brick soon enough or cheaply enough. The commissioners' decision was based primarily on these strictly economic concerns, however, because they had already relinquished to the architects the responsibility of making aesthetic judgments. Thus the struggle over the facing material masked a struggle for authority between old- and new-middle-class elites. At stake was nothing less than the very meaning of the capitol.

It fell to Bangs to spearhead the fight to get the architects to change their designs.[24] As he explained to Holabird and Root's representative, Mr. Hackett, at a meeting in July 1931, hundreds of letters in support of brick had poured into his office, most of which had remarked upon its economic advantages.[25] Bangs, however, offered some reasons of his own that were based solely on aesthetic concerns. Like the members of the New England, North Dakota, Town Criers' Club, Bangs believed that brick would be just as beautiful as stone for the capitol. "The question of a building's looks," he explained, "is one that depends upon the eye of the man that looks at it." To 90 percent of North Dakotans, he continued, "North Dakota products will be much more satisfactory than something that to an artistic eye might look more beautiful. . . . We are building a capitol for the people of North Dakota, not for the people of New York and not for some artistic gentleman to go away and talk about."[26]

Bangs went on to argue that brick would also furnish a more appropriate expression of the functions of the capitol. He had visited the Stevens Hotel in Minneapolis and the new telephone building in Indianapolis, both of which were partially faced in brick. In his view, the capitol was, like these buildings, "a plain ordinary business block." Under pressure, he conceded that the legislative wing of the capitol should be faced in stone, but never the tower. "I just can't look at the tower as peculiarly of the monumental type. It is an administrative unit of the building just as though it were 100 feet away," he explained.[27]

Not surprisingly, Hackett did not take kindly to Bangs's suggestions. He did not think brick was beautiful and he did not think he was building a hotel. Most of all, however, he questioned the commission's authority to make these kinds of aesthetic judgments. Enraged, Hackett made it perfectly clear that he was the expert and they were not. He lectured the commissioners on the precedents set throughout architectural history for using stone for monumental structures. He insulted their ability to imagine the finished product by comparing their image to a "roundhouse" and a "brewery." "You are not an architect . . . but you are a man of common sense," he taunted Bangs. Later, he asked, "Could you imagine the Lincoln Memorial made of brick?" For his trump card, Hackett attacked the commissioners' integrity, suggesting that they were allowing "some brick manufacturer" to design their building.[28]

Thus, almost as soon as it began, the debate over a facing material for the capitol flared into something much more significant—a struggle for the authority to define the meaning of the building's design. The commissioners assumed that, because they were the clients and in charge of the project's purse, they had the right to decide on the facing material. Moreover, they believed that they had the right to build a capitol that would reflect their image of the functions of government. To their minds, the tower would look just right if it were faced in ordinary brick, as so many of their businesses were, because they believed the administrative section of the government was, in fact, a business. Moreover, it was appropriate that the design of the tower should look altogether different from the more dignified legislative section, which they agreed should remain in limestone. It was, after all, the legislature that made the law; administrators only made it work.[29]

The architects were somewhat more reluctant to explain exactly what they wanted the capitol to represent. For our purposes, however, their design sketches and the completed capitol help fill in the gaps in the record. As Henry Russell-Hitchcock explained in 1934, one of the most important components of a modern building's design was its facade; sheer stone or plaster facades gave buildings the seamless continuity akin to machine technology, while irregular brick or other materials detracted from this emphasis on function and volume.[30] In the case of the North Dakota capitol, limestone siding muffled the structural differences between the administrative and legislative sections, suggesting—like the trylon and perisphere at the New York World's Fair—that the building's rounded and vertical units were best understood together. Nevertheless, when bonded in this way, the two halves were no longer equal parts. Instead, the tower, with its gridlike windows and standardized interior space, overwhelmed the more streamlined horizontal wing. Eventually, the design suggested, all of government would submit to the bureaucracy of the modern state and the once august state capitol become nothing more than a "machine for governing."

For a brief moment, it seemed as if it none of this would come to pass on the North Dakota prairie. The day after Bangs's appeal for brick, the power of the commission's purse won the battle for the authority to decide on a facing material. Probably in fear for his job, Hackett apologized profusely for his behavior and promised that Holabird and Root would draw up the designs for brick as soon as possible. Nevertheless, he had won the war. From that time on, the commissioners never again relied on aesthetic reasons for using or not using brick. Instead, they apologized for ever thinking they could judge aesthetic matters. Bangs had begun his retreat the previous day, saying over and over that he had not meant to be "stubborn or bull-headed." Commissioner Angus Fraser went even further, saying, "I really can't imagine that building in brick. I always thought of it in stone myself." And, according to commissioner Frank Conklin, no one in North Dakota (that he had ever met, anyway) had ever supported brick in the first place.[31]

After this, all that was left in the commissioners' tight corner were the economic considerations they had started with. Brick would be used now if it were cheaper than limestone, and for no other reason. So, when the Hebron Brick Company admitted they could not produce enough brick for the building until May 1932, when prices for other products would rise, the committee decided on limestone. They simply had no other choice. But, far away in Chicago, the architects must have breathed a sigh of relief. For the moment, their vision of modernism remained intact.

The third time the commissioners tried to incorporate traditional values into the new capitol, they hoped for something much less tangible than a brick facing. This time, they clung only to an ideal—a vision of classlessness based on their rhetoric of equality and community—that faded just as quickly as all the rest of their dreams had in the face of the contradictions of their culture. Nevertheless, the story of the "capitol strike" is at once the most revealing and the most rueful of all the events surrounding the construction of the North Dakota capitol.

Once they had selected a design, the commissioners set about choosing contractors for the building's construction and overseeing the negotiations between contractors and local unions. As before, the North Dakota legislature had hoped that only North Dakota labor would be used for the project. But, this time, their reasons for preferring in-state labor went beyond economic protectionism. As Conklin explained to the contractors ready to bid on parts of the project, the commissioners hoped that the construction of the capitol would provide an opportunity for the "reuniting" of capital and labor in the city of Bismarck and throughout North Dakota.[32]

Conklin's vision was based on the contradictory assortment of old-middle-class attitudes toward the working class that we have seen before. Because they preferred to think that all members of the community had equal opportunities, and that in any case they all got along, many North Dakotans were uncomfortable with open displays of conflict or discord.[33] Unions were particularly troublesome in this regard. Not only were they organized on the presumption that an employer and his employee had different interests in the workplace, but also they often took that presumption into the streets and put it on display for all to see. What many businessmen would have preferred instead were the "friendly and co-operative" negotiations that the *Fargo Forum* claimed to enjoy with the Typographic Union.[34] Nevertheless, this vision already had a kind of sentimental ring to it. In the summer of 1933, many cities in the Midwest saw their labor troubles explode into fierce, citywide street fights.[35]

If the commissioners ever could have made their dream come true, they guaranteed its failure as soon as they opened the bidding for contracts. On 20 July 1932, more than 600 people jammed the City Auditorium for the opening of bids for the construction of the new capitol. The commissioners were operating on an extremely tight budget; thus they were willing to give the major contracts to those businesses who could operate most "efficiently"—no matter how they came by their efficiency. The first bid read that day was from Ludnoff-Bicknell Company of Chicago, which came in at $1,575,00—$45,000 less if the commissioners used brick facing. This bid (and reports of the company's fine business skills) was all the commissioners needed to hear; by the end of the day, Ludnoff-Bicknell had won the contract.[36]

When the management of Ludnoff-Bicknell began to negotiate with the International Hod Carriers' Building and Common Laborers' Union of America (IHCBCLUA), the commissioners' dream started to unravel. As Ludnoff-Bicknell's representative, Mr. Norris, explained, it was of great importance to the firm that labor avoid any "disputes" with the company. The North Dakota capitol job was "small potatoes" for them, but any problems they might encounter could have a ripple effect for their other, larger projects. Under these pressures (and hardly negotiating from a position of strength when, as one legislator mentioned, thousands of migrants would be happy to have their members' jobs), the union ultimately signed a contract for wages as low as

Construction workers on strike in Bismarck (courtesy State Historical Society of North Dakota)

$.30 an hour—at least 25 percent lower than the commissioners had anticipated.[37]

Once construction got under way, it became clear that paying low wages was only one of the strategies Ludnoff-Bicknell intended to employ in order to cut their costs. According to the IHCBCLUA, the treatment of the common laborers at the project was "unjust, inhuman, and repulsive to any laborer of American ideals and standards of living." The company used "straw bosses," hired nonunion and out-of-state workers, and made unskilled laborers do skilled work for regular pay. Worst of all, however, were the hours: "[Ludnoff-Bicknell] demands unreasonable hours, often calling men to work at four or five in the morning and then very often only using them for an hour or two, or possibly working them long hours without giving them the consideration of being permitted to eat a lunch at meal time; a consideration most men give their horses."[38]

After weeks of unsuccessful negotiations with the company, the union went on strike, taking up arms in mass picketing against Ludnoff-Bicknell. Among their demands were a minimum wage of $.50 an hour and "the consideration a laborer is entitled to insofar as working conditions are concerned."[39] Appalled and frightened, the mayor of Bismarck called out the local militia. On the night of Wednesday, 24 May, the police charged the picketers, arrested several men, and effectively stopped any further demonstrations. Meanwhile, Governor Bill Langer personally conducted the negotiations for a settlement; in the end, the workers received $.40 an hour, and, after cutting costs in other areas, Ludnoff-Bicknell still met their contract.[40]

Whether the capitol strike ended in a victory for capital or for labor, it was a crushing defeat for the traditional ideal of equality and community. Far from being a unifying force, the construction of the new capitol brought out the reality of discord for everyone to see. Worse still, it attached that difference not just to an unimportant residential or commercial project, but to a building that was to represent North Dakotans and their culture to all the world. And, of course, that was exactly what it did do. The commissioners had only looked for the lowest bidder, not the lowest bidder with the best reputation among labor unions. Along with the contract, then, they handed to an outside corporation the authority to use local labor like any other cheap commodity and to leave town when the job was done. The unification of capital and labor into a community of common goals, interests, and moral values was hardly a high priority for Ludnoff-Bicknell. And, in fact, it was less important to the commissioners than meeting expenses.

By the time the people of North Dakota had built their new state capitol, they had seen a second one go up in smoke. They had envisioned a modern structure that represented their own notion of modernism—a celebration of progress that also incorporated the more traditional ideals of their culture. But the kind of modernism they got had none of these elements. Instead, the North Dakota capitol celebrated the city, bureaucracy, and technology—the very aspects of American society that most worried the people it served. Considered in this light, the

North Dakota capitol was a monument to the inability of old-middle-class Americans to find any home at all in modern society.

But the people of North Dakota never saw their capitol this way. As soon as the design left the drafting room in Chicago, North Dakotans began to reimagine it to suit themselves, relying on the same kinds of values and meanings the commissioners had abandoned. Their desire and ability to do so revealed again the way the "permanent ideals" of the old middle class had come to compensate for their diminished social and economic authority. But it also revealed just how vacuous such a compensation could be. For, as hard as they tried to make the capitol mean what they wanted it to, the people of North Dakota could not change the reality of the structure itself.

The imaginative reconstruction of the "skyscraper capitol" began in earnest just after the ground below it was broken. In their plans for a cornerstone ceremony, North Dakota officials became the first of many Dakotans to try and make the capitol more familiar, to make it their own. In fact, the way they tried to do so was both so common and so significant that it can be described as a bellwether effort for all Dakotans in the period. Just as the Masons would do in the late 1930s, Dakota officials planned a ceremony that would mythologize the pioneer past and conjoin its accomplishments to the uncertainties of the future. As Karal Ann Marling put it, they would portray the capitol as just one more part of "the mighty dream that always came true."

As they did for all kinds of celebrations, high school bands and automobile-driven notables paraded through Bismarck in front of cheering crowds, wending their way to the capitol plaza. But this time, the bands and dignitaries were only part of the entertainment. For the cornerstone ceremony, the capital's most honored guests were thousands of original settlers. Some were well-known, like Gerald Pierce, son of the territorial governor. Others had played interesting roles in the history of the state, like two bricklayers who had worked on the original capitol and the railroad telegrapher who had dispatched the first news of Custer's defeat at the Battle of the Little Big Horn. But most were just folks—men and women who personified a special past gathered together to welcome the future.[41]

During the ceremony, pioneers sat in special bleacher seats and listened to government officials continue to conjoin the past, present, and future. After an invocation by the chaplain of the American Legion, Governor George Shafer addressed the crowd. As Bangs described it later, he "paid tribute to the pioneers and asserted that the new building would be symbolic of the faith, hope and courage which they have handed down to a new generation."[42] Then he placed into the cornerstone a box filled with the sacred artifacts of their culture: an American flag, a Bible, the Compiled Laws of North Dakota, coins and stamps, a Boy Scout Handbook, and more than a dozen photographs of important people and events of the early days of statehood.[43] The box would not be opened for at least another fifty years, but, when it was, all would be intact. Like the mummies in Egyptian pyramids, the relics in the cornerstone would give the people and culture of North Dakota eternal life.

Meanwhile, editors of local newspapers provided official explanations of all the rituals and of the building itself. Generally speaking, they began by explaining the innovative design. "The tower is a bit unusual," one reporter admitted, "and not the conventional type of capitol," but "there is beauty in its simplicity and majestic grandeur in its towering limestone walls."[44] At the *Bismarck Tribune*, editors reminded the public that it was important to keep up-to-date with the latest trend in architectural design. "It took courage for the members of the capitol commission to break away from the traditional type of building . . . and they are to be congratulated for having done so. Competent critics now admit that [tower capitols] are among the most beautiful and distinguished in the country."[45]

At the same time, however, editors were careful to explain how the capitol fit into local culture. Like the commissioners, they preferred the language of business to describe the functions of the design. They admired its "clean" and "trim" lines and above all its "efficiency and durability." Needless to say, they made no mention of the workers from whom the low price for the building was won. Instead, they focused on the long-term consequences of such a "common sense" design. With any luck, they hoped, its "practicality and economy . . . [would be] emphasized in our form of government . . . for years to come."[46]

Finally, the editors spelled out the relationship between the design of the new building and the state's pioneer past. "In its towering mass

Arvard Fairbanks, "The Pioneer Family" (courtesy State Historical Society of North Dakota)

and sharp outlines," one editor wrote, "the North Dakota capitol symbolizes the spirit of a pioneer people who blazed the way for civilization and gave to the nation a great commonwealth carved out of raw prairie."[47] As the newspapermen saw it, their past was anything but history. According to the editor of the *Bismarck Tribune*, one did not even have to be a real pioneer to share in the pioneer spirit or in those basic values the pioneers personified.[48] What mattered was that the past could give the people of North Dakota a common point of reference from which to face the future.

But the most permanent and most significant addition to the capitol was not unveiled at the cornerstone ceremony; in fact, it was not dedicated until 1947. At that time, a bronze statue, the "Pioneer Family," was placed at the entrance to the capitol grounds and directly superimposed on the skyscraper.[49] From left to right, the statue included a rough-hewn but vital-looking father, plow in hand, accompanied by his equally dependable teenaged son and, to the far right, his wife, with babe in arms.[50] The statue, sponsored by the North Dakota Federation of Club Women (NDFCW) in 1927, had originally been designed as a memorial to pioneer women. As President Nina Farley Wishek put it, pioneer life was not full of fun and adventure but full of hardships and isolation; women's lives told this tale best of all.[51] As a result, she insisted that the statue not resemble an innocent young bride but a courageous, mature woman: "O Beautiful! Supreme you stand / Beloved and honored through our land—/ I know—have seen, the purging fear / in Mother's eyes, a pioneer."[52] It was a strong woman—neck, thigh, and arm muscles bulging—who accompanied the menfolk on the prairie.

Because their funds for the project dwindled in the 1930s, the NDFCW left few other clues about what they hoped the original statue would look like—nor why, when it was finally funded by a Canadian businessman, the original "Pioneer Mother" statue became but one part of the Pioneer Family statue.[53] Luckily for us, however, the clubwomen were not the only Dakotans, nor the only Dakota women, who wanted to memorialize pioneers in the Dust Bowl years. Indeed, some of the most famous women's literature from the northern plains—including Laura Ingalls Wilder's *Little House* series—was written in the Great Depression. These novels, their portrayal of domestic life, and their surprisingly ardent political agendas, provide a more complete guide to the statue's lasting meaning.

Most obviously, the "pioneer heroine" novels of the 1930s, like the Pioneer Family statue, celebrate the triumph of domestic life over the adversities and temptations of the frontier. As Ruth Ann Alexander points out, nearly all the novels' protagonists are young girls or women struggling against society's gender expectations.[54] But many of the novels also include strong secondary characters whose domestic virtues contrast with the heroines' tomboyishness and ultimately make them appear immature. Thus, even as *Land of the Burnt Thigh*'s Edith Ammons rides off to discover new frontiers, she admits that her newly married and settled sister, Ida Mary, is "serving the West in the best way for a woman."[55] Similarly, the famous "half-pint," Laura Ingalls, knows that although she "longs to travel on and on, over those miles" she must instead "be content to stay where she was, to help with the work at home and teach school."[56]

However unadventurous it may have seemed to Laura and the others, the domestic life celebrated in the novels is hardly that of chain stores and beauty parlors. On the contrary, pioneer mothers in the novels personify rural productivity, self-reliance, ingenuity, and forbearance—the very qualities Dakota women in the 1930s were beginning to question. Over and again, they are literally able to make something from nothing. Alone with an infant on the South Dakota prairie, the young wife in Rose Wilder Lane's *Let the Hurricane Roar* kills wolves and a half-frozen steer.[57] In *Land of the Burnt Thigh*, the Ammons's neighbor, Ma Wagor, remembers to save enough food from their burning home to feed them dinner.[58] Perhaps most memorably, Ma Ingalls grinds raw wheat seed into flour for bread, day and night, in *The Long Winter* in DeSmet, South Dakota. On the day before the train is due with more supplies, Ma rations out her last biscuits. In a rare display of emotion, Pa remarks, "Caroline, you're a wonder," thereby acknowledging her major role in the survival of the family.[59]

These novels ascribe to pioneer mothers not only the survival of mere individual families but also the permanent settlement of the plains. "It is pretty hard to crush the average woman's home-making instinct," wrote Edith Eudora Kohl. "The very grimness of the prairie increased their determination to raise a bulwark against it."[60] It was women, too, Kohl continued, who were responsible for social life, religion, and education on the plains, traditions from which "developed permanency . . . woman's only protection."[61] After a terrifying night of riding a horse across the plains with her baby on the saddle's pommel, the heroine of Frances Gilchrist Wood's *Turkey Red* does not shrink from her trials but rather celebrates them. "Why, I never saw the prairie so beautiful before. . . . The frontier can't abide—a quitter! . . . I'm no quitter! I'm a pioneer!"[62]

Not surprisingly, it is Wilder's series of books that most clearly conflates domesticity with permanency. Mrs. Brewster, a woman with whom Laura must board during her first term of teaching school away from home, is the only truly odious character in the entire series. She is a terrible housekeeper and cook, rude hostess, and neglectful mother. By far her worst fault, however, is a "selfish" desire to give up on the claim and return East, which she, with a butcher knife, periodically attempts to persuade her husband to do.[63] Of course, Mrs. Brewster's faults reinforce Laura's mother's virtues. Far from asking to leave the plains, Ma begs Pa to stay in South Dakota so the girls can finish school. Indeed, domesticity takes on a ritualistic quality for Ma. Whenever she is certain (often erroneously) that the family is finally settled, she takes a china woman from her chest and hangs it on a handmade bracket over the fireplace or door. Like a talisman, the doll remains unbroken, unscratched, "smiling the same smile," no matter how far she has come or what troubles she has seen.[64]

These stories of personal and collective self-reliance have become so popular and, as a result, are so much a part of Americans' shared cultural memory of pioneering that, as Anita Clair Fellman points out, they often are "not deemed 'political' in implication."[65] Politics was often just below the surface of the stories of the three best-known authors, however—Edith Eudora Kohl, Laura Ingalls Wilder, and Rose Wilder Lane. Indeed, when put in the historical context of the period in which they were written (the hard times of the 1930s), the stories no longer seem like adventure stories but like distinctly political parables. They were tales of times much like the 1930s, full of hardships, droughts, plagues, and poverties, but with an important difference: "There was no whining in those days, no yelling for help."[66] And, of course, there was no New Deal.

In each of these author's books, the overwhelming image of self-reliance is occasionally contrasted by dependence. The young wife in Lane's *Let the Hurricane Roar*, for example, worried about the effect that working for wages and "obeying another man's orders" might have on her husband's pride, "their most important asset."[67] Likewise, although the Ammons sisters profited from the Brule Indians' extravagance in spending their government checks in the sisters' store, they nonetheless joked about the Indians, who seemed to sit around as if "on a holiday" and let "other people do their work for them."[68] Wilder makes the same point. She substitutes a book of Tennyson's poems for the book of Sir Walter Scott's poems that she had in fact received for Christmas as a young woman, and she allows Laura to express disgust for the sailors in Tennyson's "The Lotus Eaters," who wish only to lie around complaining: "Wasn't that a sailor's job to ever labor up the laboring wave? / But no, they wanted their dreamful ease."[69]

None of the white settlers in the above novels depend on government support, and yet the government appears as an impediment to pioneer life nonetheless. None of the characters in any of the books mentioned, for example, consider the Homestead Act a boon or a favor but instead see it as a bet with Uncle Sam "that a man couldn't live five years on the claim without starving to death."[70] Kohl reminds readers that the entire settlement of the plains was accomplished "without a cent appropriated by state or federal government."[71] Likewise, any appearance of the government in Wilder's books is associated with red tape, foolishness, stress, or crisis. "Some blasted politicians in Washington" drive Pa from his land in Kansas; government "red-tape" nearly gets him killed at the Land Office in Brookings; government experts try to get Almanzo to grow trees "where they won't grow naturally."[72] In fact, were it up to Pa or his friend Mr. Edwards, there would be no form of organization on the frontier at all. "Pretty soon folks get to paying more attention to the organization than to what they're organized for," he complains.[73]

Strange as it may sound, evidence exists to support the idea that Wilder wrote her entire series of books as a critique of the New Deal. Whether or not that is true, Wilder's daughter, Rose Wilder Lane, was forthrightly antistatist in her works of fiction and nonfiction.[74] Like Laura's husband, Almanzo Wilder, David Beaton, a young homesteader in Lane's most famous work, *Free Land*, lies about his age to take a claim. Unlike Almanzo, however, who simply felt no shame in putting reason over rules, David exults in his feat. "He pushed back his hat and felt fine. Breaking a legality was a satisfaction, like paying something on an old grudge. A man knew instinctively that govern-

Native South Dakota illustrator Harvey Dunn's portrait of a pioneer mother in "The Prairie Is My Garden" (courtesy South Dakota Art Museum, Brookings, South Dakota)

ment was his worst enemy."[75] Nearly starving but still hard at work on the claim four years later, David and his family are bailed out—not by the state, certainly, but through the early inheritance of his father's money, based on deservedness.

Three years after writing *Free Land*, Lane put her developing antistatist, libertarian ideology in a nonfiction form. Even so, she did not forget the pioneer's role in developing and preserving American freedom and individuality. The freedom to make a living, she acknowledged, was a "double burden of toil and responsibility . . . something pioneers called 'root, hog, or die.'"[76] However dangerous, that freedom was essential to democracy and should not be taken away through centralized bureaucracies, which were merely "stupid and sluggish impediments to the whole range of human activities."[77] Thus she believed that in the Great Depression pioneer values and pioneer heroes were genuinely threatened. Luckily, however, they survived in those men and women who resisted the New Deal's beneficence. Lane lived in a small town in Missouri whose residents, for example, would be "mortally offended" if anyone told them they needed "rehabilitation."[78]

Given this cultural context, the statue of the Pioneer Family changed drastically the meaning of the skyscraper capitol. The family group literally domesticated the tower by suggesting that even this strange building could be a home, could give "a feeling of coming to anchor in a sea of grass and sky."[79] It also reminded Dakotans that hard times had existed before these, and that people had risen above their desire to flee. And yet the statue represented the time when people succeeded without help, without the very "machines for governing" that the tower had brought to bear on the prairie. In short, the statue stood and continued to stand as an eternal reminder—and an eternal warning—of the people for whom the capitol had been built and, moreover, of their most traditional values. Like Ma Ingalls's china woman, the Pioneer Family reminded Dakotans that they had come to stay.

North Dakotans, and their newspaper editors and clubwomen, struggled to revise the image of technology and bureaucracy that the capitol presented. They contended that their capitol, rather than "starting from zero" (as later modernists would claim of such a design), had started with them—with their love of progress, their practical business sense, and, most of all, their pioneer heritage. Moreover, as they celebrated, explained, and translated the form in front of them, they reminded themselves of just what it was they had and would always have in common. In their minds, the message of the capitol was seventeen stories tall: they would survive the hard times because they believed in themselves.

The story of the North Dakota capitol tells once again how the people of the Dakotas tried to protect the independent authority of their culture in the Great Depression. No longer in positions of national leadership and increasingly challenged even in their own communities, Dakotans compromised again and again until they finally fell back upon the power of their values alone. By continually giving things up—production for allotment, making things for buying them, religiosity for ritual, brick for limestone—Dakotans agreed to be transformed. Even so, they hoped never to be changed. The North Dakota capitol belonged to them because they believed it did—believed it hard enough to make it so. The irony of this enormous effort, however, was that in the end they would be the only ones who could ever see it that way. Pioneer Family or no, the skyscraper capitol was hardly a little house on the prairie.

CONCLUSION

The summer of 1938 brought the first substantial rains to the northern plains in nearly a decade. Though prices were still low, men and women harvested their crops and prayed that this was the "next year" they had been waiting for so long. Then, with the increased demand for foodstuff occasioned by the onset of World War II, prosperity returned at last. In North Dakota, total personal income rose an average of 145 percent between 1940 and 1945, compared with a 109 percent increase in the nation at large.[1] With cash in their pockets, Dakotans began to buy land again. Tenancy declined steeply, until by 1954 it neared an all-time low in South Dakota. Further, in the years after World War II, there were no more than eighteen farm foreclosures per year in that state.[2] And all the while the rain fell—not as hail, not too soon or too late, but as gentle spring showers and passing summer storms that promised a healing time.

The fall of 1938 marked a change on the political front as well. Dakota voters returned to the Republicanism they had practiced so religiously before 1932. In 1938, for example, a coalition of conservative Republicans, Democrats, and Nonpartisan Leaguers denied "Wild Bill" Langer a trip to the Senate.[3] Meanwhile, in South Dakota, Republicans ousted New Deal governor Tom Berry in 1936, even though they still preferred Franklin Roosevelt to Alf Landon by more than 30,000 votes. The "conservative resurgence" was completed in 1938 by the election to Congress of two conservative Republican senators over progressive farm Democrats.[4] In 1940 Wendell Willkie defeated Franklin Roosevelt in both states, beginning a return to Republicanism at the national level that would last twenty years and whose exceptions—like South Dakota senator George McGovern—would only win by the narrowest of margins.[5]

From this cursory perspective, it seems that many of the changes brought about by the Great Depression began to be reversed almost magically by the falling rain and the coming war. Where there had been dust, now was soil; where there had been a tenant, now stood an owner; where voters had at least tolerated an expanded federal government, now was a return to familiar antistatist ideals. The reversal was so dramatic, in fact, that some Dakotans believed it bore out what they had been saying all along: "dry spells" were inevitable cycles on the plains, nothing more, nothing less. The Great Depression had not proven that their land was unfit for farming, as some New Dealers had suggested; nor had it proven that capitalist agriculture was immoral or impractical. Indeed, the depression had proven little more than that farmers needed to learn about artificial irrigation and to be cautious about indebtedness in the future. In the 1940s, Dakotans paid off their debts and put money in the bank before they did anything else.[6]

And yet, as we have seen, the Dust Bowl years were not just another "bust" cycle, so common to the Dakotas, the American West, and industrial capitalism at large. Nor were they merely the worst of these hard times. As observers like Grace Martin Highley and Ann Marie Low knew, the Great Depression culminated a half-century during which the industrialization, professionalization, and bureaucratization of American society threatened the working lives and worldviews of small farmers and independent producers on the northern plains. Indeed, the hard times were so hard because they empowered, once and for all, the critical postproducerist, new-middle-class foundation of this transformation. In the 1930s, representatives of the new order came in all forms: county agents, advertisers, relief officials, social workers, photographers, government-sponsored club organizers, chain store managers, beauty culture advisors, morticians from Minneapolis, and architects from Chicago. They came to people whose economic desperation combined with fundamental ambivalence toward what they perceived as progress; this made an exchange between the two worldviews inequitable, confusing, and sometimes degrading. In the 1930s, Dakotans confronted the contradictions most basic to their culture. They saw that the imperatives of economics—need, want, and the power to satisfy them—could overcome even the most heartfelt loyalties to community and equality.

What power remained to the Dakotans was based in this confrontation and in its outcome. In these pages, I have recounted what Dakotans did to survive the crisis, but it is also important to recount what they did not do. Most Dakotans did not give up on their land and their communities; neither did the majority find solace in Fascist movements, as social commentators feared they might. Instead, through a myriad of strategies, Dakotans worked to make sense of the new world and to find renewed meaning in the old one. As vague as it may sound and as inadequate to the task as it very often was, such an act of cultural reconstruction was not insubstantial. The Pioneer Family statue did, in a small way at least, domesticate the skyscraper capitol. Still, the men and women of the old middle class did not succeed in turning back the clock to a time when they made their own way in the world. In fact, they did not even try to do so. However much rain might fall, the new middle class, managerial capitalism, and modernity had come to the plains to stay—in part because they were welcome there.

The long-term effects of these events are too important and too complex to discuss in sufficient detail here. I leave the following mainly as suggestions for further research. Among the most critical changes on the plains after 1935, however, was a restructuring of occupations that has, over time, significantly decreased the numerical preponderance of small producers. Despite the good times, Dakotans continued to leave the plains in huge numbers throughout the 1940s and 1950s. By 1960, in fact, nearly half of all those born in North Dakota (and still living) lived elsewhere.[7] Also, many of those who stayed behind quit farming and migrated to local cities and towns. Thus those farmers who remained owned more land, operated more highly mechanized equipment, and produced larger crops—but their absolute numbers in comparison with other workers dwindled. Whereas in 1930 nearly 63 percent of employed white males in North Dakota worked in agriculture, by 1980 this number had fallen to 18 percent.[8]

Nor is farm life, for those who stayed, exactly the same as it used to be. As we have seen, productive activities for farm women have decreased significantly in the wake of easily accessible consumer goods and an ideology that reinforces the "farm feminine mystique." Farmers spend more time on management, bookkeeping, and caring for high-tech farm equipment. This is mostly due to the continuing imperative of capitalist production to produce more and more at less and less labor cost. But the growing preponderance of paperwork over productive work can also be traced to the continued involvement of the government in agriculture. Although between 1938 and 1943 relief programs like the Works Progress Administration were officially shut down and the New Deal shifted from overt regulation to more discreet forms of Keynesian intervention, farm programs organized, developed, and sponsored by the government went on.[9] In 1988 $715 million in price supports went to South Dakota—placing the state sixth in the nation in per capita agricultural spending.[10] Not surprisingly, the frustrations of working for oneself and for government bureaucrats who have never done a day of farming also remain.[11]

Perhaps most consistent with the New Deal past is the continued intellectual imperialism of academics and other "experts" who think they know better than farmers what is best for the land and the communities of the northern plains. In good years, these currents of thought have been quiet enough. Following the farm crisis of the Reagan years and the terrific drought of 1988, however, new suggestions for the future of the Great Plains have arrived like a flood. Still, some have not seemed particularly new. According to Frank and Deborah Epstein Popper of the Rutgers University Urban Studies Department, for example, most of the plains contain land not adequately irrigated for agriculture. They suggest that 139,000 square miles of the Great Plains—including much of North and South Dakota—simply be converted into a "Buffalo Commons," a vast federally owned game preserve for its original inhabitants.[12] Neither Popper has suggested what the remaining bipeds in the Dakotas should do, where they should go, or who would grow one-third of the world's wheat in the meantime. Neither have they bothered to ask Great Plains inhabitants for suggestions—although they have remarked upon considerable resentment toward their notions—assuming, like their New Deal predecessors, that farmers are too thoroughly entrenched in the day-to-day exigencies of capitalist agricultural exploitation to see its long-term consequences.[13]

The increasing numbers of Dakotans who live in towns and cities have experienced an even greater erosion of independence. A comparison between the occupational statistics for South Dakota between 1925 and 1935 begins to show the initial realignments. In that period, all but one of the occupations to show a significant increase were working-class or white-collar occupations like garage laborer, government employee, engineer, official, secretary, and stenographer. The only increasing independent proprietorship was beauty operator. Decreasing, however, were many of the artisanal crafts and independent work done for years on the plains, including well borer, milliner, carpenter, midwife, and all the jobs related to caring for, building, or using horses and carriages.[14] (See Appendix.) In North Dakota, statistics demonstrate a continued transformation between 1940 and 1960 of the working population into blue-, pink-, and white-collar occupations: public utility, insurance and finance, mining, military, and other government employment all increased in that period.[15] By 1985, 199,000 of 402,000 employed South Dakotans and 191,000 of 372,000 employed North Dakotans held jobs classified as "managerial," "technical," "sales," or "administrative."[16] However upscale those classifications sound, they do not represent independent or even well-paying occupations but the national trend toward a service economy filled with low-status, low-paying, repetitive tasks. In 1988 the Dakotas ranked thirty-seventh and thirty-eighth in per capita disposable income and even further near the bottom in the percentage of the work force that belonged to a union.[17]

Given an economic basis that nears proletarianization, it is not surprising that the hard times of the 1980s hit small towns and cities on the plains with even more force than local farms. The drain of young people to cities has increased; the isolation of those who remain has deepened.[18] Moreover, because people in small towns have no legislative representation comparable to the farm lobby, they receive a relatively smaller share of federal funds for social service programs. As a result, rates of poverty and unemployment in small-town America have crept close to those in the nation's largest cities; domestic violence, substance abuse, and teenage pregnancy increase without even the minimal services provided in urban areas. Perhaps most frightening to residents themselves is the inadequacy of rural health care. In 1989 ten counties in North Dakota and fifteen in South Dakota had not a single physician in residence. Moreover, Dakotans are far less likely than other Americans to carry health insurance.[19] Needless to say, local charitable organizations like the Masons can do little to put such things right. Without the economic base that was relinquished in the 1930s, Masons and other townspeople still have "not much doing" in their communities.

What other historical and cultural developments on the plains might take on new meaning if put into the context of an old-middle-class struggle for survival and purpose? They range, like those I have discussed in preceding chapters, from seemingly insignificant local events to events of national importance. The creation of two of Dakota's most famous tourist attractions, for example—Mount Rushmore and the Wall Drug Store—belong to the depression era and suggest a connection between the familiar mystification of the pioneer past and its subsequent commodification. Begun in 1927, Mount Rushmore brought hundreds of thousands of tourists (and their dollars) to the Black Hills to see what Karal Ann Marling has called the symbol of "a perpetual frontier, an emblematic gateway to our historical dreams and so to the 'darkfields of the republic,' rolling ever westward, backward in time and forward in space."[20] But what did Mount Rushmore suggest about the frontier if its one-man "conqueror," Gutzon Borglum, worked with the newest, most completely mechanized, modern blasting equipment? Critics who noticed this tension between old ideals and new realities in the early 1930s suggested that Henry Ford rather than Theodore Roosevelt deserved the last spot on Cathedral Cliff.[21]

For a druggist whose business in Wall, South Dakota, was on the verge of failure, the suspicion that tourists heading toward Mount Rushmore might be hot and thirsty, and, moreover, that they might like to see a place advertised as the "geographical center of nowhere," led to a phenomenal old-middle-class success. Beginning in the mid-1930s, Ted Hustead advertised his "Free Ice Water" for miles along the highway. Once travelers were enticed to stop, he greeted them with every imaginable variety of Western souvenir, from plastic Indians to a mechanized buffalo ride. Ted Hustead understood that the image of the West—and of rural life in general—could be sold as a consumer product. As his biographer put it in 1969,

> Wall is a hick town and the natives are aware of it. Wall has the money, now, to put in parking meters and other advantages of municipal prosperity. The trouble is, the tourists drive in on purpose to see a hick town—the way it was and the way it still is—not to see a town like they came from. This makes the natives so sad they have a good cry, standing in line at the bank's deposit window.[22]

Urban travelers may have gawked and snickered at the "yokels" when they stopped for ice water and a buffalo ride, but Hustead always believed he had the last laugh. Still, we must wonder whether cashing in on one's own exploitation is really all that profitable.

The fierce midwestern isolationism of the period between 1937 and 1941 might also take on a different hue if put in the context of the immediate experiences of its proponents. The way this story is usually told, Dakotans like Senator Gerald Nye opposed entry into the growing world conflict because they believed America to be strategically impenetrable, but, more importantly, because they recalled the terrible costs of World War I. The Nye Investigations, for example, alleged, without proof, that munitions manufacturers influenced Woodrow Wilson's foreign policies, thus coercing unknowing Americans into a war for profit rather than honor.[23] But what of the impact of more recent times on Nye and others? At the very least, the experience of depression and drought might have made Dakotans hope that America's needs would be put "first." Might it not also have been possible, however, that the New Deal and its representatives exacerbated Dakotans' long-held suspicions of the state and its alliances, whatever shape they took? When he heard of the attack on Pearl Harbor, Nye did not express shock, as one might expect of someone who considered America a stronghold of safety. Instead, he expressed his gravest fear: "This is just what the British wanted," he exclaimed. "Roosevelt has manipulated us into war."[24]

A consideration of the worldview and recent experience of the old middle class might also more fully explain how people so fervently

*R. D. Berg's 1937 cartoon expressing Dakotans' fear of involvement in a foreign war in either Europe or Asia (*Dakota Farmer, *courtesy Intertec Publishing Corporation)*

against involvement in World War II could, in a matter of months, be among its most patriotic supporters. As the isolationist debate heated up, the *Dakota Farmer* sponsored an essay contest on "Americanism." Intriguingly, five of six contest winners identified Americanism as "freedom" and "liberty." J. H. Boese of Bon Homme County defined

Americanism as "something that grants every individual and every family the right to put himself on his own feet, independent and self-directing."[25] Mrs. L. A. Philbrook of Day County agreed: "Americanism is every honest man striving to solve his own problems . . . keeping us from Communism, Nazi-ism and fascism and all other isms, except Americanism."[26] Edgar Syverud, another contest winner, wrote that "Americanism admits of no superior, overlord, king, or dictator."[27] However tiny a sample, these responses suggest that Dakotans had retained their ideal of independence in the workplace and local control in government affairs, despite the realities of the day. Further, it suggests that Dakotans' ideas about what constituted "un-Americanism" might rest on the image of an overly aggressive, manipulative, even totalitarian state.[28] For the New Deal state of the World War II period, which was at once much more subtle in its interventionism and more closely attuned to the private obligations of its citizenry than its depression-era predecessor, the challenge would be to convince the Dakotans that *their* state was the friend—and *another* state, be it Nazi, Italian, or Japanese, was the foe—of liberty and freedom.[29]

Old-middle-class anticommunism also can be recast in the light of these experiences. Richard Hofstadter was the first historian to suggest that anticommunism was a response to the alienation of conservatives during the expansion of the New Deal state. Although Hofstadter lent anything but a sympathetic ear to these resentments, others have examined the old-middle-class response to liberalism more thoroughly. Jonathan Rieder has pointed out, for example, that the "tension between moral traditionalists and modern moralists in the Democratic party . . . was present from the New Deal order's earliest days."[30] He argues, moreover, that McCarthyism can be seen as a first (failed) attempt to garner all the forces for whom the New Deal had been a mixed experience at best.[31] Anticommunism also can be seen as a logical outcome of the state's manipulation of American fears of totalitarianism during World War II. In their effort to make the world safe for democracy, the government experts of "commercial Keynesianism" may well have helped make democracy at home much less secure.

Finally, these experiences—however much they have only been suggested here—may, taken as a whole, shed new light on the contemporary deradicalization of American farmers and farm organizations. As we know, anticommunism dramatically undermined democratic dissent in the American government and American culture at large during the Cold War years. It had a comparable impact on the Farmers' Union, the organization that had been so active on behalf of social democracy for dirt farmers in the depression. During the McCarthy Hearings, for example, the Farmers' Union moved quickly to denounce its previous affiliation with the American Communist party.[32] Meanwhile, its affiliation with the liberal state, at both the leadership and grass-roots levels, led to a wholesale re-working of the organization's previously proto-Populist political agendas. Rather than working against the power of big business and government, as it had for so many years, the Farmers' Union itself became a huge conglomerate, owning thousands of grain elevators and insurance programs. During the Reagan years, it was involved, in alliance with the Farm Security Administration, in massive farm foreclosures.[33] At the end of a life spent in the Farmers' Union, South Dakota Farmers' Holiday Association leader Emil Loriks did not remember that he had ever opposed Franklin Roosevelt.[34]

Not surprisingly, grass-roots organizers have found that the original spirit and actions of the farm radicals have become a nearly forgotten part of the farm past. In the early 1980s, farmers had to be taught how to protest; they had no memory of the barnyard sales, strikes, and other protests that so enlivened the depression years.[35] More critically, however, the substance of the protest has changed from one in which farmers worked for government aid on their own terms to one in which farmers try to protect the liberal status quo. They have been helped in their efforts to save the family farm by urban sympathizers, Farm Aid concerts, and a series of popular films, like *Country* and *The River*. It is telling, indeed, that the heroes and heroines of these films are shown as protectors of American ideals of self-reliance, hard work, and family life but never as recipients of federal aid. However convenient, forgetting the real events and the actual compromises made in the 1930s will prove to be the most destructive strategy of all for rural Americans. As Caroline Bird wrote in the 1960s in regard to the popular revision of the depression era by officials in the Johnson administration, "The victim of selective memory loses touch with himself."[36]

In sum, the experience of the old middle class on the northern plains in the 1930s sheds light on the tensions and struggles they faced in the years that followed. But, just as these experiences are not bound by time, perhaps they are not bound by geography. Shreds of evidence from other places suggest that Dakotans were far from alone in their struggle to come to terms with a new world, even if they do stand alone here to tell of it. We know, for example, that men and women in Colorado were at odds with many programs initiated in the 1930s.[37] We know that hundreds of thousands of Americans responded to the anti-statist ideals of Father Coughlin.[38] And yet, we also know that, in Baton Rouge, neo-populist Huey Long commissioned a modern tower capitol. What we do not know is the impact that regional, ethnic, and racial variations had on the ways in which the old middle class as a whole understood and responded to the multifaceted crisis of the Great Depression. In short, we have yet to see anything close to a full picture of the history of independent proprietorship in the early twentieth century.

We know even less about the ways in which the experience of Dakotans in the Great Depression relates to that of the many Americans who by 1930 were decidedly not in the old middle class. There are few obvious connections, for example, between the experiences of Dakotans in the field and working-class people in city factories. Yet, some aspects of other lives do resonate with familiarity. At the very least, we know that old-middle-class Americans held no monopoly on feelings of fear, shame, or ambivalence.[39] Working-class people in Baltimore and Chicago both felt enormous initial "disdain" for public relief.[40] Moreover, all kinds of Americans encountered mass culture in the 1930s—from Hollywood's political movies to the Superman comics, and even to *Gone with the Wind*—in which characters with traditional values looked for acceptance and authority in the new world.[41] Basic to Frank Capra's political films, for example, "was the rebellious cry of the individual against being trampled into an ort by massiveness— mass production, mass thought, mass education, mass politics, mass wealth, mass conformity . . . a growing resentment against being compartmentalized."[42]

Indeed, if the crisis on Main Street is reduced to a choice between traditional individualism and the liberation of the individual that modernity represents, then this was a conflict faced by each and every American in the early twentieth century. Still, the actual working independence and hegemonic culture of the Dakotans puts this choice in particularly sharp relief. The experience of the people of the Dakotas reveals, for one thing, that accommodation to modernity was less a "choice" than a cultural survival strategy for rural people in the 1930s. It suggests, likewise, that far from all aspects of mass society were unappealing to even the most conservative members of their society. At the same time, however, it suggests that even the most appealing modernist ideals—the changing nature of women's roles, for example—were also associated with loss. As Enid Bern knew, "progress" in many things is worth striving for—so long as we know what is at stake not only for those who make policy or initiate change, but also for those who live out its effects.

The old middle class may have lost the most, as Christopher Lasch contends, in the face of such "progress," but neither they nor their ideals are altogether lost: this, too, is part—the final part—of our story.[43] Whatever the effects of agricultural mechanization, the proletarianization of the small town, and the erosion of community control, North and South Dakota remain a rural enclave in the midst of modern America. Family-farm and small-town ways are still respected there. Hard work, community loyalty, faith in God, and hope in the future still abound. The ideal of a heroic "pioneer heritage" still cures many ills. Of critical importance since the 1930s, however, is that places like North and South Dakota exist in part because they have cured the ills (or perhaps obscured the realities) of people well beyond their borders. As Frank Bechhofer and Brian Elliot have written, the persistence of the old middle class is essential to the continuation of capitalism because it reassures those without a realistic hope of independence that independence is still possible.[44] In the 1930s, Americans were willing to provide massive amounts of aid to a part of the country that, Wall Drug or no, they would never stop to visit. The same is still true. Urban Americans subsidize and sentimentalize rural life because they still want to believe that the overwhelming forces of modern capitalism can be held in check by the quiet strength of traditional ways of life. Americans want to believe that somewhere in the United States the dream that inspired generations of pioneers still comes true today.

APPENDIX

Categorization of Occupations: 1925 South Dakota Census

Old Middle Class	Working Class	New Middle Class
architects	farm laborers	agents
bakers	factory workers	bookkeepers
bankers*	common laborers	engineers
barbers	millers	journalists
blacksmiths	miners	officials
boarding house owners	quarrymen	salesmen
bookbinders	railway employees*	secretaries
brick makers	servants	stenographers
butchers	stockmen	telegraph employees
cabinetmakers		
carpenters		
cigar makers*		
clergymen		
contractors		
dairymen		
dentists		
draymen		
dressmakers		
druggists		
editors		
farmers		
florists		
harness makers		
horsemen		
hotel keepers		
insurance men		
lawyers*		
machinists*		
manufacturers*		
masons		
merchants		
messengers*		
midwives		
milliners		

Old Middle Class	Working Class	New Middle Class

nurses
painters
photographers
physicians
plasterers*
printers
quarrymen*
realtors
shoemakers*
stage drivers
tailors
teachers
undertakers
well borers*

*These occupations can be in more than one category. For example, a "railway employee" could be a track layer (working class) or a station manager (new middle class). Also, some artisanal occupations (such as "harness maker"), if located in a large city like Sioux Falls or Rapid City, might not indicate independence but journeyman or even factory-work status. Finally, there were certainly some Dakotans who were in the upper class (bankers and merchants, for example), especially in the larger cities.

Socio-Economic Distribution of Gainful Workers,
All Races, 1930

Occupation	N.D.	S.D.	N.Y.	Ohio
Percentage of Males in Occupations				
Professional	2.8	3.1	5.4	4.2
Proprietors	45.0	47.0	15.0	18.0
Farmers	37.5	39.1	3.5	9.4
Owners	24.5	21.4	3.1	n/a
Tenants	13.1	17.4	.5	n/a
Retailers	3.5	3.8	6.2	4.2
Officials	3.9	4.1	6.0	4.9
Clerks	7.6	7.4	19.1	13.7
Skilled workers	7.0	7.4	20.4	21.1
Semiskilled workers	3.8	4.8	20.1	17.5
Unskilled workers	33.8	30.4	19.3	25.0
Farm	26.0	21.0	2.8	5.1
Factory	3.0	4.0	6.7	11.3
Other	3.4	4.0	5.1	6.1
Service	1.1	1.0	4.8	2.4
Percentage of Females in Occupations				
Professional	28.8	28.4	12.2	13.7
Proprietors	9.0	9.3	2.3	3.5
Farmers	5.9	5.5	.4	1.1
Owners	n/a	n/a	n/a	n/a
Tenants	n/a	n/a	n/a	n/a
Retailers	.7	1.1	1.0	1.1
Officials	2.4	2.6	.9	1.3
Clerks	20.1	23.7	36.5	34.2
Skilled workers	.3	.4	1.0	1.3
Semiskilled workers	12.0	12.8	27.3	24.5
Unskilled workers	29.8	25.4	20.0	23.0
Farm	4.0	2.9	.2	.3
Factory	.2	.6	.6	1.5
Other	.2	.5	.2	.3
Service	25.4	21.4	19.0	20.7

NOTES

ABBREVIATIONS

AREAA   *Annual Reports of Emergency Agricultural Administration*

BT   *Bismarck Tribune*

DF   *Dakota Farmer*

DOI: BSCC   Director of Institutions: Board of State Capitol Commissioners

FF   *Fargo Forum*

NDH   *North Dakota History*

NDOHP   North Dakota Oral History Project

NDSU, CES   North Dakota State University, Cooperative Extension Service

SDOHP   South Dakota Oral History Project (SDOHP citations give tape number and transcript page number.)

SFAL   *Sioux Falls Argus-Leader*

INTRODUCTION

1. L. P. Hudson, *Reapers of the Dust*, p. 8.

2. By far the best known account of the Dust Bowl remains Steinbeck's *Grapes of Wrath*. Four historical accounts have appeared since 1979: Bonnifield, *Dust Bowl*; Hurt, *Dust Bowl*; Worster, *Dust Bowl*; Gregory, *American Exodus*.

3. Mills, *White Collar*.

4. When a Kansas farmer said this, attention to rural issues in this century was probably at its peak. As quoted in Athearn, *Mythic West*, p. 84.

5. The origins, expressions, and meanings of "producerism," "republicanism," and "producer-republicanism" have been the subjects of some of the most creative and most highly charged scholarship of the past two decades. Classic accounts from social history include Johnson, *Shopkeepers' Millennium* and Ryan, *Cradle of the Middle Class*; from rural history, Henretta, "Families and Farms"; Merrill, "Cash Is Good to Eat"; and Hahn, *Roots of Southern Populism*; from labor history Foner, *Free Soil, Free Labor, Free Men*; Wilentz, *Chants Democratic*; Montgomery, *Beyond Equality*; Rodgers, *Work Ethic*;

and Gutman, *Work, Culture, and Society*. For this study, perhaps the most relevant works center on producerism and politics in the Populist era. Goodwyn, *Democratic Promise*; Hahn and Prude, eds., *Countryside in the Age of Capitalist Transformation*. On the history of republican ideology in the United States, see Wood, *Creation of the American Republic*.

6. One very good book on that shelf is David Thelen's study of Missouri farmers and townspeople in the late-nineteenth and early-twentieth centuries. See Thelen, *Paths of Resistance*.

7. Gutman, *Work, Culture, and Society*.

8. I am indebted to Robert Westbrook for his conceptualization of this shift.

9. Lingeman, *Small Town America*, p. 391.

10. Pells, *Radical Visions and American Dreams*, p. 24.

11. Ryan, *Cradle of the Middle Class*; Lewis, *Main Street*; Faragher, *Sugar Creek*; Veblen, "Country Town," p. 409; see also Lynd and Lynd, *Middletown*; Lynd and Lynd, *Middletown in Transition*; Goodwyn, *Democratic Promise*; Thomas, *Choice before Us*.

12. Wiebe, *Search for Order*; Gutman, *Work, Culture, and Society*.

13. Karl Marx, *Eighteenth Brumaire of Louis Bonaparte*, p. 47, and *Class Struggles in France*, p. 89, as quoted in Mayer, "Lower Middle Class as Historical Problem," p. 416.

14. Karl Marx, *Eighteenth Brumaire of Louis Bonaparte*, p. 22, and *Class Struggles in France*, p. 115, as quoted in Mayer, "Lower Middle Class," p. 426.

15. Hofstadter, *Age of Reform*, pp. 131–72.

16. Geiger, "Panik im Mittlestand"; Lederer, *State of the Masses*; Laswell, "Psychology of Hitlerism"; Gerth, "Nazi Party"; Sheridan, *Nazi Seizure of Power*; Shoenbaum, *Hitler's Social Revolution*. An important American counterpart to the contemporary writing in Europe was Corey, *Crisis of the Middle Class*.

17. An excellent overview of this material is found in Hamilton, *Who Voted for Hitler?*, pp. 424–51.

18. Lewis, *It Can't Happen Here*; Corey, *Crisis of the Middle Class*.

19. Ibid.

20. Brinkley, *Voices of Protest*, p. xi.

21. Curran and Burrows, "Sociology of Petit Capitalism."

22. Ibid., p. 265; see also Thompson and Leyden, "United States of America"; Bechhofer and Elliot, "Persistence and Change"; Bechhofer and Elliot, "Petty Property"; Steinmetz and Wright, "Fall and Rise of the Petty Bourgeoisie."

23. Lasch, *True and Only Heaven*, p. 17.

24. Ibid., p. 531.

25. Bechhofer and Elliot, "Petty Property," p. 184. See also Rieder, *Canarsie*.

26. Lynd and Lynd, *Middletown in Transition*; see also Bird, *Invisible Scar*; Modell, "Public Griefs and Personal Problems."

27. Mills, *White Collar.*

28. Worster, *Dust Bowl.* I do not disagree with the distinguished argument about agriculture presented here, only that Worster does not bring the same keen analytical tools to the new middle class that he does to the farmers and tenants they studied.

29. Hofstadter, *Paranoid Style in American Politics,* p. 64.

30. Athearn, *Mythic West,* pp. 89, 99–103.

31. Ibid., p. 103.

32. Susman, *Culture as History,* p. xx.

33. Brinkley, *Voices of Protest.*

34. Levine, "American Culture in the Great Depression."

35. Levine, "Hollywood's Washington," p. 191.

36. Willson, "Rural Changes," pp. 57–59; D. Robinson, *Fourth Census of South Dakota.* Further elaboration of this enumeration can be found in chap. 2 and in the appendix.

37. In 1930, 93 percent of tenant farmers believed that in five years they would be working farms of their own. Willson, "Rural Changes," p. 74.

38. *FF*, 31 Dec. 1924, p. 9.

39. Hahn, *Roots of Southern Populism,* pp. 29–39.

40. Community "boosterism" in the Dakotas, as in other midwestern towns, historically entailed competing for new industry or large state or federal institutions. In North Dakota, however, a large measure of the success or failure of a given town was in the hands of the railroad. J. Hudson, *Plains Country Towns.* For a detailed discussion of towns competing for industry and trade, see Dykstra, *Cattle Towns.*

41. Herbert T. Hoover, "South Dakota: An Expression of Regional Heritage," in Madison, ed., *Heartland,* p. 202.

42. Wright, "Varieties of Marxist Conceptions."

43. The Missouri River cuts a path through both states, dividing semiarid from arid land, more- from less-sparsely settled counties, and, according to some observers, radical from conservative voters. See McLaird, "From Bib Overalls to Cowboy Boots."

44. E. Robinson, *History of North Dakota,* pp. 199–203.

45. Cronin and Beers, *Areas of Intense Drought Distress.*

46. This concurrently broad and strict definition of class borrows from two different but equally impractical definitions now in use—a strict Marxist definition of class that ignores the ways values and ideals can cut across and beyond work experiences, and a strictly cultural definition, which uses only ideological criteria and leaves no room for an exact outlining of the boundaries of class. In the Dakotas, the old middle class, strictly defined, was a subset of all those who participated in its culture. Among other things, the changing relations between these groups is one of the most significant consequences of the depression era.

47. Several works on cultural conflict in the Midwest have used explanatory strategies other than that of class. The most innovative is R. Jensen's *Winning of the Midwest*, which proposes religious conflict—between "pietists" and "liturgicals"—to be at the heart of differences reflected in electoral politics. Although it has not been studied with care, this difference may also be found in the party affiliations of Democrats and Republicans on the northern plains. What I am suggesting is that in rural areas liturgicals and pietists (or Germans and Norwegians, for that matter) had something in common that went far beyond the particulars of electoral politics. On the northern plains, at least, Dakotans fought tooth and nail over the means but shared the ends of a society of small production.

48. U.S. National Resources Committee, *Population Statistics*, pp. 68–72. See appendix for a breakdown of occupations by gender in the 1930s.

49. Riley, "Farm Women's Roles."

CHAPTER 1

1. In his recent overview, *New Deal and the West*, p. 35, Lowitt concludes, "The greatest desolation centers were in the northern plains states—the Dakotas, eastern Montana, and large sections of Wyoming—though the states of the southern plains, where conditions were almost as critical, received more public attention." See also Worster, *Dust Bowl*, p. 35.

2. Lowitt and Beasley, eds., *One-Third of a Nation*, p. 82.

3. Low, *Dust Bowl Diary*, p. 33.

4. Saloutos, *American Farmer and the New Deal*, pp. 3–33. The other factors that contributed to the collapse were retraction of federal price supports, decline in domestic consumption due to immigration restriction, a declining birthrate, changing dietary habits, and the contraction of foreign markets.

5. E. Robinson, *History of North Dakota*, p. 375; South Dakota State Planning Board, "Mortgage Status of Farm Lands in South Dakota."

6. Tweton and Rylance, *Years of Despair*, p. 4.

7. As quoted in E. Robinson, *History of North Dakota*, p. 375.

8. Schell, *History of South Dakota*, p. 283.

9. Ibid.

10. Interview with Mrs. Esther Vaagen, NDOHP, *NDH* 44, no. 4, p. 15.

11. Interview with David Haxby and Richard Mansfield, SDOHP, no. 030, p. 25. (Hereafter, all interviews from the South Dakota Oral History Project will be followed by a tape number and transcript page number.)

12. Cronin and Beers, *Areas of Intense Drought Distress*, p. 9.

13. L. P. Hudson, *Reapers of the Dust*, p. 78. This is a collection of semiautobiographical short stories. Although some events are fictionalized, Hudson says in the preface: "The stories of all these people and all these events consti-

tute what I believe to be a true statement about a particular time which ought not to be forgotten."

14. Even in a relatively "good" year like 1935, storm damage was extensive. For reports on hail, tornadoes, and floods, see, respectively, *FF*: 1 Jan. 1935, p. 16; 12 July 1935, p. 1; 4 July 1935, p. 1; *Adams County Record*, 16 July 1936, p. 1.

15. F. F. Manfred, *Golden Bowl*, p. 6.

16. As quoted in Tweton and Rylance, *Years of Despair*, p. 5.

17. *Williston Daily Herald*: 3 July 1936, p. 1; 6 July 1936, p. 1; 10 July 1932, p. 1; *BT*, 21 Aug. 1936, p. 4.

18. Tweton and Rylance, *Years of Despair*, p. 8.

19. Interview with Althia Thom, SDOHP, no. 053, p. 23.

20. Tweton and Rylance, *Years of Despair*, p. 8.

21. Ibid.

22. Williston reported 110°, Hettinger 113°, Grafton 107°, and Grand Forks 104° on the same day. The heat wave lasted in most towns from 4 July to 18 July.

23. *Walsh County Record*, 19 July 1936, p. 10.

24. *Walsh County Record*, 9 July 1936, p. 1.

25. Low, *Dust Bowl Diary*, p. 49.

26. L. P. Hudson, *Reapers of the Dust*, p. 79; on heat-related human deaths, see death of Mrs. Julia Ruby, Zeona, S.D., and Mrs. Hilma Greij of Hettinger, N.D., as reported in the *Adams County Record*, 9 July 1936, p. 1.

27. Stegner, ed., *Report of the Lands of the Arid Region*.

28. Smith, *Virgin Land*, pp. 196–200, especially p. 199. See also Worster, *Dust Bowl*, pp. 84–87.

29. Cronin and Beers, *Areas of Intense Drought Distress*, p. 10.

30. *DF*, 22 May 1937, p. 295.

31. This description is a composite based on the following descriptions of dust storms: Lowitt and Beasley, eds., *One-Third of a Nation*, p. 92; F. F. Manfred, *Golden Bowl*, pp. 3–10, 80–91; L. P. Hudson, *Reapers of the Dust*, pp. 3–12.

32. See *Newsweek*, 19 May 1934, pp. 5–6; Low, *Dust Bowl Diary*, p. 96.

33. *Adams County Record*, 17 May 1934, p. 1.

34. *Williston Daily Herald*, 10 May 1934, p. 1; Low, *Dust Bowl Diary*, p. 101; Interview with Lillie Jenks, SDOHP, no. 709, p. 8.

35. L. P. Hudson, *Reapers of the Dust*, p. 11. See also Interview with Althia Thom, SDOHP, no. 053, p. 20.

36. Low, *Dust Bowl Diary*, pp. 152, 97.

37. Cronin and Beers, *Areas of Intense Drought Distress*, pp. 9, 13–14.

38. Ibid., pp. 16–19.

39. Ibid., p. 23.

40. Ibid., p. 29.

41. U.S. National Resources Planning Board, "Regional Planning," p. 1.

42. E. Robinson, *History of North Dakota*, p. 400.

43. F. F. Manfred, *Golden Bowl*, pp. 131–32.

44. Interview with Gilbert and Pearl Wick, NDOHP, *NDH* 44, no. 4, p. 65.

45. Interview with Mrs. Orren Merritt, SDOHP, no. 143, p. 46.

46. Lowitt and Beasley, eds., *One-Third of a Nation*, p. 57.

47. Ibid., pp. 62, 66.

48. Ibid., p. 56.

49. Ibid., pp. 60–61.

50. Ibid., pp. 69, 62.

51. Interview with Julius Albrecht, SDOHP, no. 044, pp. 16–17.

52. Interview with George Costain, SDOHP, no. 202, p. 30.

53. Lowitt and Beasley, eds., *One-Third of a Nation*, p. 84.

54. Interview with Mrs. Gene Whiting, SDOHP, no. 097, p. 33.

55. Ann Marie Low held a number of teaching jobs between 1935 and 1937. One schoolhouse in the winter was rarely more than 20° (*Dust Bowl Diary*, p. 112). For a description of teaching in a dust storm, see Interview with Mrs. Ruchdashel, SDOHP, no. 199, p. 12.

56. As quoted in Tweton and Rylance, *Years of Despair*, p. 4.

57. Hay, "Social Organizations," especially pp. 45, 50, 62, 64, 74, 75.

58. Ibid., pp. 59, 66, 87.

59. Lowitt and Beasley, eds., *One-Third of a Nation*, p. 84.

60. Kumlien, "Basic Trends of Social Change. Part 3," pp. 9–10.

61. This is an image that Frederick Manfred recalls vividly in *Golden Bowl*, especially pp. 3–6.

62. For a view of relief from an earlier period, see Atkins, *Harvest of Grief*.

63. Landis, "Rural Relief in South Dakota," p. 10; Kumlein, "Graphic Summary of the Relief Situation," pp. 18–19, 23, 54–55.

64. Landis, "Rural Relief in South Dakota," p. 10.

65. Saloutos, *American Farmer and the New Deal*, pp. 3–33; Schlesinger, *Coming of the New Deal*, p. 42. On the creation of the Agricultural Adjustment Act, see Kirkendall, *Social Scientists and Farm Politics*, especially pp. 50–60, and Campbell, *Farm Bureau and the New Deal*.

66. Landis, "Rural Relief in South Dakota," pp. 9–10; Kumlien, "Graphic Summary of the Relief Situation," p. 17.

67. Kumlien, "Graphic Summary of the Relief Situation," p. 17; E. Robinson, *History of North Dakota*, p. 406.

68. Tweton, *New Deal at the Grass Roots*, p. 83.

69. Schlesinger, *Coming of the New Deal*, p. 1.

70. Ibid., pp. 277–81. See also Lowitt and Beasley, eds., *One-Third of a Nation*, Introduction.

71. Landis, "Rural Relief in South Dakota," p. 10.

72. Lowitt and Beasley, eds., *One-Third of a Nation*, pp. 57, 69.

73. Schlesinger, *Coming of the New Deal*, pp. 284, 294–95.

74. Landis, "Rural Relief in South Dakota," pp. 14–15; Kumlien, "Graphic Summary of the Relief Situation," pp. 17–18; Schell, *History of South Dakota*, p. 292.

75. E. Robinson, *History of North Dakota*, pp. 407–8.

76. Tweton and Rylance, *Years of Despair*, p. 13.

77. Hendrickson, "Civilian Conservation Corps."

78. For a list of camps in 1935, see *FF*, 23 Feb. 1935, p. 1. One CCC camp was based on land near Ann Marie Low's family's farm. For her descriptions and complaints, see *Dust Bowl Diary*, pp. 112–58.

79. *DF*, 17 Dec. 1938, p. 514. At the same time, the National Youth Administration (NYA) paid young people up to $20 a month to work in libraries and civic buildings after school to help pay for college tuition and other school expenses. As it did elsewhere, the NYA also sponsored camps for young girls to learn home economics and personal grooming habits. Hendrickson, "National Youth Administration"; Hendrickson, "Relief for Youth."

80. Interview with Henry Timm, NDOHP, *NDH* 44, no. 4, pp. 43–44.

81. Schell, *History of South Dakota*, p. 288; Schlesinger, *Coming of the New Deal*, pp. 27–39.

82. Tweton and Rylance, *Years of Despair*, p. 9.

83. Maarten, "'Golden Opportunity'"; Saloutos, *American Farmer and the New Deal*, pp. 66–86; Davis, *Wheat and the AAA*.

84. Schell, *History of South Dakota*, p. 288.

85. Ibid., pp. 288–89.

86. *BT*, 6 Sept. 1936, p. 6.

87. Interview with David Haxby and Richard Mansfield, SDOHP, no. 030, p. 29.

88. Schell, *History of South Dakota*, p. 289.

89. Lambert, "Drought Cattle Purchase."

90. U.S. Congress, House, *Future of the Great Plains*, p. 39.

91. Ibid., pp. 63–67.

92. Saloutos, *American Farmer and the New Deal*, pp. 207, 236–53.

93. Ibid., pp. 197–206.

94. U.S. Department of Agriculture, "Land Use Planning Underway," p. 32.

95. U.S. National Resources Planning Board, "Regional Planning," p. 7.

96. Schlesinger, *Coming of the New Deal*, p. 45.

97. *DF*, 22 Oct. 1938, p. 416.

98. E. Robinson, *History of North Dakota*, p. 447.

99. Arrington, "New Deal in the West," pp. 313–14. The states that received greater per capita spending were Arizona, Montana, Nevada, New Mexico, and Wyoming.

100. Tweton, *New Deal at the Grass Roots*, p. 113.

101. For an overview of the Dakota economy in World War II, see E. Robinson, *History of North Dakota*, pp. 424–27; and Schell, *History of South Dakota*, pp. 302, 355.

102. Tweton and Rylance, *Years of Despair*, p. 16; Schell, *History of South Dakota*, p. 362; Slocum, "Migrants from Rural South Dakota Families, pp. 16–17.

103. Marie Braught Johnson's family left South Dakota for Oregon after wind had blown them out year after year and then grasshoppers ate the one good corn crop they had. They heard that out West "the grass [was] up to the cow's belly, and there was fruit free for the picking." Today, Marie goes back to South Dakota every once in a while to visit, but she would never live there again: "No Way! No Way! I just get that feeling every time I go back, like it used to be. I know it's not quite that bad any more, but . . . no way." Ganzel, *Dust Bowl Descent*, p. 27.

104. E. Robinson, *History of North Dakota*, pp. 397, 409. In South Dakota, some Democrats, like Governor Tom Berry, called themselves "New Deal Democrats." Nevertheless, even Berry believed that "too much government did more harm than good." O'Rourke, "South Dakota Politics," p. 238.

105. Avery, "Some South Dakotans' Opinions," p. 309. Two volunteers for the Otter Tail County Historical Society "were struck by the reluctance of people to talk about the 1930s." Tweton, *New Deal at the Grass Roots*, p. vii.

106. Interview with Althia Thom, SDOHP, no. 053, p. 15. Eric Severeid also recalled the period as one in which people survived "with damn little help from anybody but their neighbors." As quoted in Athearn, *Mythic West*, p. 236.

107. *One Hundred Years in Grant County*. See also Interview with Ella Boschma in Wolff and Cash, comps. and eds., "South Dakotans Remember the Great Depression," p. 234.

CHAPTER 2

1. Interview with Rueben Taralseth, NDOHP, *NDH* 43, no. 2, p. 57.

2. E. Robinson, *History of North Dakota*, pp. 173, 171.

3. Estimated from the 1925 Census (see below), this figure is particularly significant in comparison with David Montgomery's calculation that, in 1875, more than two-thirds of the American work force were wage-laborers. Montgomery, *Beyond Equality*, pp. 28–30.

4. Although it is beginning to change with works like Faragher's *Sugar Creek* and Nelson's *After the West Was Won*, the literature of the agricultural trans-Mississippi West is still preoccupied with the experience of settling, not with the settled places themselves. Even the rich new literature on women in the West examines the role of women on the trail and in frontier society more often than their roles through subsequent generations. See, for example, Faragher, *Women and Men on the Overland Trail*; Schlissel, *Women's Diaries*;

Stratton, *Pioneer Women*. Moreover, in those settled places that have been examined, historians have rarely engaged class as an essential ingredient in understanding social relations there. For example, Lewis Atherton, the best-known historian of the midwestern small town, describes a "middle-class code" that informed the ideals but not the structures of local society. See Atherton, *Main Street on the Middle Border*, pp. 72–76, 100–105, 278–80. Likewise, Richard Lingeman confines his discussion of class to a single chapter of *Small Town America*. Finally, it seems that historians of the American West—new or old—have yet to discover the northern plains as a laboratory for book-length studies at all. With the exception of Schell and Robinson's classic histories, Howard Lamar's *Dakota Territory*, John Hudson's *Plains Country Towns*, Paula Nelson's work, and some dated studies of farm politics, the shelf is nearly bare. Nevertheless, many excellent journal articles and unpublished manuscripts await compilation or completion.

5. Schell, *History of South Dakota*, pp. 158–74.

6. E. Robinson, *History of North Dakota*, pp. 137–40. See also Woodward, *Checkered Years*.

7. According to Rachel Ann Rosenfeld, when family farming won out over large-scale corporate farming in North Dakota, petty production became anything but "an anachronism left over from a previous era." Rosenfeld, *Farm Women*, p. 13.

8. Nelson, *After the West Was Won*; Kohl, *Land of the Burnt Thigh*.

9. E. Robinson, *History of North Dakota*, p. 157.

10. Willson, "Rural Changes," pp. 57–59.

11. E. Robinson, *History of North Dakota*, p. 158.

12. The best treatment to date of Norwegian immigration is Gjerde, *From Peasants to Farmers*. Gjerde tries to bridge the "salt-water curtain" by examining the migration experience from both sides of the Atlantic.

13. Andrew R. L. Cayton and Peter S. Onuf have recently argued that the "bourgeois vision" of society, fostered by most pioneers to the Old Northwest, had begun to crumble by the late nineteenth century—just the moment when mass migration from those states to the Dakotas began (*Midwest and the Nation*, esp. p. 103).

14. Interview with David Haxby, SDOHP, no. 030, p. 40.

15. Interview with Jacob Eisenmenger, SDOHP, no. 194, especially pp. 2–3.

16. Interview with Carl Swanson, SDOHP, no. 111, p. 22.

17. Ruth Carothers to Stock, Aug. 1978.

18. Schlissel, Gibboen, and Hampsten, *Far from Home*.

19. The influence of the railroad on patterns of settlement and the chances for a town's survival has been skillfully documented in J. Hudson, *Plains Country Towns*.

20. These years are covered in the general histories of the two states, as

well as in the histories of the Populist movement. See for example Schell, *History of South Dakota*, pp. 223–41; E. Robinson, *History of North Dakota*, pp. 217–34; Fite, *Farmers' Frontier*; and Hicks, *Populist Revolt*.

21. Schell, *History of South Dakota*, p. 224.

22. Lamar, *Dakota Territory*; E. Robinson, *History of North Dakota*, pp. 230–31.

23. South Dakota State Planning Board, *Land Ownership*; Cap and Brown, "Farm Tenancy and Rental Contracts."

24. Willson, "Rural Changes," p. 74.

25. D. Robinson, *Fourth Census of South Dakota*, pp. 115–50.

26. See appendix for complete listing of occupations and classifications.

27. Lynd and Lynd, *Middletown*.

28. Rodgers, *Work Ethic*, p. xi.

29. Riley, "Farm Women's Roles," 96–98.

30. Interview with Alice Conitz, NDOHP, *NDH* 43, no. 2, p. 53.

31. James Shikany to Stock, 3 Aug. 1978.

32. Mittelstaedt, ed., "General Store Era."

33. Interview with Dr. Leonard Tobin, SDOHP, no. 885, p. 3.

34. Interview with Dr. M. G. Flath, NDOHP, *NDH* 43, no. 2, pp. 38, 39.

35. Rodgers, *Work Ethic*.

36. *SFAL*, 3 Jan. 1925, p. 12.

37. Ruth McNicol Finch to Stock, 10 Aug. 1978.

38. Geraldine M. Robbins to Stock, 10 Aug. 1978.

39. *SFAL*, 3 Jan. 1925, p. 12.

40. *Lake Norden Enterprise* as quoted in *SFAL*, 3 Apr. 1925, p. 12.

41. *Forbes* as quoted in *BT*, 31 Dec. 1929, p. 4; 16 Jan. 1929, p. 4. Simon seems suspicious of government planners and other intellectuals in the late 1920s, writing on 16 Jan. 1929 that "it's all right to entertain ideas, but it's better to give them a stiff kick."

42. *FF*, 20 Feb. 1925, p. 8.

43. *SFAL*, 3 Jan. 1925, p. 12; 13 Jan. 1925, p. 6; 29 July 1925, p. 6; 10 Sept. 1925, p. 6.

44. *Mitchell Gazette* as quoted in *SFAL*, 13 Jan. 1925, p. 6.

45. Ibid.

46. *SFAL*, 7 Dec. 1928, p. 16.

47. Ibid.

48. *SFAL*, 5 Oct. 1925, p. 6.

49. Interview with Althia Thom, SDOHP, no. 053, p. 20.

50. Allen Brigham, *Alpena Journal*, as quoted in *South Dakota Offers Better Opportunities*, p. 11.

51. For estimates on the number of migrants and speculators as opposed to settlers in different parts of the Dakotas, see Willson, "Rural Changes," and Kumlien, "Standard of Living of Farm and Village Families," pp. 46–48.

52. The best argument for "community" life on the frontier is presented by Faragher, *Sugar Creek*, pp. 130–42. See also Hine, *Community on the American Frontier*. For a complete discussion of the idea of community in American life, as well as a critical overview of the historical literature on community, see Bender, *Community and Social Change*.

53. *SFAL*, 10 Sept. 1925, p. 6; 29 July 1925, p. 6.

54. Ruth Carothers to Stock, Aug. 1978.

55. Grace Campbell to Stock, 7 Aug. 1978.

56. Interview with Ada Engsten, NDOHP, *NDH* 44, no. 4, p. 34.

57. Ruth Carothers to Stock, Aug. 1978.

58. See, for example, descriptions of community life in *South Dakota Offers Better Opportunities*, pp. 11, 23, 25, 31, 33.

59. Ibid., pp. 47–49.

60. *SFAL*, 10 Sept. 1925, p. 6. The disparity between the existence of class difference and the language of classlessness is one of the best known qualities of small-town life. See description and discussion in Lingeman, *Small Town America*, pp. 393–440.

61. Hahn, *Roots of Southern Populism*, chap. 2, especially pp. 50–52.

62. Hine, *Community on the American Frontier*, pp. 93–126.

63. Ruth McNicol Finch to Stock, 10 Aug. 1978.

64. Huey, "Making Music," p. 7.

65. For a discussion of the role of state fairs in rural culture see Marling, *Blue Ribbon*.

66. Faragher, *Sugar Creek*, p. 170.

67. Hay, "Social Organizations," pp. 40–50; Kumlien, "Social Problem of the Church"; Kumlien, "Basic Trends of Social Change. Part 8."

68. Hay, "Social Organizations," p. 43.

69. Kumlien, "Social Problem of the Church," especially p. 3.

70. Faragher, *Sugar Creek*, p. 170.

71. Hay, "Social Organizations," pp. 50–76; Kumlien, "Basic Trends of Social Change. Part 3."

72. South Dakota State Planning Board and Day County Planning Board, *Economic and Social Survey*, pp. 20–24.

73. Helen Parkman interview, 24 July 1986.

74. *FF*, 4 Jan. 1925, p. 8.

75. Martinson, "Some Memoirs of a Nonpartisan League Organizer"; Remele, "North Dakota's Forgotten Farmers' Union." On the idea that nineteenth-century political parties, and the Populist party in particular, forged a culture or a community of its own altogether different from the atomizing experience of modern-day politics, see Goodwyn, *Democratic Promise*.

76. *FF*, 31 Dec. 1924, p. 9.

77. *SFAL*, 28 Jan. 1926, p. 6.

78. *FF*, 31 Dec. 1924, p. 9.

CHAPTER 3

1. Interview with Benjamin Wangsness, SDOHP, no. 1152, p. 2.

2. Wolff and Cash, comps. and eds., "South Dakotans Remember the Great Depression," pp. 243–47.

3. See, for example, Lynd and Lynd, *Middletown*; Lynd and Lynd, *Middletown in Transition*; Warner, *Yankee City*; West, *Plainville*.

4. Lingeman, *Small Town America*, p. 401; West, *Plainville*, p. xii.

5. Ruth McNicol Finch to Stock, 10 Aug. 1978.

6. Ibid.; Grace Campbell interview, 30 July 1986.

7. Rambow, "Ku Klux Klan in the 1920s."

8. Harwood, "Ku Klux Klan in Grand Forks."

9. Ibid.

10. Ibid.

11. Several very useful sources on immigration to and ethnic cultures in the Dakotas have recently been published. Sherman, *Prairie Mosaic*; Berg, ed., *Ethnic Heritage*; Ostergren, "European Settlement and Ethnicity Patterns"; Myers, "An Immigrant Heritage." An older source on South Dakota is still very helpful: Johansen, *Immigrant Settlements and Social Organization*.

12. E. Robinson, *History of North Dakota*, p. 282.

13. Ibid., pp. 282–83, 290.

14. Peterson, "Norwegian Farm Homes," p. 4.

15. The history of German-Russian migration is covered in several different accounts. See, for example, E. Robinson, *History of North Dakota*, pp. 282–88; Isenmenger, "McIntosh German-Russians"; Aberle, *From the Steppes to the Prairies*; John E. Pfeiffer, "German-Russians and their Immigration to South Dakota," in Blakely, ed., *Selected Papers*, pp. 200–211. One of the best primary sources on life in a German-Russian town is Wishek, *Along the Trails of Yesterday*.

16. The isolation of German-Russians until 1930 is described in several sources. See, for example, Isenmenger, "McIntosh German-Russians," pp. 11–17.

17. Ibid., p. 11; see also E. Robinson, *History of North Dakota*, pp. 287–88.

18. Welsch, "Germans from Russia."

19. Watne, "Public Opinion."

20. Petry, "Morality Legislation."

21. Easton, "Women's Suffrage"; E. Robinson, *History of North Dakota*, pp. 259, 287; Myers, "Immigrant Heritage." See also Blackorby, "Political Factional Strife in North Dakota."

22. Richard Jensen contends that the political differences between Republicans and Democrats in the Midwest in the late nineteenth century can be traced to the religious and cultural differences between "pietists" and "liturg-

icals." Although the Dakotas are not included in his study, these distinctions may be applicable there as well. See R. Jensen, *Winning of the Midwest*.

23. The published literature on populism in North and South Dakota has grown considerably in recent years due to revived interest in the subject among social historians in general. For an overview of northern plains populism, see Hicks, *Populist Revolt*; Hendrickson, "Political Aspects of the Populist Movement"; Dibbern, "Who Were the Populists?"

24. The published writings on the NPL have also increased in recent years. See E. Robinson, *History of North Dakota*, pp. 327–51; Morlan, *Political Prairie Fire*; and Larry Remele, "Power to the People: The Nonpartisan League," in Howard, ed., *North Dakota Political Tradition*, pp. 66–92.

25. Kathleen Moum, "Social Origins of the Nonpartisan League."

26. D. Jerome Tweton, "The Anti-League Movement: The IVA," in Howard, ed., *North Dakota Political Tradition*, pp. 93–122.

27. See also David Danbom, "North Dakota: The Most Midwestern State," in Madison, ed., *Heartland*, pp. 112–14.

28. Ibid., p. 96.

29. Helen Parkman interview, 24 July 1986.

30. *BT*, 7 Nov. 1928, p. 1.

31. *SFAL*, 13 Apr. 1925, p. 2.

32. For actual maps of the different ways in which the railroad cut towns into two "sides," see J. Hudson, *Plains Country Towns*, p. 88.

33. Unless otherwise indicated, the following account is drawn from Interview with Theodore Straub, SDOHP, no. 1034, incomplete transcript, or Straub, *Autobiography*.

34. In his recent work, John Bodnar discusses the role of middle-class businessmen in immigrant communities. See Bodnar, *Transplanted*, pp. 117–37.

35. Straub, *Autobiography*, p. 66.

36. For a brief discussion of the professionalization of the funeral business in the United States, see B. Bledstein, *Culture of Professionalism*, pp. 4–5.

37. Straub, *Autobiography*, p. 69.

38. For Theodore, however, German-Russian custom was little more than an irritant. It required, for example, that he embalm a body in a bedroom where family members could appear periodically from behind a dividing sheet or curtain to see how he was faring. (Soon he learned to attach a handkerchief soaked in ether to the curtain to make sure they would go away.) As long as he was only his father's assistant, Theodore tried to be patient. His father had asked him to promise not to "upset the pattern in which he had run the business from its inception" (*Autobiography*, p. 68).

39. Ibid., p. 79.

40. Ibid., p. 130.

41. Ibid., pp. 133–34.

42. Ibid., p. 124.

43. Interview with Theodore Straub, SDOHP, no. 1034, incomplete transcript.

44. *Eureka!*, p. 280.

45. Interview with Theodore Straub, SDOHP, no. 1034, incomplete transcript.

46. "Eureka, S.D., was once the World's Wheat Mart," *Life*, Aug. 1937, pp. 20–33.

47. The new interest in American folk cultures was inspired in part by the publication of three classic anthropological works: Robert Redfield's *Tepoztlan*, Ruth Benedict's *Patterns of Culture*, and Robert and Helen Lynd's *Middletown*. It had widespread popular repercussions as well, including an interest in regionalist painters, regionalist fiction, and the WPA's American Guide series. See Susman, *Culture as History*, chap. 4; Pells, *Radical Visions and American Dreams*; Marling, *Wall-to-Wall America*.

CHAPTER 4

1. Interview with Grace Martin Highley, SDOHP, no. 790, pp. 2–3; Wolff and Cash, comps. and eds., "South Dakotans Remember the Great Depression," pp. 257–58.

2. Interview with Grace Martin Highley, SDOHP, no. 790, pp. 2–3.

3. Although political and economic studies have dominated scholarship, a few historians have pointed to the cultural implications of the disaster. Best of all of these is Susman, *Culture as History*, especially chaps. 9 and 10 and the introduction. See also McElvaine, *Great Depression*.

4. Lowitt and Beasley, eds., *One-Third of a Nation*, p. 93.

5. Interview with Mr. and Mrs. E. B. Dwight, SDOHP, no. 391, p. 13.

6. *BT*, 11 Sept. 1936, p. 3; see also editor of *Traill County Tribune*, who tells readers to have "more faith in nature, in ourselves, and in our country." As quoted in *FF*, 7 July 1934, p. 4.

7. Hay, "Problems of Rural Youth," especially p. 1.

8. Kumlien, "Basic Trends of Social Change. Part 2," p. 23.

9. Kumlien, "What Farmers Think of Farming."

10. Hay, "Problems of Rural Youth," pp. 35–38.

11. Ibid., p. 1.

12. Low, *Dust Bowl Diary*, p. 52.

13. Ibid., pp. 184–85.

14. One of the things Dakotans remember most fondly about the depression is the ways in which neighbors tried, despite the obvious difficulties, to help one another. As Mrs. Orren Merritt remembered it, "[People] tried to make the best of things and were, oh, happy, good neighbors," she said. "[They] helped each other out whenever they could. . . . If someone had a good gar-

den, they'd share it with you." Interview with Mrs. Orren Merritt, SDOHP, no. 142, p. 48.

15. Interview with Oscar Fosheim, SDOHP, no. 002, p. 2.

16. Lois Phillips Hudson suggested that "people who had lived for three generations under the homesteaders' law of unconditional hospitality to those in need now began to live there under another law—the law of the desert" (*Reapers of the Dust*, p. 78).

17. Lantis, "Rural Socio-Economic Conditions in Ward County," p. 85.

18. L. P. Hudson, *Bones of Plenty*, p. 424.

19. Landis, "Rural Relief in South Dakota," pp. 42–44.

20. Interview with Hugh O'Connor, NDOHP, *NDH* 44, no. 4, p. 49.

21. As quoted in Lowitt and Beasley, eds., *One-Third of a Nation*, p. 67. Like O'Connor and the North Dakota administrators, most Dakotans believed that the dole could destroy both individual and community self-reliance. Over and over again, editors of Dakota newspapers and other social leaders issued the same kinds of warnings. "An important job for the future is that of rebuilding self-reliance," wrote Charles Day at the *SFAL*, 20 June 1933, p. 6. See also 4 Apr. 1933, p. 6. Even Tom Berry, the "New Deal governor" of South Dakota, included this warning in his inaugural address: "We must get away from living on the government and commence to start living under it." *SFAL*, 29 June 1933, p. 6.

22. Interview with Steve Hakl, SDOHP, no. 759, p. 34.

23. Interview with Hugh O'Connor, NDOHP, *NDH* 44, no. 4, p. 49.

24. As quoted in *FF*, 21 Feb. 1935, p. 4.

25. Interview with O. Leonard Orvedal, NDOHP, *NDH* 44, no. 4, p. 72.

26. Interview with Homer Ayres, SDOHP, no. 187, p. 16. Worse still, however, were the ways shopkeepers handled their relief customers, refusing to sell them tobacco or pepper, for example, "because they said [it] would just give them an appetite and they'd just eat that much more" (p. 15).

27. L. P. Hudson, *Bones of Plenty*, pp. 420–21.

28. L. P. Hudson, *Reapers of the Dust*, p. 8.

29. Stine, "Development of Social Welfare in North Dakota."

30. Interview with Al J. Vohs, NDOHP, *NDH* 44, no. 4, p. 44.

31. *FF*, 1 Mar. 1935, p. 1.

32. *BT*, 1 Sept. 1936, p. 4.

33. *FF*, 27 Jan. 1935; 28 Jan. 1935; 29 Jan. 1935; 1 Feb. 1935.

34. Wolff and Cash, comps. and eds., "South Dakotans Remember the Great Depression," pp. 251–55.

35. Sannes, "Organizing Teamsters in South Dakota in the 1930s."

36. *BT*, 1 Sept. 1936, p. 4.

37. *FF*, 27 Jan. 1935, p. 16.

38. *FF*, 7 July 1935, p. 18.

39. L. P. Hudson, *Bones of Plenty*, pp. 428–29.

40. L. P. Hudson, *Reapers of the Dust*, p. 8.

41. Lowitt and Beasley, eds., *One-Third of a Nation*, pp. 95–96.

42. Susman, *Culture as History*, p. xx.

43. Low, *Dust Bowl Diary*, p. 117

44. Ibid., p. 149.

45. Ibid., pp. 102–5.

46. Ibid., p. 124.

47. Ibid., p. 129.

48. Ibid., p. 15

49. Schlesinger, *Coming of the New Deal*, pp. 16–18; Finegold and Skocpol, "Capitalists, Farmers, and Workers in the New Deal."

50. Finegold, "From Agrarianism to Adjustment," pp. 20–23.

51. Agnew, "A Touch of Class," p. 70; see also Ehrenreich and Ehrenreich, "Professional-Managerial Class"; Mills, *White Collar*.

52. Agnew, "A Touch of Class," p. 72.

53. Susman, *Culture as History*, p. xx.

54. Skowronek, *Building a New American State*, chap. 1.

55. Karl, "Presidential Planning and Social Research."

56. Kirkendall, *Social Scientists and Farm Politics*.

57. As Agnew sees it, it was not until the 1930s that the new middle class really discovered itself either. "Touch of Class," p. 62.

58. Herman Kahn as quoted in Schlesinger, *Coming of the New Deal*, p. 17.

59. Ibid., p. 18.

60. As quoted in Westbrook, "Tribune of the Technostructure," p. 400.

61. Agnew, "A Touch of Class," p. 62. A number of books in the 1930s and early 1940s discussed the changing nature of middle-class work relations. See Burnham, *Managerial Revolution*; Corey, *Crisis of the Middle Class*; Soule, *Coming American Revolution*.

62. Stott, *Documentary Expression*, introduction, chap. 1.

63. As quoted in Agnew, "A Touch of Class," p. 65.

64. As quoted in Westbrook, "Tribune of the Technostructure," p. 403.

65. Fite, "Farmer Opinion," p. 673.

66. *DF*, 8 Oct. 1938, p. 388.

67. As quoted in Schlesinger, *Coming of the New Deal*, p. 46.

68. Kirkendall, *Social Scientists and Farm Politics*, p. 43.

69. Schapsmeier and Schapsmeier, *Henry Wallace of Iowa*; Kirkendall, "Mind of a Farm Leader."

70. The term "service intellectual" is taken from Kirkendall, *Social Scientists and Farm Politics*, preface.

71. Finegold, "From Agrarianism to Adjustment," p. 21; Saloutos, *American Farmer and the New Deal*, pp. 40–55.

72. Finegold, "From Agrarianism to Adjustment," p. 21.

73. Ibid., pp. 22–25; Schlesinger, *Coming of the New Deal*, p. 38. One South Dakotan was directly involved in drafting the legislation for the AAA. See Williams, "W. R. Ronald."

74. Fite calls the AAA the farmers' "unwanted child." "Farmer Opinion," p. 673.

75. U.S. Congress, House, *Future of the Great Plains*, pp. 63–67.

76. Curtis, *Mind's Eye, Mind's Truth*, p. 25.

77. Ibid., p. vii.

78. Ibid., p. 71.

79. Thomas Stokes as quoted in Schlesinger, *Coming of the New Deal*, p. 18.

80. *DF*, 2 May 1934, p. 215.

81. Lowitt and Beasley, eds., *One-Third of a Nation*, pp. 63–66, 83. In Huron, South Dakota, for example, she met with men from the local Kiwanis Club who told her, "We don't want any dole. All we want is a chance to carry ourselves through the winter so we'll be able to become self-supporting next year if we have half a chance" (p. 83).

82. Lowitt and Beasley, eds., *One-Third of a Nation*, p. 53.

83. Ibid., p. 76.

84. *SFAL*, 7 Apr. 1933, p. 6.

85. *DF*, 26 Feb. 1938, p. 94.

86. *SFAL*, 27 July 1933, p. 6; 29 July 1933, p. 6.

87. As quoted in *SFAL*, 30 Mar. 1933, p. 1.

88. As quoted in *FF*, 25 Apr. 1934, p. 10.

89. *DF*, 6 Jan. 1934, p. 10.

90. *DF*, 12 May 1934, p. 215.

91. *DF*, 29 Jan. 1938, p. 53.

92. *DF*, 26 Feb. 1938, p. 94.

93. *SFAL*, 14 Apr. 1933, p. 6.

94. *DF*, 3 Aug. 1935, p. 282.

95. *FF*, 27 June 1934, p. 12.

96. *FF*, 19 July 1934, p. 4; see also *DF*, 27 Apr. 1935, p. 153.

97. *BT*, 11 July 1936, p. 4.

98. *DF*, 10 June 1933.

99. As quoted in *FF*, 4 July 1934, p. 8.

100. Susman, *Culture as History*, pp. 158–60.

101. M. Catalina to Eleanor Roosevelt, 21 Apr. 1934, Box 2190, E. Roosevelt Papers.

102. E. Robinson, *History of North Dakota*, pp. 399–404.

103. *SFAL*, 21 Apr. 1933, p. 6.

104. *SFAL*, 16 Apr. 1933, p. 6.

105. David Danbom, "North Dakota: The Most Midwestern State," in Madison, ed., *Heartland*, p. 112.

106. A very helpful and perceptive study of resistance to and acceptance of new ideas in farming is Danbom, *Resisted Revolution*.

107. *DF*, 9 Jan. 1932, p. 3. See also Fite, "Transformation of South Dakota Agriculture," p. 283.

108. Kumlien, "Basic Trends of Social Change. Part 2," p. 11.

109. On the popularity of the automobile, see E. Robinson, *History of North Dakota*, pp. 379–80.

110. Wasson, "Use of Time."

111. *DF*, 1 Feb. 1930, p. 112.

112. *DF*, 12 Mar. 1938, p. 128.

113. *SFAL*, 24 Oct. 1926, p. 4. Roy Alden Atwood makes a similar argument about the reactions of Iowans to Rural Free Delivery in "Routes of Rural Discontent."

114. Bern, "Memoirs of a Prairie Schoolteacher," p. 16.

115. See, for example, Avery, "Some South Dakotans' Opinions"; Nash, *American West*.

116. Vyzralek, "Dakota Images."

117. Mills, *White Collar*; see also "Professional Ideology of Social Pathologists," in Mills, *Power, Politics, and People*, pp. 525–52. It may well be that Mills overstated his case here. In fact, it is more important that the new middle class shared the *ideals* of the old middle class than that they came from the same background. Likewise, even though the New Dealers may have been more nostalgic about than sympathetic toward the rural past, they did anything but diminish its significance. On the difference between "nostalgia" and "memory," see Lasch, *True and Only Heaven*.

118. Barrett, *Memories of a County Agent*; Baker *County Agent*; Danbom, "Agricultural Experiment Station and Professionalization."

119. Kirkendall, *Social Scientists and Farm Politics*, chap. 1.

120. A great body of literature describes the "conservative" consequences of New Deal reform. For the path-breaking essay and an early historiographic overview, see Bernstein, "New Deal"; Auerbach, "New Deal, Old Deal, or Raw Deal."

121. Bremer, "Along the 'American Way.'"

122. Reid, ed., *Picturing Minnesota, 1936–1943*, p. 2.

123. *BT*, 28 Aug. 1936, p. 1.

124. Nellie Fitzgerald to Eleanor Roosevelt, 21 Jan. 1937, Box 2233, p. 1, E. Roosevelt Papers.

125. The letters from every state can be found in the "Clergy Letters" Collection, President's Personal Files, 21a, Franklin D. Roosevelt Library, Hyde Park, N.Y. The letters are filed by state; together they fill eighty-one boxes. The "N.D." and "S.D." refer to the box in which each state's letters are filed. Photocopies of the letters from North Dakota can be found in the "New Deal

Clergy" Collection, MS. 588, Orin G. Libby Manuscript Collection, Department of Special Collections, Chester Fritz Library, University of North Dakota.

126. These letters have been analyzed before but hardly with much concern for subtext. See Billington and Clark, "Clergy Reaction to the New Deal."

127. Rosenman, *Public Papers and Addresses of Franklin D. Roosevelt*, p. 370.

128. Oliver Seim to FDR, 29 Oct. 1935, N.D., "Clergy Letters" Collection.

129. H. Holzhausen to FDR, 23 Oct. 1935, N.D., p. 4, "Clergy Letters" Collection.

130. Madison, "Reformers and the Rural Church"; for contemporary works here, see Brunner, *Churches of Distinction*; Fry, *Diagnosing the Rural Church*; Douglass and Brunner, *Protestant Church as a Social Institution*.

131. Kumlien, "Basic Trends of Social Change. Part 8," p. 17. For more on the relationship between clergy and their reformers, see Stock, "FDR and the Forgotten Class."

132. Frederick Errington to FDR, 22 Oct. 1935, N.D., "Clergy Letters" Collection.

133. Most of the time, the clergy did not reveal their own desperate circumstances to FDR. This kind of information is easily uncovered, however, in church and community histories. See, for example, *Diamond Jubilee*, p. 133. (Kinzler's church was not finally completed until 1955.) and "History of the Carrington Congregational Church" from the "Church History" Collection.

134. Hacktor Moe to FDR, 22 Oct. 1935, S.D., "Clergy Letters" Collection, p. 2. "Your Letter of September 24 was duly received. I wish to thank you for the confidence you show in my calling. It is the first time to my knowledge that the President of the U.S. has asked the clergy for information."

135. Ibid.

136. John Drewelow to FDR, 3 Nov. 1935, N.D., "Clergy Letters" Collection.

137. W. W. Gunter to FDR, 15 Jan. 1936, N.D., "Clergy Letters" Collection.

138. N. W. Stoa to FDR, 14 Nov. 1935, N.D., "Clergy Letters" Collection.

139. See O. E. Kinzler to FDR, 16 Oct. 1935, N.D., "Clergy Letters" Collection; C. S. Pederson to FDR, 23 Oct. 1935, N.D., "Clergy Letters" Collection; Wendell Walton to FDR, 20 Oct. 1935, S.D., "Clergy Letters" Collection.

140. V. H. Dissen to FDR, 24 Oct. 1935, N.D., "Clergy Letters" Collection.

141. C. E. Peters and H. M. Anderson to FDR, 22 Oct. 1935, S.D., "Clergy Letters" Collection.

142. Felix Hummer to FDR, 24 Oct. 1935, N.D., "Clergy Letters" Collection; Lorenz Weber to FDR, 16 Oct. 1935, N.D., "Clergy Letters" Collection.

143. Monseigneur Grabig to FDR, n.d., S.D., "Clergy Letters" Collection.

144. O. E. Kinzler to FDR, 16 Oct. 1935, N.D., "Clergy Letters" Collection.

CHAPTER 5

1. *Dickinson Daily Press*, 9 Feb. 1933, p. 4, quoted in Remele, "Public Opinion," p. 58.

2. It has been generally understood, if not thoroughly documented, that the farmers of the Holiday Association were owners, owners' children, and tenants who had recently lost their land. Shover, *Cornbelt Rebellion*, chap. 1; Karr, "Farm Rebels of Plymouth County, Iowa," especially pp. 641–43. Even local officials of the Communist party acknowledged that the FHA was an example of "petty-bourgeois" not working-class revolutionism, though it hoped nonetheless to "point out to the agrarian petty bourgeoisie the robber side of finance capital, its alliance with the rich farmer capitalist against the poor and middle farmers . . . its role as governmental oppressor, tax-looter and warmaker, and win the passive or active support of the poor and middle farmer for the proletarian revolution." Whittaker Chambers, as quoted in Shover, *Cornbelt Rebellion*, p. 67.

3. Although they have missed many other developments on the northern plains in the twentieth century, historians have not neglected the Farmers' Holiday Association. Nonetheless, scholars are divided as to the relative merits and political orientation of the organization. Those who have associated the FHA with potentially antidemocratic causes include Hofstadter, *Age of Reform* and Schlesinger, *Politics of Upheaval*. The other camp includes scholars who place the FHA within the history of radical farm movements that attempted to retain a more (not less) democratic and/or "republican" way of life. Shover, *Cornbelt Rebellion*, pp. 33, 215–16; Shover, "Populism in the 1930s"; Pratt, "Radicals, Farmers, and Historians"; Brinkley, *Voices of Protest*. Regional historians have also begun to document the work of the FHA in the northern plains states. Among the earliest of these was Saloutos and Hicks, *Agricultural Discontent*. More recent works, some as yet unpublished, include: Remele, "North Dakota Farm Strike"; Miller, "Restrained, Respectable Radicals"; Pratt, "Farm Revolt on the Northern Plains."

4. Morlan, *Political Prairie Fire*. For shorter histories of the movement, see E. Robinson, *History of North Dakota*, chap. 15; Remele, "Power to the People: The Nonpartisan League," in Howard, ed., *North Dakota Political Tradition*, pp. 66–92.

5. The following account is taken, except where otherwise noted, from Shover, *Cornbelt Rebellion*, pp. 28–33, and Saloutos and Hicks, *Agricultural Discontent*, pp. 436–41. See also Dileva, "Frantic Farmers Fight Law"; Davenport, "Get Away from those Cows," pp. 10–11.

6. Shover, *Cornbelt Rebellion*, p. 29.

7. On the relationship between the FBF and the Agricultural Colleges and United States Department of Agriculture in general in this period, see Campbell, *Farm Bureau and the New Deal*.

8. As quoted in Saloutos and Hicks, *Agricultural Discontent*, p. 439. For more on Reno, see White, *Milo Reno*.

9. Saloutos and Hicks, *Agricultural Discontent*, p. 440.

10. On this initial meeting, see Shover, *Cornbelt Rebellion*, pp. 37–40.

11. Williams, *Emil Loriks*, pp. 35–61. Loriks's own account of the development of South Dakota's FHA can be found in several places, including: Interview with Emil Loriks, SDOHP, no. 001, pp. 17–20; Terkel, *Hard Times*, p. 227; Emil Loriks, "Great Depression: The Early Thirties and the Farmers' Holiday Movement," in Blakely, ed., *Selected Papers*, pp. 497–501.

12. As quoted in Conrad and Conrad, *Fifty Years*, pp. 35–36.

13. Miller, "Restrained, Respectable Radicals," p. 444.

14. *McKenzie County Farmer*, 25 Aug. 1932, p. 4, quoted in Remele, "Public Opinion," p. 35. According to the editor of the *Bismarck Capitol* (reprinted in the *Hebron Herald*, 25 Aug. 1932), "Unlike usual strikes, this one seems to have aroused the editors of the most conservative and respected papers to make comment on the justice of the move if not exactly approving the method" (Remele, "Public Opinion," pp. 37–38).

15. Emil Loriks, WNAX radio, 20 Sept. 1932, as quoted in Williams, *Emil Loriks*, p. 28.

16. The North Dakota resolutions are discussed and reprinted in Dodd, "Farmer Takes a Holiday," pp. 19–32, appendix. They are also discussed in detail in the *Dunn County Journal* (also known as the *Dunn County Farmer's Press*), 11 Aug. 1932, p. 1. In 1934, the *Dunn County Journal* became the *Farmer-Labor Defender and the Dunn County Journal*, then the official organ of the FHA, with Usher Burdick as editor.

17. Shover, *Cornbelt Rebellion*, pp. 38–39.

18. John Simpson, president of the National Farmers' Union, was accorded more time at these hearings than any other witness. See U.S. Senate, Committee on Agriculture and Forestry, *Agricultural Emergency Act*, pp. 104–18, 119–28, 164–72. On Simpson himself, see Fite, "John A. Simpson."

19. U.S. Senate, Committee on Agriculture and Forestry, *Agricultural Emergency Act*, pp. 109, 111.

20. Ibid., pp. 116–17.

21. *Minot Daily News*, 20 Aug. 1932, p. 3, quoted in Remele, "Public Opinion," p. 39. See also *Parshall Plainsman*, 25 Aug. 1932, p. 4, quoted in Remele, "Public Opinion," pp. 39–40.

22. U.S. Senate, Committee on Agriculture and Forestry, *Agricultural Emergency Act*, p. 123.

23. Ibid., pp. 111–12.

24. Anderson, "Metamorphosis of American Agrarian Idealism." On the increasing importance of consumption to farm leaders, I have taken my lead from Casper, "'A Plain Business Proposition.'"

25. As quoted in Williams, *Emil Loriks*, p. 155.

26. Remele, "Public Opinion," p. 40.

27. U.S. Senate, Committee on Agriculture and Forestry, *Agricultural Emergency Act*, p. 119.

28. Ibid., pp. 120–21.

29. This was one of Loriks's favorite rhetorical rally-calls during the FHA campaign and later on as well. See Williams, *Emil Loriks*, p. 157.

30. For a complete discussion of the strike, see Shover, *Cornbelt Rebellion*, pp. 41–57; Remele, "North Dakota Farm Strike."

31. *Dunn County Journal*, 20 Oct. 1932, p. 1.

32. As quoted in Williams, *Emil Loriks*, p. 81.

33. Remele, "North Dakota Farm Strike," p. 11; Remele, "Public Opinion," chap. 3.

34. This kind of mediation was so effective in South Dakota, historically a more politically conservative state than North Dakota, that far fewer "penny sales" actually occurred there. See Miller, "Restrained, Respectable Radicals," p. 440.

35. Williams, *Emil Loriks*, p. 27; see also Miller, "Restrained, Respectable Radicals," pp. 440–41.

36. Dodd, "Farmer Takes a Holiday," pp. 49–50.

37. Conrad and Conrad, *Fifty Years*, p. 37.

38. Dodd, "Farmer Takes a Holiday," p. 48; Dodd also suggests that the FHA had a kind of unwritten moral code that guided their decisions on who to help in the community. In general, it seems, the farmers would not help "those who did not help themselves" or were "bad farmers" to begin with (pp. 50–51).

39. Williams, *Emil Loriks*, pp. 45–52.

40. Ibid., p. 154.

41. Several historians have tried to capture the colorful—and long—career of the "fighting governor." See Holzworth, *Fighting Governor*; Rylance, "William Langer"; "Political Crisis," in Tweton and Rylance, *Years of Despair*.

42. As quoted in Conrad and Conrad, *Fifty Years*, p. 38.

43. Dodd, "Farmer Takes a Holiday," appendix.

44. Rylance, "William Langer." Langer was indicted for the misappropriation of Civilian Works Administration funds and yet was reelected by a wide margin. Subsequently, his election was recalled, as were the elections of several of his replacements. Altogether, there were five governors in a seven-month period in the state, a record for any state government. Despite all of this, Langer served as a U.S. senator from North Dakota for nearly twenty years.

45. See Hjalmervik, "William Langer's First Administration," pp. 15–19; Shover, *Cornbelt Rebellion*, p. 153; Saloutos and Hicks, *Agricultural Discontent*, pp. 482–84.

46. As quoted in Shover, *Cornbelt Rebellion*, pp. 161–62.

47. As quoted in Saloutos and Hicks, *Agricultural Discontent*, p. 486; see also *DF*, 25 Nov. 1933, p. 349.

48. As quoted in Williams, *Emil Loriks*, p. 57.

49. On Reno and Kennedy's continued radicalism, see Shover, *Cornbelt Rebellion*, pp. 187–99. For Brinkley's consideration of that particular ideology, see Brinkley, *Voices of Protest*.

50. On the Townsend Plan, see letters to *DF*, 6 June 1936, p. 298. This plan advocated pensions for all Americans of retirement age as a way to prime the economic pump.

51. An early evaluation of the response of farmers, nationwide, to the AAA is Fite, "Farmer Opinion," pp. 656–73. To Fite, the issue in farm legislation was the means, not the end, of federal support, as farmers preferred cost of production nearly two-to-one over domestic allotment.

52. NDSU, CES, *AREAA*: 1933.

53. Tontz, "Membership of General Farmers' Organizations"; Tucker, "Populism Up-to-Date."

54. Danbom, *Resisted Revolution*.

55. Barrett, *Memories of a County Agent*, pp. 67–73

56. NDSU, CES, *AREAA*: 1933, Stark County, p. 36.

57. Ibid., Ransom County, p. 1; Benson County, p. 1.

58. Ibid., Nelson County, p. 5; Renville County, p. 3.

59. Ibid., Sioux County, n.p.

60. Ibid., Sheridan County, p. 2.

61. Ibid., Sioux County, n.p.

62. Ibid., Renville County, p. 4.

63. Ibid., Renville County, p. 5.

64. Ibid., Ransom County, n.p.

65. Ibid., Renville County, p. 3

66. Ibid., Benson County, p. 11

67. Ibid., Ransom County, n.p.

68. Ibid., Sioux County, n.p.

69. Ibid., Nelson County, exhibits 2, 3.

70. Ibid., Ransom County, n.p. One local columnist was well aware of the ways in which the government borrowed from the farmers' traditional language of cooperation. As T. E. Hayes wrote, "If the [new AAA] gets past the Supreme Court, our farmers will be back under the old Feudal System—wards of the government; no longer the sons of freedom, for their liberty will be gone if they cooperate with the government (Cooperate! What a misnomer; what a shame that a word capable of the best meaning should be used to destroy the liberty given in our constitution.)" (*DF*, 15 Jan. 1938, p. 26).

CHAPTER 6

1. The differences between the roles of "farm wives," "women farmers," and "farm housewives" is described in Boulding, "Labor of U.S. Farm Women," p. 269; another typology used by Carolyn Sachs, as developed by Jessica Pearson, delineates farm women's roles into these four: independent producers, agricultural partners, agricultural helpers, and homemakers. Sachs, *Invisible Farmers*, p. 81.

2. Sachs, *Invisible Farmers*.

3. In 1930, poultry experts recommended flocks of fifty birds to maintain food for a family, and up to five hundred for profitable sale. See Kleinegger, "Out of the Barns," p. 99.

4. Ward, *Farm Woman's Problems*, pp. 10–11. Ward distinguishes between the western and central states and includes the Dakotas in the central region.

5. Kleinegger, "Out of the Barns," p. 117.

6. "Crucialness" is a term used to quantify the economic impact of women's production on the farm household by Bush in "Barn Is His."

7. *DF*, 5 Dec. 1936, pp. 598–99.

8. Lane, *Free Land*, p. 227.

9. This has been a sin of omission as much as one of commission; few students of the old middle class have considered distinguishing between male and female ways of generating class location, thus leaving the impression that all are afforded the same title. See, for example, Steinmetz and Wright, "Fall and Rise of the Petty Bourgeoisie."

10. Rosenfeld, *Farm Women*, p. 24; Sachs, *Invisible Farmers*, p. 29.

11. Ward, *Farm Woman's Problems*, p. 11.

12. Westin, *Making Do*, p. 78. On the history of childbirth and birth control in the early twentieth century, see Leavitt, *Brought to Bed*; Reed, *From Private Vice to Public Virtue*.

13. Cott, *Grounding of Modern Feminism*, pp. 185, 186–87.

14. Riley, *Female Frontier*, p. 2.

15. Schlissel, *Women's Diaries*; Jeffrey, *Frontier Women*; Riley, *Frontierswomen*; Schlissel, Gibboens, and Hampsten, *Far From Home*.

16. Lane, *Let the Hurricane Roar*, especially pp. 88–90.

17. Nelson, *After the West Was Won*, pp. 61–80.

18. *DF*, 13 Apr. 1935, p. 142.

19. Schwieder, "South Dakota Farm Women."

20. Ware, *Holding Their Own*, p. 3; see also Bird, *Invisible Scar*, pp. 22–69; Milkman, "Women's Work and Economic Crisis."

21. Schwieder, "South Dakota Farm Women," p. 11.

22. *DF*, 20 June 1936, p. 328.

23. Westin, *Making Do*, p. ix.

24. One woman tells of giving birth in subzero temperatures without a doctor present because she had back bills. See *DF*, 6 Jan. 1934, p. 15.

25. D. Robinson, *Fourth Census of South Dakota*, pp. 115–52. There were also 28,000 females listed as students. In 1925, more than 80 percent of South Dakota women were employed in the following ten occupations (listed in order of frequency): student, farmer, teacher, stenographer, laborer, nurse, servant, salesman, bookkeeper, telephone employee. All but two of these occupations would increase in number between 1925 and 1935, despite the movement against female employment. As Nancy Cott has noted, the "Depression moved women down in the labor market, not out of it" (*Grounding of Modern Feminism*, p. 224). The 1925 South Dakota census numbered 107,699 "housewives."

26. *DF*, 21 Nov. 1936, p. 585.

27. On the concern over married women working, see Scharf, *To Work or To Wed*; Shallcross, *Should Married Women Work?*; Cott, *Grounding of Modern Feminism*, pp. 209–25; Milkman, "Women's Work," p. 84. On the bias against women and girls in New Deal relief, see Ware, *Beyond Suffrage*; Abramowitz, *Regulating the Lives of Women*, pp. 215–36. In South Dakota, there were 3,176 women on relief programs in 1937, compared to 55,531 men. *DF*, 15 Jan. 1938, pp. 18–19.

28. Humphries, "Women," p. 113.

29. Several important studies were funded in the 1930s to examine the effect of the depression on family life. See, for example, Komarovsky, *Unemployed Man and His Family*; Bakke, *Citizens without Work*; Lynd and Lynd, *Middletown in Transition*.

30. Westin, *Making Do*, p. 77.

31. Ibid., p. 127.

32. *DF*, 19 Jan. 1935, p. 26.

33. *DF*, 13 Apr. 1935, p. 142.

34. *DF*, 15 Jan. 1930, p. 65.

35. J. Hudson, *Plains Country Towns*.

36. Hargreaves, "Women in the Agricultural Settlement," p. 187.

37. Strasser, *Satisfaction Guaranteed*; see also Sklar, *Corporate Reconstruction of American Capitalism*.

38. Strasser, *Never Done*; Humphries, "Women," p. 111.

39. *DF*, 1 May 1930, p. 481.

40. Zimmerman, *Challenge of Chain Store Distribution*, pp. 26–72; see also Zimmerman, *Super Market*.

41. Strasser, *Never Done*, pp. 260–61; Lebhar, *Chain Store in America*.

42. *DF*, 1 May 1930, p. 481.

43. According to Christine Kleinegger, "Historical evidence abounds which indicates that advertisers were eager to attract farm women as consumers

early in the twentieth century" ("Out of the Barns," p. 128). See also Marchand, *Advertising the American Dream*, pp. 285–334.

44. See, for example, *DF*, 16 Feb. 1935, p. 63.

45. Ehrenreich and English, *For Her Own Good*, p. 2.

46. Ibid., p. 128; see also Baker, "Women in the U.S. Department of Agriculture."

47. Ehrenreich and English, *For Her Own Good*, pp. 141, 146.

48. True, "Statistics of Cooperative Extension Work," pp. 12–13. See also Ward, "Status and Results of Home Demonstration Work."

49. Cott, *Grounding of Modern Feminism*, p. 163.

50. Willard, "That Kitchen!," p. 2.

51. Ibid., p. 3.

52. "4-H Club Girl."

53. Schwieder, "South Dakota Farm Women," p. 14.

54. *DF*, 24 Oct. 1936, p. 536.

55. *DF*, 29 Aug. 1936, p. 425.

56. Farm women did not always accept the advice of experts; in fact, they often found the home management experts to be "cut-and-dried," if not arrogant, in their attempts to teach them things—like preserving—that they already knew (*DF*, 28 Apr. 1934, p. 200). On the whole, however, Dakota women's relationships with the new-middle-class experts were somewhat less fraught than their husbands' were, perhaps because the paternalistic relationships between male experts and women clients so closely mirrored those between women and men at large, and perhaps because some of those experts, particularly doctors, improved the real quality (and length!) of women's lives. On the passive and active relationship of women to experts, see Ehrenreich and English, *For Her Own Good*, pp. 10–11; Leavitt, *Brought To Bed*, introduction.

57. *DF*, 26 May 1934, p. 248.

58. *DF*, 4 July 1934, p. 176.

59. *DF*, 22 June 1935, p. 242.

60. *DF*, 18 Aug. 1934, p. 362.

61. *DF*, 22 June 1935, p. 242.

62. *DF*, 25 May 1936, p. 202; see also 5 Jan. 1935, p. 10; 16 Feb. 1935, p. 64.

63. *DF*, 25 May 1936, p. 202.

64. *DF*, 5 Jan. 1935, p. 10.

65. Ehrenreich and English, *For Her Own Good*, pp. 167–97; Strasser, *Never Done*, pp. 225–41.

66. *DF*, 19 Jan. 1935, p. 26.

67. Molly Ladd-Taylor, *Raising a Baby the Government Way*, p. 43.

68. *DF*, 29 Aug. 1936, p. 426.

69. *DF*, 28 Apr. 1934, p. 200.

70. According to Strasser, "Truly scientific motherhood . . . required that

mothers not merely study their children but read and follow the advice of scientifically trained experts . . . who knew something mothers did not" (*Never Done*, pp. 232–34).

71. *DF*, 18 Aug. 1934, p. 362.

72. Reports on the Dionnes were regularly given in all major Dakota newspapers. On the (almost incredible) story of the famous quints, see Berton, *Dionne Years*.

73. *DF*, 28 Mar. 1936, p. 170.

74. *DF*, 1 Aug. 1936, p. 384; 23 May 1936, p. 278.

75. *DF*, 4 July 1936, p. 346.

76. *DF*, 18 July 1936, p. 368; The debate on this topic went on so long (nearly nine months), that some readers began to ask Mabel Sensor "to please change the subject." Still, the letters poured in. Finally, she summarized many of the remaining opinions in an extra-long "Home Page," 16 Jan. 1937, pp. 40–41.

77. *DF*, 18 July 1936, p. 368.

78. Cowan, *More Work for Mother*.

79. *DF*, 26 Sept. 1936, pp. 480–81.

80. *DF*, 18 July 1936, p. 368.

81. The term "farm feminine mystique" is used by Kleinegger ("Out of the Barns," p. 175) but is an obvious play on Betty Friedan's term, the "feminine mystique," whose foundations were laid in the 1920s and 1930s. Cowan, "Two Washes in the Morning"; Marsh, *Suburban Lives*; on image, cosmetics, and attitude, see Cowan, "Two Washes in the Morning," pp. 152–55. In the early 1920s, home economists were already thinking that "efficiency" wasn't enough for a farm woman, but that she should be shown how to "give attention to the attractiveness and comfort of her home, the training and companionship of her children, the enjoyment of books and neighbors, and the building up of recreational, social, and educational life in her community" (Ward, "Farm Woman's Problems," p. 24).

82. *DF*, 20 June 1936, p. 328.

83. See, for example, *DF*, 13 Mar. 1937, p. 157.

84. See, for example, *DF*, 27 Feb. 1937, p. 120.

85. *DF*, 16 Jan. 1937, pp. 40–41.

86. *DF*, 24 Oct. 1936, p. 537.

87. *DF*, 22 May 1937, p. 311.

88. *DF*, 23 Oct. 1937, p. 569.

89. *DF*, 16 Jan. 1937, pp. 40–41.

90. *DF*, 2 Jan. 1937, p. 16.

91. *DF*, 7 Nov. 1936, p. 560.

92. *DF*, 24 Oct. 1936, p. 537.

93. Seena B. Kohl, *Working Together: Women and Family in Southwestern Saskatchewan*, as quoted in Rosenfeld, *Farm Women*, p. 277.

94. Bush, "Barn Is His"; Kleinegger, "Out of the Barns," pp. 155–210.

95. Rosenfeld, *Farm Women*, p. 271. Boulding, "Labor of U.S. Farm Women," pp. 278–81. The last of women's productive activities to move into men's sphere was poultry production. Even so, Kleinegger finds, the bigger and more profitable a woman's flock was, the more likely it was first to be "hers," then "ours," then "his" (Kleinegger, "Out of the Barns," p. 90).

96. One writer to *DF* anticipated this shift, writing, "The modern housewife is not expected to go out in the barn and do chores. . . . The man is the sole proprietor of the barnyard, and whatever he has out there is his own business" (16 Jan. 1937, pp. 40–41); see also Rosenfeld, *Farm Women*, p. 24; Sachs, *Invisible Farmers*, p. 29; Kleinegger, "Out of the Barns," p. 208.

97. Rosenfeld, *Farm Women*, p. 184.

98. Ehrenreich and English, *For Her Own Good*, p. 11.

99. Ehrenreich and English, *For Her Own Good*.

100. Rosenfeld, *Farm Women*, pp. 267–68.

101. Ware, *Holding Their Own*, p. xx.

CHAPTER 7

1. Perhaps the best example here comes from Walsh County, North Dakota, where voters debated the merits of accepting Public Works Administration funds for a new courthouse. They rejected the government's first proposal in July 1935 because they did not want "to be bribed into mortgaging their own future . . . by the government offer of generous assistance" (*Walsh County Record*, 18 July 1935, p. 8). Three years later, however, they accepted an even more generous offer. This time many people believed that "if this community does not avail themselves [*sic*] of this offer, then another community will. In the end we will have to pay our share and get nothing in return for it" (*Walsh County Record*, 11 July 1935, p. 8; 22 Sept. 1938, p. 12).

2. Dumenil, *Freemasonry and American Culture*, p. xi.

3. Although the memberships of urban lodges included more men with white-collar occupations than with independent employment (Dumenil, *Freemasonry and American Culture*, pp. 11–13, 225), in rural North Dakota the Masons were still solidly old-middle-class. There, the Masonic ranks were filled by "the very best type of citizenry . . . professional men of high intelligence . . . leaders in business in their communities . . . artisans whose manual skill has given them a conspicuous place in their material constructiveness of their towns and cities, [and] farmers with an horizon besides that of their fields—in short, a worthy portion of the general community, the practical, the trained, and the cultured portion of it" (*BT*, 4 Nov. 1929, p. 4).

4. Clawson, "Nineteenth-Century Women's Auxiliaries," p. 41. See also Clawson, *Constructing Brotherhood*; Carnes, *Secret Ritual and Manhood in Victorian America*.

5. *Proceedings*, 1924, p. 69; *BT*, 4 Nov. 1929, p. 4.

6. General histories of Freemasonry in North Dakota come in a variety of forms. Individual lodges have printed their own histories, and these can be found in the collections at the University of North Dakota and the State Historical Society of North Dakota in Bismarck. Two syntheses are also available, one in manuscript form in Box 41, File 6, Libby Papers, the other published in Pond, *Masonry in North Dakota*.

7. Dumenil, *Freemasonry and American Culture*, p. 88.

8. Ibid., pp. 31–32.

9. Ibid., pp. 38–39.

10. A complete compilation of membership figures appears in *Proceedings*, 1986, pp. 233–34.

11. Dumenil, *Freemasonry and American Culture*, p. xi.

12. *Proceedings*, 1922, p. 23.

13. Generally speaking, these difficulties were common to lodges around the country. Dumenil, *Freemasonry and American Culture*, p. xiii.

14. *Proceedings*, 1922, pp. 23, 30, 60, 89–90.

15. Ibid., 1926, p. 82.

16. Ibid., 1922, p. 89; 1927, p. 26.

17. Ibid., 1922, p. 59.

18. Ibid., 1925, p. 58.

19. For a discussion of this point on a national level, see Dumenil, *Freemasonry and American Culture*, part II.

20. Brunner's team of sociologists published three important accounts of rural life based on their 1924, 1930, and 1937 observations of 140 small towns throughout America. Brunner, Hughes, and Patten, *American Agricultural Villages*; Brunner and Kolb, *Rural Social Trends*; Brunner, *Rural Trends in Depression Years*. The manuscript surveys from three of the four North Dakota towns studied (Grafton, Mayville, Casselton, and Oakes) are available at the North Dakota Institute for Regional Studies, North Dakota State University, Fargo, N.D.

21. On changing trends in club activities, see especially Brunner and Kolb, *Rural Social Trends*, pp. 268–69. See also "Grafton, North Dakota," 1930, "Note."

22. "Grafton, North Dakota," 1924, pp. 31–32.

23. Ibid., 1930, p. 7; see also Fass, *Damned and the Beautiful*.

24. *Proceedings*, 1922, pp. 24, 68.

25. Ibid., 1924, p. 69.

26. Ibid., 1922, p. 45.

27. Ibid., 1924, p. 70.

28. Ibid., 1922, p. 44.

29. Ibid., 1924, p. 70.

30. Ibid., 1922, p. 85.

31. Ibid., 1925, p. 59.

32. Dumenil, *Freemasonry and American Culture*, pp. 37–39.

33. Ibid., p. 32.

34. *Proceedings*, 1922, p. 44.

35. Ibid., 1922, p. 45.

36. Ibid., 1931, p. 17.

37. Ibid., 1939, p. 70.

38. "Grafton, North Dakota," 1930, "Note."

39. *Proceedings* 1930, p. 27.

40. W. L. Stockwell to John Robinson, 24 Dec. 1934, Box 1, File 19, Robinson Papers.

41. *Proceedings*, 1930, p. 27.

42. Ibid., 1937, p. 70.

43. Each annual report listed the membership losses for various categories in the General Secretary's address. See also *Proceedings*, 1937, p. 25.

44. The first discussion of how *little* Masonic work had been done appears in *Proceedings*, 1930, p. 11.

45. The Masons were particularly perplexed by the impact of the Social Security Act on their charitable activities (*Proceedings*, 1936, p. 34; 1937, pp. 27, 54–55), but general issues of the role of Masonic relief in the age of government reform plagued them as well. Leaders were concerned, for example, that members were counting on Masonic relief too much and beginning to see Masonic relief as something they wanted to receive for themselves rather than give to others (*Proceedings*, 1937, p. 44; 1938, p. 35).

46. Brunner, *Rural Trends in Depression Years*, p. 284; Hay, "Social Organizations," pp. 23–26, 85–87.

47. *Proceedings*, 1938, p. 78. For a similar argument brought up to the recent past, see Emmett, *Freemasonry in Manitoba*, pp. 63–64.

48. *Proceedings*, 1933, p. 85.

49. Ibid., 1931, p. 10.

50. Ibid., 1933, pp. 10, 85–86.

51. Ibid., 1931, p. 11.

52. Ibid., 1938, p. 20; 1937, p. 18.

53. Ibid., 1933, p. 35.

54. Ibid., 1938, p. 20; 1939, p. 29. See also "Proclamation," (1938), Box 1, File 25, Robinson Papers.

55. Dumenil, *Freemasonry and American Culture*, pp. 12–13.

56. As Charles Starke put it, "Suspensions [for unpaid dues] . . . is [*sic*] merely an elimination of those whom we could not assimilate and no cause of worry. Our strength does not lie in numbers, but in a well organized body of good men, thinking alike on all great social and moral problems" (*Proceedings*, 1931, p. 9).

57. Ibid., 1933, p. 20.

58. Ibid., 1934, pp. 18–19.

59. J. Robinson to all members, 1 Oct. 1932, Box 1, File 28, Robinson Papers. For his own part, Robinson compiled a list of the names and addresses of delinquents from his home lodge in Garrison. The list reveals a part of the problem that leaders did not discuss openly: some of the Masons were not just delinquent—they were gone. One Garrison member, Floyd C. Agnew, for example, owed the lodge $11 but listed his current address in care of the Kenyon Beauty Parlor in Palo Alto, Ca. In some of the worst drought years, the only Grand Lodge in the country that increased its membership was the Grand Lodge of California. J. Robinson to Stockwell, 26 Oct. 1935, Box 1, File 22, Robinson Papers.

60. *Proceedings*, 1937, p. 9.

61. "Proclamation," (1938), Box 1, File 25, Robinson Papers.

62. *Proceedings*, 1938, p. 85. See also ibid., 1986, p. 235, for a list of all Masonic Grand Masters. By the 1960s and 1970s, nearly every leader, all of whom presumably joined the craft some time after 1925, has a Nordic or a German surname.

63. Harold Rease to J. Robinson, 16 Nov. 1939, Box 1, File 26, Robinson Papers.

64. I am assuming here that when the Masons said they invited "families" and other "non-members" to informal social functions, they meant to include women. See, for example, *Proceedings*, 1938, p. 20. See also the participation of the women's auxiliary in preparing meals at annual communications, including the Golden Jubilee. "Golden Jubilee," Box 1, File 28, Robinson Papers. Of course, women's auxiliaries did not just act as support structures for the male organizations; to the contrary, they sometimes had (perhaps unintended) feminist implications. See Clawson, "Nineteeth-Century Women's Auxiliaries," especially pp. 56–58; Dumenil, *Freemasonry and American Culture*, pp. 25–26, 196–97.

65. *Proceedings*, 1938, p. 19.

66. Ibid.

67. Ibid., 1932, p. 10.

68. Fabian, "Speculation and Gambling on the Chicago Board of Trade." See also Fabian, *Card Sharps, Dream Books, and Bucket Shops*.

69. *Proceedings*, 1937, p. 44

70. Ibid., 1931, p. 25.

71. Ibid., p. 25.

72. Ibid., 1938, p. 60.

73. Ibid., 1930, p. 27.

74. Ibid., 1935, p. 20.

75. Ibid., p. 153.

76. Much of Libby's work is documented through correspondence in Box 41, Libby Papers.

77. *Proceedings*, 1930, p. 174.

78. Ibid.

79. Ibid., 1930, p. 170.

80. Ibid., p. 174.

81. Ibid., 1935, p. 148.

82. Ibid., 1935, p. 95.

83. Ibid., 1935, pp. 115–16.

84. "Lewis and Clark Memorial," Box 1, File 20, Robinson Papers.

85. *Proceedings*, 1939, pp. 141–45.

86. Ibid., p. 7.

87. Ibid., p. 8.

88. Ibid., 1927, p. 27.

89. "Important Business and Legislation," Box 1, File 28, Robinson Papers.

90. In 1935 Mark Forkner hosted "Reconsecration Night"; in 1936 L. K. Thompson held "Forward Together, Brethren Night"; and in 1937 William Hutchinson convened "Rededication Night."

91. *Proceedings*, 1935, p. 31.

92. Ibid., p. 174.

93. Ibid. As William Hutchinson put it by quoting Elihu Root, "Not what ultimate object we can attain in our short lives, but what tendencies toward higher standards of conduct we can aid in our generation is the test that determines our duty of service" (*Proceedings*, 1937, p. 20).

94. Ibid., 1936, pp. 28–29.

95. Ibid., 1945, p. 28.

CHAPTER 8

1. John Robinson to all Masons, 1 Oct. 1932, Box 1, File 28, Robinson Papers.

2. Ibid.

3. Although the opportunity to build a new capitol fell only to the people of North Dakota, the conflicts it represented were felt by people in both states. Likewise, there are artifacts of the built environment in South Dakota—Mount Rushmore and Wall Drug, for example—that speak to these conflicts in their own ways. (See conclusion.) More generally, several modernist architectural styles became popular in South Dakota in this period. See Torma, "Building Diversity."

4. Scholarly treatments of the North Dakota Capitol are few and far between; many fewer studies have been done on the tower in Bismarck than on that in Lincoln. For one study, and a good bibliography of contemporary commentary, see Russell-Hitchcock and Seale, *Temples of Democracy*, pp. 284–87. For an historical study, see Melhouse, "Construction of the North Dakota Capitol." To date, however, the most thorough essay on the Capitol is an un-

published piece, "North Dakota Capitol," by the former state architectural historian, L. Martin Perry.

5. The North Dakota Capitol is an important early example of a new style of design that appeared on the American landscape between World Wars I and II after having been first introduced in Europe. To my mind, it combines what historian Jeffrey Meikle calls the "zig-zag" or "exposition-style" modernism of the late 1920s and the more streamlined style of the 1930s. Meikle, *Twentieth Century Limited*, pp. 3–4. In either case, however, its single tower with flat roof and unornamented, regimented, and standardized sidings abruptly opposes the prairie that surrounds it—not to mention the traditional, sometimes antistatist ideals of those who built it. North Dakotans suggest that the tower is not out of place because it expresses the innovation of the pioneers; likewise, they say that it looks like a grain elevator or silo, and thus does in some small way resemble their landscape. As I have tried to point out in this text, progress and innovation were an important part of the old-middle-class creed, but they were defined on terms specific to the culture of the small producer. The tower design, however, defines innovation according to the technological, professional-managerial ethos. Similarly, progress and technology were welcomed by Dakotans much more often in the business sphere than in the political sphere. Even the distinctly innovative Nonpartisan League fought to maintain traditional, small-producerist ideals.

6. Report of the Board of State Capitol Commissioners to the Governor, 1 Dec. 1932, p. 11, DOI: BSCC. For a summary of the actions of the legislature, see pp. 7–9. The vast majority of primary sources on the Capitol are found in DOI: BSCC. All references to DOI: BSCC are to materials found in series 270–95; citations are as complete as possible but reflect some inconsistencies in cataloguing. See also Russell-Hitchcock and Seale, *Temples of Democracy*, p. 285.

7. The commissioners were well aware of the changing trends in modern architecture, particularly in the construction and design of public monuments. In the early stages of the selection process, they visited the Nebraska and Louisiana Capitols (also tower designs), as well as new skyscraper designs in Minneapolis and Indianapolis. Ultimately, this kind of expenditure cost the commissioners their posts when a new, economy-minded governor, Bill Langer, was elected. On their trips and their reasons for supporting a modern design, see Report to the Governor, 1932, DOI: BSCC; Report of Gen. G. A. Fraser and Frank L. Anders, 22 Dec. 1931, DOI: BSCC. On the differences among the three tower Capitols, see Russell-Hitchcock and Seale, *Temples of Democracy*, pp. 227–87.

8. As quoted in Report to the Governor, 1932, p. 10, DOI: BSCC.

9. These reasons are laid out clearly in T. B. Wells to George Bangs, 6 Apr. 1931, ser. 278, Architect Selection Files, DOI: BSCC. See also George Bangs,

"Memo re: Selection of Architect for North Dakota Capitol," 20 Aug. 1931, pp. 4–5, DOI: BSCC.

10. A thorough study of the professionalization of architecture has yet to be done, but there are some general works on the topic. See, for example, Wolfe, *From Bauhaus to Our House*, pp. 33–36.

11. Ramsey, "Emergence of the Architectural Profession on the Upper Great Plains."

12. North Dakota architects often had to convince businessmen that they needed an architect's help in the first place. See, for example, Joseph De-Remer's pamphlet, "The Architect," that explains what an architect is and does (ser. 278, Architect Selection Files, Box 1, DeRemer Application, DOI: BSCC).

13. Ibid., p. 5.

14. DeRemer, untitled address, 7 July 1931, ser. 278, Architect Selection Files, Box 1, DeRemer Application, pp. 2, 3, 4, DOI: BSCC. DeRemer had, in fact, designed the Masonic temple in Grafton, N.D., that was visited by Edmund Brunner's sociologists.

15. DeRemer clearly knew that he was fighting an uphill battle. He both defended the merits of a small firm and tried to capitalize on his connections to big firms in Minneapolis. He also admitted to the board that he knew there were people who thought his firm was not big enough to handle the job. As a result, he was willing even to take out a bond to guarantee his work or to do it without pay until it was completed (ibid., pp. 4–9, 11–14).

16. DeRemer, untitled address, ibid., p. 11. See also Wells to Bangs, 6 Apr. 1931, ibid.

17. Report to the Governor, 1932, p. 10, DOI: BSCC.

18. Conklin noted, for example, that a firm from Denver gave "a clean-cut presentation . . . brought together in a ship-shape manner." But when Gilbert Horton of Jamestown forgot to index his specifications, the commissioners called the error "not excusable in anyone classing themselves up-to-date." Likewise, Braseth and Houkon of Fargo just seemed "a little slow in their mental processes . . . [for] a work of this magnitude" ("Architect Ratings Book," ser. 278, Architect Selection Files, Box 1, DOI: BSCC).

19. In 1927, John Holabird and John Wellborn Root, Jr., formed a partnership to continue the work of their fathers, both famous and prolific architects of the Chicago school. A great deal has been written about the progenitors, little on the progeny. See Condit, *Chicago School of Architecture*. See also "Holabird and Root Application," ser. 278, Architect Selection Files, DOI: BSCC.

20. DeRemer, untitled address, ser. 278, Architect Selection Files, Box 1, DeRemer Application, p. 12, DOI: BSCC.

21. *Minutes*, vol. 1, ser. 270, pt. 69, p. 21, DOI: BSCC.

22. Most scholars agree that the Capitol was almost entirely a product of Holabird and Root's office. See, for example, Perry, "Construction of the North Dakota Capitol," p. 1; Russell-Hitchcock and Seale, *Temples of Democracy*, p. 286; also, Ronald Ramsey interview, 26 Sept. 1986. On the "disappearance" of DeRemer, see *Minutes*, 8 Aug. 1933 and 31 Aug. 1933, vol. 3, ser. 270, DOI: BSCC.

23. The North Dakota Capitol has much in common with two of Holabird and Root's most famous works from this period, the Racine County Courthouse and the Forest Products Laboratory, Madison, Wisconsin.

24. The transcripts of this meeting and its continuation the following day are found in *Minutes*, 19 Sept. 1931, vol. 1, ser. 270, pt. 69, pp. 26–38 and 63–75, DOI: BSCC.

25. Letters came to Bangs from individuals, social clubs, and business associations. The Hebron Lions Club, for example, wrote, "Brick manufactured in North Dakota . . . [would] make North Dakotans more state-conscious. The new capitol would then become a symbol of the possibilities of our state and the use of brick would give an impetus to the brick industry in North Dakota and make all North Dakotans more alert to the possibilities for further development and give more favorable advertising and publicity to the industry than you could give it in one hundred years." Letters like this one can be found in several different collections. The largest number are in General Correspondence, "Brick," ser. 271, Box 1, DOI: BSCC. Others, though, are included in ser. A-19, Box 27, File 19, Langer Papers.

26. *Minutes*, vol. 1, ser. 270, pt. 69, p. 35, DOI: BSCC.

27. Ibid., pt. 69, pp. 29, 30.

28. Ibid., pt. 69, pp. 28, 27, 32, 34.

29. Ibid., pt. 69, p. 31.

30. Russell-Hitchcock and Johnson, *International Style*, pp. 50–55.

31. *Minutes*, vol. 1, ser. 270, pt. 69, pp. 33, 66, 76, DOI: BSCC.

32. *Minutes*, 23 Feb. 1932, vol. 2, ser. 270, DOI: BSCC.

33. The great exception here, of course, is political difference—even that based on different kinds of work within the old middle class, such as that which underscored the conflict between the Nonpartisan League and the Independent Voter's Association. Few farmers, however, would have said that the difference between their needs and those of townspeople was based on class.

34. See chap. 3.

35. A fictional account of labor strife in a middle western state in the 1930s can be found in Sandoz, *Capitol City*. The Minneapolis truckers' strike of 1933 was a particularly violent nonfictional episode.

36. *Minutes*, 20 July 1932, vol. 2, ser. 270, DOI: BSCC.

37. Ibid., 8 Aug. 1932. See also Russell-Hitchcock and Seale, *Temples of Democracy*, p. 286.

38. "The Facts of Capitol Strike at Bismarck," ser. A-19, Box 27, File 18, Langer Papers. See also the letter from George Madison to Dick Johnson of Strandburg, S.D., telling him how to get on the work crews at the Capitol.

39. Ibid.

40. Ibid. Also, Russell-Hitchcock and Seale, *Temples of Democracy*, p. 286.

41. The most complete description of the cornerstone ceremony and parade is in Bangs, *Autobiography of George Bangs*, pp. 67–73.

42. Ibid., p. 69.

43. Ibid., pp. 71–72.

44. As quoted, ibid., p. 64.

45. *BT*, Feb. 1933, as found in Box 9, File 10, Anders Papers.

46. Ibid.

47. As quoted in Bangs, *Autobiography*, p. 63.

48. During the cornerstone ceremony, many of the shopkeepers in Bismarck displayed historical paraphernalia in their windows. Some of them had just borrowed their history from the Historical Society, however. This didn't bother the editors; in fact, they said they admired the newcomers to the past all the more. Then they explained, "Tradition is a good thing. It heightens community spirit and gives our community a caste above those which, like Topsy, 'jest grewed'" (*BT*, 11 Oct. 1932, p. 4).

49. As quoted in *Minutes*, "Memo from Anna Stevens," 23 Mar. 1932, ser. 1, Box 4, File 10, North Dakota Federation of Women's Clubs Papers.

50. The statue of the Pioneer Family was given by Harry McLean, a wealthy Canadian businessman.

51. The records of the Pioneer Mother Project are a fascinating part of the papers of the North Dakota Federation of Women's Clubs. For information on the statue, see ser. 1, Box 1, File 6; ser. 1, Box 7, File 9; ser. 1, Box 4, File 10, all in North Dakota Federation of Women's Clubs Papers.

52. Nina Farley Wishek, "Pioneer Mother," *North Dakota Clubwoman* 17, no. 3 (Dec. 1933): 1.

53. Without knowing the details of the negotiations between the clubwomen and their benefactor, it is hard to know whose idea it was to expand the statue from mother to family. However, knowing as we do that women's work shifted significantly away from production to child care and consumption by the 1940s, the shift is not altogether surprising.

54. Alexander, "South Dakota Women Writers."

55. Kohl, *Land of the Burnt Thigh*, p. 287.

56. Wilder, *These Happy Golden Years*, p. 153.

57. Lane, *Let the Hurricane Roar*.

58. Kohl, *Land of the Burnt Thigh*, pp. 256–90.

59. Wilder, *Long Winter*, p. 319.

60. Kohl, *Land of the Burnt Thigh*, p. 25.

61. Ibid., p. 134.

62. Frances Gilchrist Wood, *Turkey Red*, as quoted in Alexander, "South Dakota Women Writers," p. 295.

63. Wilder, *These Happy Golden Years*, pp. 7, 23.

64. Wilder, *On the Banks of Plum Creek*, p. 123; see also Wilder, *Little House in the Big Woods*, p. 62. Similar images of domesticity, self-reliance, and forbearance can be found in the paintings done by Harvey Dunn beginning in the late 1930s. A native of Kingsbury County, South Dakota, Dunn became a well-known illustrator and teacher in Philadelphia and Teaneck, New Jersey, in the 1910s and 1920s. In the 1930s, he began to return to South Dakota for summer vacations and to devote much of his time to portraits of the land and its people during the pioneer period. Schell, *History of South Dakota*, p. 397.

65. Fellman, "Laura Ingalls Wilder and Rose Wilder Lane," p. 561.

66. Laura Ingalls Wilder to Rose Wilder Lane as quoted in Fellman, "Laura Ingalls Wilder and Rose Wilder Lane," p. 556.

67. Lane, *Let the Hurricane Roar*, pp. 60, 77.

68. Kohl, *Land of the Burnt Thigh*, p. 235.

69. Wilder, *Little Town on the Prairie*, p. 235; see also Fellman, "Laura Ingalls Wilder and Rose Wilder Lane," p. 557.

70. Wilder, *These Happy Golden Years*, p. 119; Kohl, *Land of the Burnt Thigh*, p. 30; Lane, *Free Land*, p. 264.

71. Kohl, *Land of the Burnt Thigh*, pp. 42, 204.

72. Wilder, *Little House on the Prairie*, p. 316; Wilder, *By the Shores of Silver Lake*, pp. 234–35; Wilder, *These Happy Golden Years*, p. 171.

73. Wilder, *Little Town on the Prairie*, p. 214; Wilder, *Long Winter*, p. 112.

74. Fellman, "Laura Ingalls Wilder and Rose Wilder Lane," p. 558.

75. Lane, *Free Land*, p. 29.

76. Lane, *Give Me Liberty*, p. 29.

77. Ibid., p. 61.

78. Ibid., p. 60.

79. Kohl, *Land of the Burnt Thigh*, p. 14.

CONCLUSION

1. E. Robinson, *History of North Dakota*, p. 424.

2. Schell, *History of South Dakota*, p. 303.

3. Ibid., p. 413. He was elected to that post in 1940 with only 38 percent of the vote.

4. O'Rourke, "South Dakota Politics," p. 267.

5. In his initial bid for a Senate seat in 1960, George McGovern lost to Karl Mundt by 15,000 votes. When he ran again in 1962 to fill the seat vacated by the death of Francis Case, he won by 597 votes. See Schell, *History of South Dakota*, p. 316.

6. E. Robinson, *History of North Dakota*, pp. 426–27.

7. Ibid., p. 443.

8. U.S. National Resources Committee, *Population Statistics*, pp. 68–72; *United States Twentieth Census*, 36:52. There are, of course, many farmers in the Dakotas who are neither white nor male, but for purposes of comparison with the data from 1930 this categorization was most applicable. A great deal of the decrease in the numbers of farmers in the Dakotas is due to the near disappearance of seasonal farm labor and to increased mechanization. The percentage of all those engaged in agriculture who are farm owner/operators may actually have increased since the 1930s. The fact remains, however, that relative to other workers the number of farmers decreased dramatically.

9. Brinkley, "New Deal and the Idea of the State," in Fraser and Gerstle, eds., *Rise and Fall of the New Deal Order*, pp. 85–121.

10. U.S. Bureau of the Census, *Statistical Abstracts*, p. 651.

11. Rhodes, *Farm*, p. 179.

12. "The Poppers and the Plains," *New York Times*, 24 June 1990, section 6, p. 24.

13. Ibid., p. 47.

14. D. Robinson, *Fourth Census of South Dakota*; Fox, *Fifth Census of South Dakota*.

15. "Progress Report to the North Dakota Economic Development Commission."

16. U.S. Bureau of the Census, *Twentieth Census*.

17. U.S. Bureau of the Census, *Statistical Abstracts*, p. xvii.

18. "Rural Population Falling in Midwest," Rochester, N.Y., *Democrat and Chronicle*, 2 Sept. 1988, p. 5a.

19. U.S. Congress, Office of Technology Assessment, *Health Care*, especially pp. 6–7, 244.

20. Marling, *Colossus of Roads*, p. 89. See also S. Lee, "Traveling the Sunshine State."

21. "In the Driftway," quoted in Marling, *Colossus of Roads*, p. 87.

22. Jennings, *Free Ice Water*, p. 48.

23. See, for example, Schact, ed., *Three Faces of Midwestern Isolationism*.

24. As quoted in Leonard, "Nye Committee," pp. 20–28. On Nye, see also Leonard, "From County Politics to the Senate," pp. 14–23; Fuller, "Press and the 1938 North Dakota Election," p. 29.

25. *DF*, 16 July 1938, p. 293.

26. *DF*, 7 May 1938, p. 205.

27. *DF*, 7 May 1938, p. 205.

28. See, for example, *DF*, 7 May 1935, p. 206.

29. Fraser and Gerstle, eds., *Rise and Fall of the New Deal Order*; Westbrook, "'I Want a Girl Just Like the Girl That Married Harry James.'"

30. This quote is actually a paraphrasing by Fraser and Gerstle of Rieder's

essay, "Rise of the Silent Majority," in Fraser and Gerstle, eds., *Rise and Fall of the New Deal Order*, pp. 243–68. For the quote itself, see p. xxii.

31. Ibid., pp. 245–48.

32. Miller, "McCarthyism before McCarthy," pp. 1–21; Usher Burdick, "Attempt to 'Smear' the North Dakota Farmers' Union," in Remele, "Public Opinion"; Dyson, *Red Harvest*, pp. 197–99.

33. On the history and development of the Farmers' Union after 1945, see Williams, *Emil Loriks*, chaps. 5 and 6; Conrad and Conrad, *Fifty Years*, chaps. 8–12.

34. Williams, *Emil Loriks*, pp. 146–47.

35. Pratt, "Midwest Farm Protest—Then and Now," in *Plowing up a Storm*. Also, Joseph Amato interview, 10 June 1985; William Pratt interview, 21 Oct. 1987.

36. Bird, *Invisible Scar*, p. xvi.

37. Wickens, *Colorado in the Great Depression*.

38. Brinkley, *Voices of Protest*.

39. McElvaine, *Great Depression*, pp. 170–95; Bird, *Invisible Scar*.

40. Argersinger, *Toward a New Deal in Baltimore*, pp. xvi, xviii; see also Cohen, *Making a New Deal*.

41. Susman, *Culture as History*; Levine, "Hollywood's Washington."

42. Frank Capra, as quoted in Levine, "Hollywood's Washington," p. 189.

43. Lasch, *True and Only Heaven*.

44. Bechhofer and Elliot, "Persistence and Change," pp. 75, 98–99.

BIBLIOGRAPHY

Oral Histories, Personal Interviews, and Correspondence

North Dakota Oral History Project, as published in *North Dakota History* 43, no. 2 (Spring 1976): 8–100, and *North Dakota History* 44, no. 4 (Fall 1977): 8–87.

South Dakota Oral History Project. 75 interviews with South Dakotans describing pioneer days and/or their experiences in the Great Depression. South Dakota Oral History Center, University of South Dakota, Vermillion, S.D.

Twenty-one responses to July 1978 questionnaire on women's folklore and childhood in North and South Dakota. These are:

Evelyn Abley to Catherine Stock. 15 July 1978.

Everett and Mildred Bogue to Catherine Stock. July 1978; June 1985.

Grace Campbell to Catherine Stock. 7 Aug. 1978.

Isabel Campbell to Catherine Stock. 12 July 1978.

Ruth Carothers to Catherine Stock. Aug. 1978.

Mary Parsons Davis to Catherine Stock. July 1978.

Isabel Evensen to Catherine Stock. July 1978.

Gertrude Ferguson to Catherine Stock. July 1978.

Gerald and Esther Finch to Catherine Stock. 12 July 1978.

Ruth McNicol Finch to Catherine Stock. 10 Aug. 1978.

M. W. and Helen Gault to Catherine Stock. 15 July 1978.

Helen Gerjets to Catherine Stock. July 1978.

Eleanor Sarles Goodman to Catherine Stock. 14 July 1978.

Roger Hale to Catherine Stock. July 1978.

Dorothy Healy Hupper to Catherine Stock. 10 Aug. 1978.

Eleanor Kelly to Catherine Stock. July 1978.

Luverne C. Larsen to Catherine Stock. 14 July 1978.

Geraldine M. Robbins to Catherine Stock. 10 Aug. 1978.

Georgia Schlosser to Catherine Stock. July 1978.

Ruth Schmitt to Catherine Stock. 16 July 1978.

James Shikany to Catherine Stock. 1 July 1978.

Joseph Amato interview. 10 June 1985.

Grace Campbell interview. 30 July, 1986.

Helen Parkman interview. 24 July 1986.

William Pratt interview. 21 Oct. 1987.

Ronald Ramsey interview. 26 Sept. 1986.

Ornelle Thrane interview. 15 July 1990.

Manuscript Collections

Anders, Frank. Papers. MS. 1417. North Dakota Institute for Regional Studies, North Dakota State University, Fargo, N.D.

Chisolm, Henry. Collection of Western Americana. Richardson Archives, I. D. Weeks Library, University of South Dakota, Vermillion, S.D.

Christopherson, Charles A. Papers. Richardson Archives, I. D. Weeks Library, University of South Dakota, Vermillion, S.D.

"Church History" Collection. MS. A89. North Dakota Heritage Center, North Dakota State Historical Society, Bismarck, N.D.

"Clergy Letters" Collection. President's Personal Files, 21a, Franklin D. Roosevelt Collection, Franklin D. Roosevelt Library, Hyde Park, N.Y.

Coe, William Robertson. Collection. Western Americana Collection, Beineke Rare Book Library, Yale University, New Haven, Conn.

Director of Institutions: Board of State Capitol Commissioners, ser. 270–95. North Dakota State Archives, State Historical Society of North Dakota, Bismarck, N.D.

"Grafton, North Dakota." (MS. surveys from 1924, 1930, 1936.) SC 369. North Dakota Institute for Regional Studies, North Dakota State University, Fargo, N.D.

Ku Klux Klan in North Dakota. MS. 598. Orin G. Libby Manuscript Collection, Department of Special Collections, Chester Fritz Library, University of North Dakota, Grand Forks, N.D.

Langer, William. Papers. Orin G. Libby Manuscript Collection, Department of Special Collections, Chester Fritz Library, University of North Dakota, Grand Forks, N.D.

Libby, Orin G. Papers. MS. A85. State Historical Society of North Dakota, Bismarck, N.D.

"New Deal Clergy" Collection. MS. 588. Orin G. Libby Manuscript Collection, Department of Special Collections, Chester Fritz Library, University of North Dakota, Grand Forks, N.D. (The "New Deal Clergy" Collection contains photocopies of the North Dakota letters found in the "Clergy Letters" Collection in the Franlin D. Roosevelt Library, Hyde Park, N.Y.)

North Dakota Church History. MS. 441. Orin G. Libby Manuscript Collection, Department of Special Collections, Chester Fritz Library, University of North Dakota, Grand Forks, N.D.

North Dakota Federal Emergency Relief Administration Publications. MS. 475. Department of Special Collections, Chester Fritz Library, University of North Dakota, Grand Forks, N.D.

North Dakota Federation of Women's Clubs. Papers. MS. A202. State Historical Society of North Dakota, Bismarck, N.D.

North Dakota Promotional Literature. MS. 444. Department of Special

Collections, Chester Fritz Library, University of North Dakota, Grand
Forks, N.D.

North Dakota State University. Cooperative Extension Service. *Annual Reports of the Emergency Agricultural Agents for 1933.* No collection number. North Dakota Institute for Regional Studies, North Dakota State University, Fargo, N.D.

Peterson, August. Papers. Richardson Archives, I. D. Weeks Library, University of South Dakota, Vermillion, S.D.

Proceedings of the Grand Lodge A. F. and A. M. of North Dakota. Department of Special Collections, Chester Fritz Library, University of North Dakota, Grand Forks, N.D.

Robinson, John. Papers. MS. 618. Orin G. Libby Manuscript Collection, Department of Special Collections, Chester Fritz Library, University of North Dakota, Grand Forks, N.D.

Roosevelt, Eleanor. Papers. Personal Correspondence. Franklin D. Roosevelt Memorial Library, Hyde Park, N.Y.

WPA Historical Records Survey for South Dakota. Richardson Archives, I. D. Weeks Library, University of South Dakota, Vermillion, S.D.

Newspapers and Periodicals

Adams County Record. 1934–36.
Bismarck Tribune. 1924–36.
Dakota Farmer. 1927–38.
Dunn County Journal. 1931–35.
Fargo Forum. 1924–36.
Life. 1936–38.
The New Republic. 1932–40.
Newsweek. 1932–36.
North Dakota Clubwoman. 1928–34.
Sioux Falls Argus-Leader. 1924–36.
Walsh County Record. 1934–36.
Williston Daily Herald. 1934–36.

U.S. Government Documents

Cronin, Francis, and Edward Beers. *Areas of Intense Drought Distress, 1930–1936.* WPA Research Bulletin, ser. 5, no. 1. Washington, D.C.: Government Printing Office, 1937.

Farmers in a Changing World. USDA Yearbook of Agriculture. Washington, D.C.: Government Printing Office, 1940.

True, A. C. "Statistics of Cooperative Extension Work, 1920–21." USDA Circular 140. Washington, D.C.: Government Printing Office, Nov. 1920.

U.S. Bureau of the Census. *1980 Census of Population.* Vol. 1, *Characteristics of the Population.* Chap. C, *General Social and Economic Characteristics.* Pt. 36, North Dakota; Pt. 34, South Dakota. Washington, D.C.: Government Printing Office, 1983.

U.S. Bureau of the Census. *Statistical Abstracts of the U.S., 1990.* Washington, D.C.: Government Printing Office, 1990.

U.S. Congress. House. *The Future of the Great Plains.* Report of the Great Plains Committee. 75th Cong., 1st sess., 1936. H. Doc. 114.

U.S. Congress. Office of Technology Assessment. *Health Care in Rural America.* Washington, D.C.: Government Printing Office, Sept. 1990.

U.S. Department of Agriculture. "Land Use Planning Underway." Washington, D.C.: Government Printing Office, July 1940.

U.S. National Resources Committee. *Population Statistics, Vol. 1: National Data.* Washington, D.C.: Government Printing Office, 1937.

U.S. National Resources Planning Board. "Regional Planning, Part 9: The Northern Plains." Washington D.C.: Government Printing Office, 1940.

U.S. Senate. Committee on Agriculture and Forestry. *Agricultural Emergency Act to Increase Farm Purchasing Power.* 73rd Cong., 1st sess., 1933. Hearings of H. R. 3835.

U.S. Senate. Committee on Agriculture and Forestry. *To Abolish the Federal Farm Board and Secure for the Farmer the Cost of Production.* 72nd Cong., 1st sess., 1932. Hearings of S. 3133.

Ward, Florence. *The Farm Woman's Problems.* USDA Circular 148. Washington, D.C.: Government Printing Office, Nov. 1920.

———. "Status and Results of Home Demonstration Work, Northern and Western States, 1919." USDA Circular 141. Washington, D.C.: Government Printing Office, Jan. 1921.

Bulletins and Pamphlets

Diamond Jubilee, 75th Anniversary of Napoleon, N.D. Napoleon, N.D.: n.p., 1959.

Emmett, Robert E. *Freemasonry in Manitoba: Part 2, 1925–1974.* Winnepeg: Research and Education Committee of the Grand Lodge of Manitoba, A.F. and A.M., 1975.

Eureka!. Eureka, S.D.: n.p., 1937.

"The 4-H Club Girl, Her Book." Circular 66. Feb. 1925. Junior Extension

Work, Agricultural Extension Division, North Dakota Agricultural College, Fargo, N.D.

Fox, Lawrence. *Fifth Census of the State of South Dakota: Taken in the Year 1935.* N.p., n.d.

Hay, Donald G. "Problems of Rural Youth in Selected Areas of North Dakota." Bulletin 293. June 1940. Agricultural Experiment Station, North Dakota Agricultural College, Fargo, N.D.

————. "Social Organizations and Agencies in North Dakota: A Study of Trends, 1926 to 1936." Bulletin 288. July 1937. Agricultural Experiment Station, North Dakota Agricultural College, Fargo, N.D.

Johansen, John Peter. "Immigrant Settlements and Social Organization." Bulletin 313. June 1937. Dept. of Rural Sociology, Agricultural Experiment Station, South Dakota State College, Brookings, S.D.

Kumlien, W. F. "Basic Trends of Social Change in South Dakota. Part 2: Rural Life Adjustments." Bulletin 357. Dec. 1941. Dept. of Rural Sociology, Agricultural Experiment Station, South Dakota State College, Brookings, S.D.

————. "Basic Trends of Social Change in South Dakota. Part 3: Community Organization." Bulletin 356. Dec. 1941. Dept. of Rural Sociology, Agricultural Experiment Station, Brookings, S.D.

————. "Basic Trends of Social Change in South Dakota. Part 8: Religious Organization." Bulletin 348. May 1941. Dept. of Rural Sociology, Agricultural Experiment Station, South Dakota State College, Brookings, S.D.

————. "A Graphic Summary of the Relief Situation in South Dakota, 1930–1935." Bulletin 310. May 1937. Dept. of Rural Sociology, Agricultural Experiment Station, South Dakota State College, Brookings, S.D.

————. "Mortgage Status of Farm Lands in South Dakota." Brookings: Central Office, 1938.

————. "Rural Population, 1928–1935. Mobility in South Dakota." Bulletin 315. Jan. 1938. Dept. of Rural Sociology, Agricultural Experiment Station, South Dakota State College, Brookings, S.D.

————. "The Social Problem of the Church in South Dakota." Bulletin 294. Mar. 1935. Dept. of Rural Sociology, Agricultural Experiment Station, South Dakota State College, Brookings, S.D.

————. "The Standard of Living of Farm and Village Families in Six South Dakota Counties." Bulletin 320. Mar. 1935. Dept. of Rural Sociology, Agricultural Experiment Station, South Dakota State College, Brookings, S.D.

————. "What Farmers Think of Farming." 1927. Dept. of Rural Sociology, Agricultural Experiment Station, South Dakota State College, Brookings, S.D.

Landis, Paul. "Rural Relief in South Dakota." Bulletin 289. 1934. Dept. of Rural Sociology, Agricultural Experiment Station, South Dakota State College, Brookings, S.D.

Miller, Cap, and Willard Brown. "Farm Tenancy and Rental Contracts in North Dakota." Bulletin 289. Nov. 1937. Agricultural Experiment Station, North Dakota Agricultural College, Fargo, N.D.

"Progress Report to the North Dakota Economic Development Commission: Research on Industrial Market Potentials for Selected North Dakota Agricultural Commodities." 1 Jan. 1959. Department of Agricultural Economics, Agricultural Experiment Station, North Dakota Agricultural College, Fargo, N.D.

Robinson, Doane, dir. *Fourth Census of the State of South Dakota: Taken in the Year 1925.* Sioux Falls, S.D.: Press of Mark D. Scott, n.d.

Slocum, Walter. "Migrants from Rural South Dakota Families, Their Geographic and Occupational Distribution." Bulletin 359. Apr. 1942. Dept. of Rural Sociology, Agricultural Experiment Station, South Dakota State College, Brookings, S.D.

South Dakota State Planning Board. "Land Ownership in South Dakota." Brookings, S.D.: Central Office, 1937.

South Dakota State Planning Board. "Mortgage Status of Farm Lands in South Dakota." Brookings, S.D.: Central Office, 1935.

South Dakota State Planning Board and Day County Planning Board. *Economic and Social Survey of Day County.* Brookings, S.D.: Central Office, 1936.

Wasson, Grace. "The Use of Time by South Dakota Farm Homemakers." Bulletin 247. Mar. 1930. Dept. of Home Economics, Agricultural Experiment Station, South Dakota State College, Brookings, S.D.

Willard, Ruth. "That Kitchen!" Home Extension Division. Circular 63:5. 1924. North Dakota Agricultural College, Fargo, N.D.

Willson, E. A. "Incomes and Costs of Living of Farm Families in North Dakota, 1923–1931." Bulletin 271. June 1933. Agricultural Experiment Station, North Dakota Agricultural College, Fargo, N.D.

———. "Rural Changes in Western North Dakota." Bulletin 214. Jan. 1928. Agricultural Experiment Station, North Dakota Agricultural College, Fargo, N.D.

Wilner, Stanley. "A Statistical Analysis of Land Ownership in North Dakota, 1935." Bulletin 6. July 1939. Agricultural Experiment Station, North Dakota Agricultural College, Fargo, N.D.

Books and Articles

Aberle, George. *From the Steppes to the Prairies: The Story of the Germans . . . and their Resettlement in the Americas—North and South America and Canada.* Bismarck, N.D.: Bismarck Tribune Co., 1963.

Abramowitz, Mimi. *Regulating the Lives of Women: Social Welfare Policy from Colonial Times to the Present*. Boston: South End Press, 1988.

Agnew, Jean-Christophe. "A Touch of Class." *Democracy* 3 (Spring 1983): 59–72.

Alexander, Ruth Ann. "South Dakota Women Writers and the Blooming of the Pioneer Heroine, 1922–1939." *South Dakota History* 14, no. 4 (Winter 1984): 283–307.

Anderson, Clifford B. "The Metamorphosis of American Agrarian Idealism in the 1920s and 1930s." *Agricultural History* 35 (Oct. 1961): 182–88.

Argersinger, Jo Ann. *Toward a New Deal in Baltimore: People and Government in the Great Depression*. Chapel Hill: University of North Carolina Press, 1988.

Arrington, Leonard J. "The New Deal in the West: A Preliminary Statistical Inquiry." *Pacific Historical Review* 38 (Aug. 1969): 311–16.

———. "The Sagebrush Resurrection: New Deal Expenditures in the Western States, 1933–1939." *Pacific Historical Review* 52 (Feb. 1983): 1–16.

Athearn, Robert G. *The Mythic West in Twentieth-Century America*. Lawrence: University Press of Kansas, 1986.

Atherton, Lewis. *Main Street on the Middle Border*. 1957. Reprint. Bloomington: Indiana University Press, 1982.

Atkins, Annette. *Harvest of Grief: Grasshopper Plagues and Public Assistance in Minnesota, 1873–1878*. St. Paul: Minnesota Historical Society Press, 1984.

Atwood, Roy Alden. "Routes of Rural Discontent: Cultural Contradictions of Rural Free Delivery in Southeast Iowa, 1899–1977." *Annals of Iowa* 48, nos. 5 and 6 (Summer/Fall 1986): 264–73.

Auerbach, Jerrold S. "New Deal, Old Deal, or Raw Deal: Some Thoughts on New Left Historiography." *Journal of Southern History* 35 (Feb. 1969): 18–30.

Avery, Inda. "Some South Dakotans' Opinions about the New Deal." *South Dakota History* 7, no. 3 (Summer 1977): 309–24.

Baker, Gladys. *The County Agent*. Chicago: University of Chicago Press, 1939.

———. "Women in the U.S. Department of Agriculture." *Agricultural History* 50, no. 1 (Jan. 1976): 190–201.

Bakke, E. Wright. *Citizens without Work*. New Haven: Yale University Press, 1940.

Bangs, Cyrilla. *The Autobiography of George Bangs*. Indianapolis: n.p., 1949.

Barrett, Ben. *Memories of a County Agent*. Fargo, N.D.: n.p., 1964.

Bechhofer, Frank, and Brian Elliot. "Persistence and Change: The Petite Bourgeoisie in Industrial Society." *Archives Européennes de Sociologie* 17 (1976): 74–99.

———. "Petty Property: The Survival of a Moral Economy." In *The Petite Bourgeoisie: Comparative Studies of the Uneasy Stratum*, edited by Frank Bechhofer and Brian Elliot. London: Macmillan, 1981.

Bender, Thomas. *Community and Social Change in America*. New Brunswick, N.J.: Rutgers University Press, 1978.

Berg, Francis M., ed. *Ethnic Heritage in North Dakota*. Washington, D.C.: Attiyeh Foundation, 1983.

Bern, Enid. "Memoirs of a Prairie Schoolteacher." *North Dakota History* 42, no. 3 (Summer 1975): 5–18.

Bernstein, Barton. "The New Deal: Conservative Achievements of Liberal Reform." In *Toward a New Past: Dissenting Essays in American History*, edited by Barton Bernstein. New York: Pantheon Books, 1968.

Berton, Pierre. *The Dionne Years: A Thirties Melodrama*. Toronto: McClelland and Stewart, 1977.

Billington, Monroe. "The Alabama Clergy and the New Deal." *Alabama Review* 32 (July 1979): 214–25.

———. "Roosevelt, the New Deal and the Clergy." *Mid-America* 53–54 (1971–72): 20–33.

Billington, Monroe, and Cal Clark. "Clergy Reaction to the New Deal: A Comparative Study." *The Historian* 48 (1985–86): 214–25.

Bird, Caroline. *The Invisible Scar*. New York: Van Rees Press, 1966.

Blackorby, Edward. *Prairie Rebel: The Public Life of William Lemke*. Lincoln: University of Nebraska Press, 1955.

Blakely, H. W., ed. *Selected Papers of the First Nine Dakota History Conferences, 1969–1977*. The Karl Mundt Historical and Educational Foundation Series, no. 8. Madison: South Dakota State College, 1981.

Bledstein, Burton J. *The Culture of Professionalism: The Middle Class and the Development of Higher Education in America*. New York: W. W. Norton, 1976.

———. "Discussing Terms: Professions, Professionals, Professionalism." *Prospects* 10 (1985): 1–15.

Blumin, Stuart. *The Emergence of the Middle Class: Social Experience in the American City, 1760–1900*. New York: Cambridge University Press, 1989.

Bonnifield, Paul. *The Dust Bowl: Men, Dirt and Depression*. Albuquerque: University of New Mexico Press, 1979.

Boulding, Elise. "The Labor of U.S. Farm Women: A Knowledge Gap." *Sociology of Work and Occupations* 7, no. 3 (Aug. 1980): 261–90.

Braeman, John, ed. *The New Deal, State and Local Levels*. Columbus: Ohio State University Press, 1975.

Bremer, William. "Along the 'American Way': The New Deal's Work Relief Programs for the Unemployed." *Journal of American History* 42, no. 3 (Dec. 1975): 636–52.

Brinkley, Alan. *Voices of Protest: Huey Long, Father Coughlin and the Great Depression.* New York: Vintage Books, 1983.

Brunner, Edmund deS. *Churches of Distinction in Town and Country.* New York: Doran, 1923.

———. *Rural Trends in the Depression Years: A Survey of Village Centered Agricultural Communities, 1930–1936.* New York: Columbia University Press, 1937.

Brunner, Edmund deS., Gwendolyn S. Hughes, and Marjorie Patten. *American Agricultural Villages.* New York: Doran, 1927.

Brunner, Edmund deS., and J. H. Kolb. *Rural Social Trends.* New York: McGraw-Hill, 1933.

Burnham, James. *The Managerial Revolution: What Is Happening in the World.* New York: John Day, 1941.

Bush, Corlan G. "The Barn Is His, the House Is Mine: Agricultural Technology and Sex Roles." In *Energy and Transport: Historical Perspectives on Policy Issues,* edited by George Daniels and Mark Role. Beverly Hills: Sage Publications, 1982.

Campbell, Christiana. *The Farm Bureau and the New Deal: A Study of the Making of National Farm Policy, 1933–1940.* Urbana: University of Illinois Press, 1962.

Carlson, Paul, and Steve Porter. "South Dakota Congressmen and the Hundred Days of the New Deal." *South Dakota History* 8, no. 4 (Fall 1978): 327–39.

Carnes, Mark. *Secret Ritual and Manhood in Victorian America.* New Haven: Yale University Press, 1989.

Cayton, Andrew R. L., and Peter S. Onuf. *The Midwest and the Nation: Rethinking the History of an American Region.* Bloomington: University of Indiana Press, 1990.

Clawson, Mary Ann. *Constructing Brotherhood: Class, Gender, and Fraternalism.* Princeton: Princeton University Press, 1989.

———. "Nineteenth-Century Women's Auxiliaries and Fraternal Orders." *Signs: Journal of Women in Culture and Society* 12, no. 1 (1986): 40–61.

Cohen, Lizabeth. *Making a New Deal: Industrial Workers in Chicago, 1919–1939.* New York: Cambridge University Press, 1990.

Condit, Carl W. *The Chicago School of Architecture: A History of the Commercial and Public Buildings in the Chicago Area, 1875–1925.* Chicago: University of Chicago Press, 1964.

Conkin, Paul. *FDR and the Origins of the Welfare State.* New York: Thomas Y. Crowell, 1967.

Conrad, Charles, and Joyce Conrad. *Fifty Years of the North Dakota Farmers' Union.* N.p., 1976.

Corey, Lewis. *The Crisis of the Middle Class.* New York: Covici-Friede, 1935.

Cott, Nancy F. *The Grounding of Modern Feminism*. New Haven: Yale University Press, 1987.

Cowan, Ruth Schwartz. *More Work for Mother: The Ironies of Household Technology from the Open Hearth to the Microwave*. New York: Basic Books, 1983.

———. "Two Washes in the Morning and a Bridge Party at Night: The American Housewife between the Wars." *Women's Studies* 3 (1976): 147–72.

Curran, James, and Roger Burrows. "The Sociology of Petit Capitalism: A Trend Report." *Sociology* 20, no. 2 (May 1986): 265–79.

Curtis, John. *Mind's Eye, Mind's Truth: FSA Photography Reconsidered*. Philadelphia: Temple University Press, 1989.

Danbom, David. "The Agricultural Experiment Station and Professionalization: Scientists' Goals for Agriculture." *Agricultural History* 60, no. 2 (Spring 1986): 246–55. .

———. *The Resisted Revolution: Urban America and the Industrialization of Agriculture, 1900–1930*. Ames: Iowa State University Press, 1979.

Davenport, Walter. "Get Away from Those Cows." *Colliers* 74 (24 Feb. 1932): 10–11.

Davis, Joseph S. *Wheat and the AAA*. Washington, D.C.: Brookings Institute, 1935.

Dibbern, John. "Who Were the Populists? A Study of Grass-Roots Alliancemen in Dakota." *Agricultural History* 56, no. 4 (Oct. 1982): 677–91.

Dileva, Frank. "Frantic Farmers Fight Law." *Annals of Iowa* 32 (Oct. 1953): 81–109.

Douglass, H. Paul, and Edmund deS. Brunner. *The Protestant Church as a Social Institution*. New York: Harper and Brothers, 1935.

Drache, Hiram M. *Day of the Bonanza*. Fargo: North Dakota Institute for Regional Studies, 1964.

———. "Midwest Agriculture: Changing with Technology." *Agricultural History* 50, no. 1 (Jan. 1976): 290–302.

Dumenil, Lynn. *Freemasonry and American Culture, 1880–1930*. Princeton: Princeton University Press, 1984.

Dykstra, Robert. *The Cattle Towns*. New York: Knopf, 1968.

Dyson, Lowell. *Red Harvest: The Communist Party and American Farmers*. Lincoln: University of Nebraska Press, 1982.

Easton, Patricia O'Keefe. "Women's Suffrage in South Dakota: The Final Decade, 1911–1920." *South Dakota History* 13 (1983): 206–26.

Ehrenreich, Barbara, and John Ehrenreich. "The Professional-Managerial Class." In *Between Capital and Labor: The Professional Middle Class*, edited by Pat Walker. Boston: South End Press, 1979.

Ehrenreich, Barbara, and Deirdre English. *For Her Own Good: 150 Years of* the Experts' Advice to Women. Garden City, N.J.: Anchor, Doubleday, 1978.

Fabian, Ann Vincent. Card Sharps, Dream Books, and Bucket Shops: Gambling in Nineteenth-Century America. Ithaca: Cornell University Press, 1990.

Faragher, John Mack. Sugar Creek: Life on the Illinois Prairie. New Haven: Yale University Press, 1986.

———. Women and Men on the Overland Trail. New Haven: Yale University Press, 1979.

Fass, Paula. The Damned and the Beautiful: American Youth in the 1920s. New York: Oxford University Press, 1977.

Fellman, Anita Clair. "Laura Ingalls Wilder and Rose Wilder Lane: The Politics of a Mother-Daughter Relationship." Signs 15, no. 1 (Spring 1990): 535–61.

Finegold, Kenneth. "From Agrarianism to Adjustment: The Political Origins of New Deal Agricultural Policy." Politics and Society 11, no. 1 (1981): 1–11.

Fite, Gilbert. American Farmers: The New Minority. Bloomington: Indiana University Press, 1981.

———. "Farmer Opinion and the Agricultural Adjustment Act, 1933." Mississippi Valley Historical Review 48, no. 4 (Mar. 1962): 656–73.

———. The Farmers' Frontier: 1865–1900. New York: Holt, Rinehart, Winston, 1966.

———. George N. Peek and the Fight for Farm Parity. Norman: University of Oklahoma Press, 1954.

———. "John A. Simpson: The Southwest's Militant Farm Leader." Mississippi Valley Historical Review 35 (Mar. 1949): 563–84.

———. "The Pioneer Farmer: A View over Three Centuries." Agricultural History 50, no. 1 (Jan. 1976): 275–89.

———. "The Transformation of South Dakota Agriculture: The Effects of Mechanization, 1939–1964." South Dakota History 19, no. 3 (Fall 1989): 278–305.

Foner, Eric. Free Soil, Free Labor, Free Men: The Ideology of the Republican Party before the Civil War. New York: Oxford University Press, 1970.

Fox, Richard Wightman, and T. J. Jackson Lears, eds. The Culture of Consumption. New York: Pantheon, 1983.

Fraser, Stephen, and Gary Gerstle, eds. The Rise and Fall of the New Deal Order, 1930–1980. Princeton: Princeton University Press, 1989.

Fry, C. Luther. Diagnosing the Rural Church: A Study in Method. New York: Doran, 1924.

Fuller, John F. "The Press and the 1938 North Dakota Election." North Dakota History 35, no. 1 (Winter 1968): 28–56.

Ganzel, Bill. *Dust Bowl Descent*. Lincoln: University of Nebraska Press, 1984.

Geiger, Theodor. "Panik im Mittlestand." *Die Arbeit* 7 (1930): 637–54.

Gerth, Hans. "The Nazi Party: Its Leadership and Composition." *American Journal of Sociology* 45 (1940): 517–41.

Giddens, Anthony. *The Class Structure of Advanced Societies*. New York: Harper and Row, 1973.

Gjerde, Jon. *From Peasants to Farmers: The Migration from Balestrand, Norway, to the Upper Middle West*. New York: Cambridge University Press, 1985.

Goodwyn, Lawrence. *Democratic Promise: The Populist Moment in America*. New York: Oxford University Press, 1976.

Gouldner, Alvin W. *The Future of Intellectuals and the Rise of the New Class*. New York: Seabury Press, 1979.

Gregory, James. *American Exodus: The Dust Bowl Migration and Okie Culture in California*. New York: Oxford University Press, 1989.

Guimond, James. *American Photography and the American Dream*. Chapel Hill: University of North Carolina Press, 1991.

Gutman, Herbert. *Work, Culture, and Society in Industrializing America: Essays in American Working-Class and Social History*. New York: Knopf, 1975.

Hahn, Steven. *The Roots of Southern Populism: Yeomen Farmers and the Transformation of the Georgia Upcountry, 1850–1890*. New York: Oxford University Press, 1983.

Hahn, Steven, and Jonathan Prude, eds. *The Countryside in the Age of Capitalist Transformation: Essays in the Social History of Rural America*. Chapel Hill: University of North Carolina Press, 1985.

Halttunen, Karen. *Confidence Men and Painted Women: A Study of Middle-Class Culture in America, 1830–1870*. New Haven: Yale University Press, 1982.

Hamilton, Richard. *Who Voted for Hitler?* Princeton: Princeton University Press, 1982.

Hampsten, Elizabeth. *Read This Only to Yourself: The Private Writings of Midwestern Women, 1880–1910*. Bloomington: Indiana University Press, 1982.

Hargreaves, Mary M. W. "Women in the Agricultural Settlement of the Northern Plains." *Agricultural History* 50, no. 1 (Jan. 1976): 179–89.

Harwood, William. "The Ku Klux Klan in Grand Forks, North Dakota." *South Dakota History* 1, no. 4 (Fall 1971): 301–35.

Hearn, Charles. *The American Dream in the Great Depression*. Westport, Conn: Greenwood Press, 1977.

Hendrickson, Kenneth E., Jr. "The Civilian Conservation Corps in South Dakota." *South Dakota History* 11, no. 1 (Winter 1980): 1–20.

————. "The National Youth Administration in South Dakota: Youth and the New Deal, 1935–1943." *South Dakota History* 9, no. 2 (Spring 1978): 131–51.

————. "Relief for Youth: The Civilian Conservation Corps and the National Youth Administration in North Dakota." *North Dakota History* 48, no. 4 (Fall 1981): 4–16.

————. "Some Political Aspects of the Populist Movement in South Dakota." *North Dakota History* 34, no. 1 (Winter 1967), 77–92.

Henretta, James. "Families and Farms: Mentalité in Pre-Industrial America." *William and Mary Quarterly* 35 (1978): 3–32.

Hicks, John D. *The Populist Revolt*. Lincoln: University of Nebraska Press, 1961.

Hine, Robert. *Community on the American Frontier: Separate but Not Alone*. Norman: University of Oklahoma Press, 1980.

Hofstadter, Richard. *Age of Reform: From Bryan to F. D. R.* New York: Knopf, 1955.

————. *The Paranoid Style in American Politics and Other Essays*. Chicago: University of Chicago Press, 1964.

Hollingshead, A. B. "The Life Cycle of Nebraska Rural Churches." *Rural Sociology* 2 (1937): 180–91.

Holt, James. "The New Deal and the American Anti-Statist Tradition." In *The New Deal: The National Level*, edited by John Braemman, Robert H. Bremner, and David Brody. Columbus: Ohio State University Press, 1975.

Holzworth, John Michael. *The Fighting Governor*. Chicago: Pointer Press, 1938.

Hooks, Gregory M. "A New Deal for Farmers and Social Scientists: The Politics of Rural Sociology in the Depression Era." *Rural Sociology* 48, no. 3 (1983): 386–408.

Hoover, Herbert. "Farmers Fight Back: A Survey of Rural Political Organizations, 1873–1983." *South Dakota History* 13 (1983): 122–57.

Howard, Thomas, ed. *The North Dakota Political Tradition*. Ames: Iowa State University Press, 1981.

Hudson, John. *Plains Country Towns*. Minneapolis: University of Minnesota Press, 1985.

Hudson, Lois Phillips. *The Bones of Plenty*. St. Paul: Minnesota Historical Society Press, 1984.

————. *Reapers of the Dust: A Prairie Chronicle*. St. Paul: Minnesota Historical Society Press, 1984.

Huey, William G. "Making Music: Brass Bands on the Northern Plains, 1860–1930." *North Dakota History* 54, no. 1 (Winter 1987): 3–13.

Humphries, Jane. "Women: Scapegoats and Safety Valves in the Great Depression." *Review of Radical Political Economics* 8, no. 1 (Spring 1976): 98–121.

Hurt, R. Douglas. *The Dust Bowl: An Agricultural and Social History*. Chicago: Nelson-Hall, 1981.

Irons, Peter. *New Deal Lawyers*. Princeton: Princeton University Press, 1982.

Isenmenger, Gordon. "The McIntosh German-Russians: The First Fifty Years." *North Dakota History* 51, no. 3 (Summer 1984): 4–23.

Jaher, Frederick Cople. *The Urban Establishment: Upper Strata in Boston, New York, Charleston, Chicago, and Los Angeles*. Urbana: University of Illinois Press, 1982.

Jeffrey, Julie Roy. *Frontier Women: The Trans-Mississippi West, 1840–1880*. Albuquerque: University of New Mexico Press, 1979.

Jennings, Dana Close. *Free Ice Water: The Story of Wall Drug*. Aberdeen, S.D.: North Plains Press, 1969.

Jensen, Joan. "I've Worked, I'm Not Afraid of Work: Farm Women in New Mexico, 1920–1940." *New Mexico Historical Review* 61 (Jan. 1980): 27–52.

Jensen, Richard. *The Winning of the Midwest: Social and Political Conflict, 1888–1896*. Chicago: University of Chicago Press, 1971.

Johnson, Paul. *A Shopkeepers' Millenium*. New Haven: Yale University Press, 1979.

Jones, Alfred Haworth. "The Search for a Usable American Past in the New Deal Era." *American Quarterly* 23 (Dec. 1971): 710–24.

Karl, Barry. "Presidential Planning and Social Research: Mr. Hoover's Experts." *Perspectives in American History* 3 (1969): 347–409.

Karolevitz, Robert. *Challenge: The South Dakota Story*. Sioux Falls, S.D.: Brevet Press, 1975.

Karr, Rodney. "Farm Rebels of Plymouth County, Iowa, 1932–1933." *Annals of Iowa* 47, no. 7 (Winter 1985): 637–45.

Kirkendall, Richard. "The Mind of a Farm Leader." *Annals of Iowa* 47, no. 2 (Fall 1983): 138–53.

———. *Social Scientists and Farm Politics in the Age of Roosevelt*. Columbia: University of Missouri Press, 1966.

Kirschner, Donald. *City and Country: Rural Responses to Urbanization in the 1920s*. Westport, Conn.: Greenwood Press, 1970.

Kohl, Edith Eudora. *Land of the Burnt Thigh*. St. Paul: Minnesota Historical Society Press, 1986.

Komarovsky, Mirra. *The Unemployed Man and His Family*. New York: Institute of Social Research, 1940.

Kraenzel, Carl. *The Great Plains in Transition*. Norman: University of Oklahoma Press, 1954.

Kramer, Dale. *The Wild Jackasses: The American Farmer in Revolt*. New York: Hastings House, 1956.

Ladd-Taylor, Molly. *Raising a Baby the Government Way*. New Brunswick, N.J.: Rutgers University Press, 1986.

Lamar, Howard. *Dakota Territory, 1861–1899: A Study in Frontier Politics.* New Haven: Yale University Press, 1956.

———. "Public Values and Private Dreams: South Dakotans' Search for Identity, 1850–1900." *South Dakota History* 8, no. 2 (Spring 1978): 117–42.

———. *The Reader's Encyclopaedia of the American West.* New York: Thomas Y. Crowell, 1977

Lambert, C. Roger. "The Drought Cattle Purchase, 1934–1935: Problems and Complaints." *Agricultural History* 52, no. 1 (Winter 1978): 3–31.

Lane, Rose Wilder. *Free Land.* Lincoln: University of Nebraska Press, 1966.

———. *Give Me Liberty.* New York: Longmans, Green, and Co., 1936.

———. *Let the Hurricane Roar.* New York: Longmans, Green, and Co., 1933.

Lasch, Christopher. *The True and Only Heaven: Progress and Its Critics.* New York: W. W. Norton, 1991.

Laslett, Peter. *The World We Have Lost.* New York: Scribner, 1965.

Laswell, Harold. "The Psychology of Hitlerism." *Political Quarterly* 4, no. 3 (1933): 373–84.

Leavitt, Judith Walzer. *Brought to Bed: Childbearing in America, 1750 to 1950.* New York: Oxford University Press, 1985.

Lebhar, Godfrey. *The Chain Store in America, 1859–1959.* New York: Chain Store Publishing Corp., 1959.

Lederer, Emil. *State of the Masses: The Threat to the Classless Society.* New York: W. W. Norton, 1940.

Lee, R. Alton. "McCarthyism at the University of South Dakota." *South Dakota History* 19, no. 3 (Fall 1989): 424–38.

Lee, Shebby. "Traveling the Sunshine State: The Growth of Tourism in South Dakota, 1914–1939." *South Dakota History* 19, no. 2 (Summer 1989): 194–223.

Leonard, Robert James. "From Country Politics to the Senate: The Learning Years for Senator Nye." *North Dakota History* 39, no. 3 (Summer 1972): 14–23.

———. "The Nye Committee: Legislating against War." *North Dakota History* 41, no. 4 (Fall 1974): 20–28.

Leuchtenberg, William. *Franklin D. Roosevelt and the New Deal, 1932–1940.* New York: Harper and Row, 1963.

Levine, Lawrence. "American Culture in the Great Depression." *Yale Review* 74 (Winter 1985): 196–223.

———. "Hollywood's Washington: Film Images of National Politics during the Great Depression." *Prospects* 10 (1985): 169–96.

Lewis, Sinclair. *Babbitt.* New York: New American Library, 1961.

———. *It Can't Happen Here.* New York: New American Library, 1961.

———. *Main Street.* New York: New American Library, 1961.

Lingeman, Richard. *Small Town America: A Narrative History, 1620–the Present*. New York: G. P. Putnam's Sons, 1980.

Lord, Russell. *The Wallaces of Iowa*. Boston: Houghton Mifflin, 1947.

Low, Ann Marie. *Dust Bowl Diary*. Lincoln: University of Nebraska Press, 1984.

Lowitt, Richard. *The New Deal and the West*. Bloomington: Indiana University Press, 1984.

Lowitt, Richard, and Maurine Beasley, eds. *One-Third of a Nation: Lorena Hickok Reports on the Great Depression*. Urbana: University of Illinois Press, 1981.

Luebke, Frederick. *Ethnicity on the Great Plains*. Lincoln: University of Nebraska Press, 1982.

Lynd, Robert S., and Helen Merrell Lynd. *Middletown: A Study in Modern American Culture*. New York: Harcourt, Brace and World, 1929.

———. *Middletown in Transition: A Study in Cultural Conflicts*. New York: Harcourt Brace, 1937.

Maarten, James. "'A Golden Opportunity': The South Dakota Agricultural Extension Service and the Agricultural Adjustment Administration, 1933–1935." *South Dakota History* 12, nos. 2 and 3 (Summer/Fall 1982): 163–81.

McConnell, Grant. *The Decline of Agrarian Democracy*. Berkeley: University of California Press, 1953.

McCoy, Donald R. *Angry Voices: Left-of-Center Politics in the New Deal Era*. Lawrence: University Press of Kansas, 1958.

McDean, Harry C. "Dust Bowl Historiography." *Great Plains Quarterly* 6, no. 2 (Spring 1986): 117–21.

McElvaine, Robert S. *The Great Depression: America, 1929–1941*. New York: Times Books, 1984.

McLaird, James D. "From Bib Overalls to Cowboy Boots: East River/West River Differences in South Dakota." *South Dakota History* 19, no. 4 (Winter 1989): 454–91.

Madison, James H. "Reformers and the Rural Church, 1900–1950." *Journal of American History* 73, no. 3 (Dec. 1986): 645–68.

Madison, James H., ed. *Heartland*. Bloomington: University of Illinois Press, 1988.

Malcolm, Andrew. *Bitter Harvest*. New York: Times Books, 1986.

Manfred, Frederick Feikema. *The Golden Bowl: A Novel*. Albuquerque: University of New Mexico Press, 1944.

———. *The Wind Blows Free: A Reminiscence*. Sioux Falls, S.D.: Center for Western Studies, 1979.

Manfred, James. *Isolationism in America, 1935–1941*. Ithaca, N.Y.: Cornell University Press, 1966.

Marchand, Roland. *Advertising the American Dream: Making Way for Modernity, 1920–1940*. Berkeley: University of California Press, 1985.

Marling, Karal Ann. *Blue Ribbon: A Social and Pictorial History of the Minnesota State Fair*. St. Paul: Minnesota Historical Society Press, 1990.

———. *The Colossus of Roads: Myth and Symbol along the American Highway*. Minneapolis: University of Minnesota Press, 1984.

———. *Wall-to-Wall America: A Cultural History of Post Office Murals in the Great Depression*. Minneapolis: University of Minnesota Press, 1982.

Marsh, Margaret. *Suburban Lives*. New Brunswick, N.J.: Rutgers University Press, 1990.

Martinson, Henry. "Some Memoirs of a Nonpartisan League Organizer." *North Dakota History* 42, no. 2 (Spring 1975): 18–21.

Mayer, Arno. "The Lower Middle Class as Historical Problem." *Journal of Modern History* 47 (1975): 409–36.

Meikle, Jeffrey. *Twentieth Century Limited: Industrial Design in America, 1925–1939*. Philadelphia: Temple University Press, 1979.

Melhouse, James. "The Construction of the North Dakota Capitol." *Plains Talk* (Summer 1970), 1–6.

Merrill, Michael. "Cash Is Good to Eat: Self-Sufficiency and Exchange in the Rural Economy of the United States." *Radical History Review* 4 (1977): 42–71.

Milkman, Ruth. "Women's Work and Economic Crisis: Some Lessons of the Great Depression." *Review of Radical Political Economics* 8, no. 1 (Spring 1976): 73–97.

Miller, John. "McCarthyism before McCarthy: The 1938 Election in South Dakota." *Heritage of the Great Plains* 15 (Summer 1982): 1–21.

———. "Restrained, Respectable Radicals: The South Dakota Farm Holiday." *Agricultural History* 59, no. 3 (July 1985): 429–47.

Mills, C. Wright. *Power, Politics, and People: The Collected Essays of C. Wright Mills*. New York: Oxford University Press, 1963.

———. *White Collar: The American Middle Classes*. New York: Columbia University Press, 1951.

Mittelstaedt, Robert, ed. "The General Store Era: Memoirs of Arthur and Harold Mittelstaedt." *South Dakota History* 9, no. 1 (Winter 1978): 36–60.

Modell, John. "Public Griefs and Personal Problems: An Empirical Inquiry into the Impact of the Great Depression." *Social Science History* 9, no. 4 (Fall 1985): 399–427.

Montgomery, David. *Beyond Equality*. Urbana: University of Illinois Press, 1981.

———. "Class, Capitalism, and Contentment." *Labor History* 30 (Winter 1989): 125–37.

Morlan, Robert. *Political Prairie Fire: A History of the Nonpartisan*

League, 1915–1922. 1955. Reprint. St. Paul: Minnesota Historical Society Press, 1985.

Moum, Kathleen. "The Social Origins of the Nonpartisan League." *North Dakota History* 53, no. 2 (Spring 1986): 18–22.

Myers, Rex C. "An Immigrant Heritage: South Dakota's Foreign-Born in the Era of Assimilation." *South Dakota History* 19, no. 2 (Summer 1989): 134–55.

Nash, Gerald. *The American West in the Twentieth Century: A Short History of an Urban Oasis.* Englewood Cliffs, N.J.: Prentice-Hall, 1973.

Nelson, Paula. *After the West Was Won: Homesteaders and Town-Builders in Western South Dakota, 1900–1917.* Iowa City: University of Iowa Press, 1986.

One Hundred Years in Grant County, South Dakota, 1878–1978. Pierre: State Publishing Co., 1979.

O'Rourke, Paul A. "South Dakota Politics during the New Deal Years." *South Dakota History* 1, no. 3 (Summer 1971): 231–71.

Ostergren, Robert. "European Settlement and Ethnicity Patterns on the Agricultural Frontiers of South Dakota." *South Dakota History* 13, nos. 1 and 2 (Spring/Summer 1983): 49–82.

Patterson, James. *The New Deal and the States: Federalism in Transition.* Princeton: Princeton University Press, 1969.

Paul, Rodman. *The Great Plains in Transition, 1859–1900.* New York: Harper and Row, 1988.

Pells, Richard. *Radical Visions and American Dreams: Culture and Social Thought in the Depression Years.* New York: Harper and Row, 1973.

Peterson, Fred W. "Norwegian Farm Homes in Steele and Traill Counties, North Dakota: The American Dream and the Retention of Roots, 1890–1914." *North Dakota History* 51, no. 1 (Winter 1984).

Plowing up a Storm: The History of Midwestern Farm Activism. Lincoln: Nebraska Educational Network, 1985.

Pond, Harold Sachett. *Masonry in North Dakota, 1804–1964.* Grafton, N.D.: The Record Printers, 1964.

Pratt, William C. "Radicals, Farmers, and Historians: Some Recent Scholarship about Agrarian Radicalism in the Upper Midwest." *North Dakota History* 52, no. 4 (Fall 1985): 12–25.

Rambow, Charles. "The Ku Klux Klan in the 1920s: A Concentration on the Black Hills." *South Dakota History* 14 (1984): 1–30.

Reed, James. *From Private Vice to Public Virtue: The Birth Control Movement in American Society since 1830.* New York: Basic Books, 1978.

Reid, Robert, ed. *Picturing Minnesota, 1936–1943: Photographs from the Farm Security Administration.* St. Paul: Minnesota Historical Society Press, 1989.

Remele, Larry. "The North Dakota Farm Strike of 1932." *North Dakota History* 41, no. 4 (Fall 1974): 4–19.

———. "North Dakota's Forgotten Farmers' Union." *North Dakota History* 45, no. 2 (Spring 1978): 4–21.

Rhodes, Richard. *Farm*. New York: Simon and Schuster, 1989.

Rieder, Jonathan. *Canarsie: The Jews and Italians of Brooklyn against Liberalism*. Cambridge: Harvard University Press, 1985.

Riley, Glenda. "Farm Women's Roles in the Agricultural Development of South Dakota." *South Dakota History* 13, nos. 1 and 2 (Spring/Summer 1983): 83–121.

———. *The Female Frontier*. Lawrence: University Press of Kansas, 1988.

———. *Frontierswomen: The Iowa Experience*. Ames: Iowa State University Press, 1981.

Robinson, Elwyn. *History of North Dakota*. 1966. Reprint. Lincoln: University of Nebraska Press, 1982.

Rodgers, Daniel T. *The Work Ethic in Industrial America, 1850–1920*. Chicago: University of Chicago Press, 1978.

Rogin, Paul. *The Intellectuals and McCarthy: The Radical Specter*. Cambridge: M.I.T. Press, 1967.

Rosenfeld, Rachel Ann. *Farm Women: Work, Farm, and Family in the United States*. Chapel Hill: University of North Carolina Press, 1985.

Rosenman, Samuel I. *The Public Papers and Addresses of Franklin D. Roosevelt*. Vol. 4. New York: Random House, 1938.

Russell-Hitchcock, Henry, and Philip Johnson. *The International Style: Architecture since 1922*. New York: W. W. Norton, 1966.

Russell-Hitchcock, Henry, and William Seale. *Temples of Democracy*. London: Harcourt Brace Jovanovich, 1976.

Ryan, Mary. *Cradle of the Middle Class: The Family in Oneida County, New York, 1790–1865*. Cambridge: Cambridge University Press, 1981.

Rylance, Daniel. "William Langer and the Themes of North Dakota History." *South Dakota History* 3, no. 1 (Winter 1972): 41–62.

Sachs, Carolyn. *The Invisible Farmers: Women in Agricultural Production*. Totowa, N.J.: Rowman and Allanheld, 1983.

Saloutos, Theodore. *The American Farmer and the New Deal*. Ames: Iowa State University Press, 1982.

Saloutos, Theodore, and John D. Hicks. *Agricultural Discontent in the Middle West, 1900–1939*. Madison: University of Wisconsin Press, 1951.

Sandoz, Mari. *Capital City*. Lincoln: University of Nebraska Press, 1939.

Saposs, David J. "The Role of the Middle Class in Social Development: Fascism, Populism, Communism, Socialism." In *Economic Essays in Honor of Wesley Clair Mitchell*. New York: Columbia University Press, 1935.

Scase, Richard. "The Petty Bourgeoisie and Modern Capitalism: A Consideration of Recent Theories." In *Social Class and the Division of Labour: Essays in Honor of Ilya Neustadt*, edited by Anthony Giddens and Gavin Mackenzie. Cambridge: Cambridge University Press, 1982.

Schact, John N., ed. *Three Faces of Midwestern Isolationism*. Iowa City: The Center for the Study of Recent History of the United States, 1981.

Schapsmeier, Edward L., and Frederick H. Schapsmeier. *Henry Wallace of Iowa: The Agrarian Years, 1910–1940*. Ames: Iowa State University Press, 1968.

Scharf, Lois. *To Work or To Wed: Female Employment, Feminism, and the Great Depression*. Westport, Conn.: Greenwood Press, 1976.

Schell, Herbert. *History of South Dakota*. 3d ed. Lincoln: University of Nebraska Press, 1975.

Schlesinger, Arthur. *The Coming of the New Deal*. Boston: Houghton Mifflin, 1959.

———. *The Politics of Upheaval*. Boston: Houghton Mifflin, 1960.

Schlissel, Lillian. *Women's Diaries of the Westward Journey*. New York: Schocken Books, 1982.

Schlissel, Lillian, Byrd Gibboens, and Elizabeth Hampsten. *Far from Home: Families of the Westward Journey*. New York: Schocken Books: 1989.

Schwieder, Dorothy. "South Dakota Farm Women in the Great Depression." *Journal of the West* 24, no. 4 (Oct. 1985): 6–18.

Shallcross, Ruth. *Should Married Women Work?*. Washington: National Association of Business and Professional Women, 1940.

Sheridan, William Allen. *The Nazi Seizure of Power: The Experience of a Single German Town, 1930–1935*. Chicago: University of Chicago Press, 1965.

Sherman, William. *Prairie Mosaic: An Ethnic Atlas of Rural North Dakota*. Fargo: North Dakota Institute for Regional Studies, 1983.

Shoenbaum, David. *Hitler's Social Revolution: Class and Status in Nazi Germany, 1933–1939*. Garden City, N.J.: Doubleday, 1966.

Shortridge, James. *The Middle West: Its Meaning in American Culture*. Lawrence: University Press of Kansas, 1989.

Shover, John. *Cornbelt Rebellion: The Farmers' Holiday Association*. Urbana: University of Illinois Press, 1965.

———. "Populism in the 1930s: The Battle for the AAA." *Agricultural History* 39 (Jan. 1965): 17–24.

Sklar, Martin J. *The Corporate Reconstruction of American Capitalism, 1890–1916*. New York: Cambridge University Press, 1988.

Skocpol, Theda. "Political Responses to Capitalist Crisis: Neo-Marxist Theories of the State and the New Deal." *Politics and Society* 10, no. 2 (1980): 155–201.

Skowronek, Steven. *Building a New American State: The Expansion of National Administrative Capacities, 1877–1920*. New Haven: Yale University Press, 1986.

Smith, Henry Nash. *Virgin Land: The American West as Symbol and Myth*. Cambridge: Harvard University Press, 1950.

Soule, George. *The Coming American Revolution*. New York: Macmillan, 1934.

South Dakota Offers Better Opportunities to Home-Builders and Home-Seekers. Pierre: Hipple Printing, 1927.

Stegner, Wallace, ed. *Report of the Lands of the Arid Region of the United States*. Cambridge: Harvard University Press, 1962.

Steinbeck, John. *The Grapes of Wrath*. New York: Viking Press, 1939.

Steinmetz, George, and Erik Olin Wright. "The Fall and Rise of the Petty Bourgeoisie: Changing Patterns of Self-Employment in the Postwar United States." *American Journal of Sociology* 94, no. 5 (Mar. 1989): 973–1018.

Sternsher, Bernard. *Hitting Home: The Great Depression in Town and Country*. Chicago: Quadrangle Books, 1970.

Stott, William. *Documentary Expression and 1930s America*. New York: Oxford University Press, 1973.

Strasser, Susan. *Never Done: A History of American Housework*. New York: Pantheon Books, 1982.

———. *Satisfaction Guaranteed: The Making of the American Mass Market*. New York: Pantheon Books, 1989.

Stratton, Joanna. *Pioneer Women: Voices from the Kansas Frontier*. New York: Simon and Schuster, 1981.

Straub, Theodore Friedrich. *The Autobiography of Theodore Friedrich Straub: The Life of a Furniture Dealer in South Dakota, 1908–1980*. Eureka, S.D.: n.p., 1981.

Susman, Warren. *Culture as History: The Transformation of American Society in the Twentieth Century*. New York: Pantheon Books, 1984.

Terkel, Studs. *Hard Times: An Oral History of the Great Depression*. New York: Pantheon Books, 1970.

Thelen, David. *Paths of Resistance: Tradition and Dignity in Industrializing Missouri*. New York: Oxford University Press, 1986.

Thomas, Norman. *The Choice before Us: Mankind at the Crossroads*. New York: Macmillan, 1934.

Thompson, J. H., and D. R. Leyden. "The United States of America." In *The Small Firm: An International Survey*, edited by D. J. Story. London: Croom Helm, 1983.

Tontz, Robert L. "Membership of General Farmers' Organizations, United States, 1874–1960." *Agricultural History* 38 (July 1964): 143–56.

Torma, Carolyn. "Building Diversity: A Photographic Survey of South Dakota Architecture, 1913–1940." *South Dakota History* 19, no. 2 (Summer 1989): 156–93.

Tucker, W. P. "Populism Up-to-Date: The Story of the Farmers' Union." *Agricultural History* 21 (Oct. 1947): 198–208.

Tweton, D. Jerome. "John M. Gillette: The Rural Sociologist as Reformer." *North Dakota Quarterly* 49 (Summer 1981): 5–25.

———. *The New Deal at the Grass Roots: Programs for the People in Otter Tail County, Minnesota.* St. Paul: Minnesota Historical Society Press, 1988.

———. "'Taking Pictures of the History of Today': The Federal Government Photographs North Dakota, 1936–1942." *North Dakota History* 57, no. 3 (Summer 1990): 3–13.

Tweton, D. Jerome, and Daniel F. Rylance. *The Years of Despair: North Dakota in the Depression.* Grand Forks, N.D.: Oxcart Press, 1973.

Veblen, Thorstein. "The Country Town." In *The Portable Veblen*, edited by May Lerner. New York: Viking Press, 1948.

Vidich, Arthur, and Joseph Bensman. *Small Town in Mass Society: Class, Power, and Religion in a Rural Community.* Princeton: Princeton University Press, 1968.

Vidich, Arthur, and Stanford M. Lyman. *American Sociology: Worldly Rejections of Religion and Their Directions.* New Haven: Yale University Press, 1985.

Vyzralek, Frank E. "Dakota Images: Early Photographers and Photography in North Dakota, 1853–1925." *North Dakota History* 57, no. 3 (Summer 1990): 25–37.

Ware, Susan. *Beyond Suffrage: Women in the New Deal.* Cambridge: Harvard University Press, 1981.

———. *Holding Their Own: American Women in the 1930s.* Boston: Twayne, 1982.

Warner, W. Lloyd. *Yankee City.* New Haven: Yale University Press, 1963.

Watne, Joel Andrew. "Public Opinion toward Non-Conformists and Aliens during 1917." *North Dakota History* 34, no. 1 (Winter 1967): 5–29.

Webb, Walter Prescott. *The Great Plains.* Boston: Ginn and Co., 1931.

Welsch, Robert. "Germans from Russia: A Place to Call Home." In *Broken Hoops and Plains People*, Nebraska Curriculum Development Center. Lincoln: University of Nebraska Printing and Duplicating Services, 1976.

West, James (Carl Withers). *Plainville, U.S.A.* New York: Columbia University Press, 1945.

Westbrook, Robert B. "'I Want a Girl Just Like the Girl That Married Harry James': American Women and the Problem of Political Obligation in World War II." *American Quarterly* 42 (1990): 587–614.

———. *John Dewey and American Democracy.* Ithaca: Cornell University Press, 1991.

———. "Tribune of the Technostructure: The Popular Economics of Stuart Chase." *American Quarterly* 32, no. 4 (Fall 1980): 387–408.

Westin, Jeanne. *Making Do: How Women Survived the '30s.* Chicago: Follett, 1976.

Wheeler, Wayne. *Social Stratification in a Plains Community*. Minneapolis: n.p., 1949.

White, Roland. *Milo Reno: Farmers' Union Pioneer*. Ames, Iowa: Athens Press, 1941. Reprint. New York: Arno Press, 1975.

Wickens, James F. *Colorado in the Great Depression*. New York: Garland Press, 1979.

Wiebe, Robert. *The Search for Order, 1877–1920*. New York: Hill and Wang, 1967.

Wilder, Laura Ingalls. *By the Shores of Silver Lake*. New York: Harper and Row, 1939.

———. *Farmer Boy*. New York: Harper and Row, 1933.

———. *Little House in the Big Woods*. New York: Harper and Row, 1932.

———. *Little House on the Prairie*. New York: Harper and Row, 1935.

———. *Little Town on the Prairie*. New York: Harper and Row, 1938.

———. *The Long Winter*. New York: Harper and Row, 1940.

———. *On the Banks of Plum Creek*. New York: Harper and Row, 1937.

———. *These Happy Golden Years*. New York: Harper and Row, 1943.

Wilentz, Sean. *Chants Democratic*. New York: Oxford University Press, 1984.

Williams, Elizabeth Evenson. *Emil Loriks: Builder of a New Economic Order*. Sioux Falls, S.D.: Center for Western Studies, 1987.

———. "W. R. Ronald: Prairie Editor and an AAA Architect." *South Dakota History* 1, no. 3 (Fall 1974): 272–91.

Wishek, Nina Farley. *Along the Trails of Yesterday: A Story of McIntosh County*. Ashley, N.D.: Ashley Tribune, 1941.

Wolfe, Tom. *From Bauhaus to Our House*. New York: Farrar, Straus, Giroux, 1981.

Wolff, Gerald W., and Joseph H. Cash, comps. and eds. "South Dakotans Remember the Great Depresison." *South Dakota History* 19, no. 2 (Summer 1989): 224–58.

Wood, Gordon. *The Creation of the American Republic, 1776–1787*. New York: W. W. Norton, 1969.

Woodward, Mary Dodge. *The Checkered Years: A Bonanza Farm Diary, 1884–1888*. St. Paul: Minnesota Historical Society Press, 1989.

Worster, Donald. *Dust Bowl: The Southern Plains in the 1930s*. New York: Oxford University Press, 1979.

Wright, Erik Olin. "Varieties of Marxist Conceptions of Class Structure." *Politics and Society* 9, no. 3 (1980): 323–70.

Wright, Erik Olin, Cynthia Costello, David Hachen, and Joey Sprague. "The American Class Structure." *American Sociological Review* 47 (Dec. 1982): 709–26.

Zimmerman, M. M. *The Challenge of Chain Store Distribution*. New York: Harper and Brothers, 1931.

————. *Super Market: Spectacular Exponents of Mass Distribution*. New York: Super Market Publishing Co., 1937.

Zunz, Oliver. *Making America Corporate, 1870–1920*. Chicago: University of Chicago Press, 1990.

Unpublished Works

Blackorby, Edward. "Political Factional Strife in North Dakota from 1920 to 1932." Master's thesis, University of North Dakota, 1938.

Casper, Scott. "'A Plain Business Proposition': The McNary-Haugen Debate of 1924 and the Position of Jeffersonian Ideology in a Consumer Society." Unpublished seminar paper, Yale University, 1987.

Dodd, James. "The Farmer Takes a Holiday." Master's thesis, North Dakota State University, 1960.

Fabian, Ann Vincent. "Speculation and Gambling on the Chicago Board of Trade." Paper presented at the Organization of American Historians, Reno, Nevada, Mar. 1988.

Finegold, Kenneth, and Theda Skocpol. "Capitalists, Farmers, and Workers in the New Deal: The Ironies of Government Intervention." Paper presented to the Conference Group on the Political Economy of Advanced Industrial Societies, Annual Meeting of the American Political Science Association, Washington, D.C., Aug. 1980.

Hjalmervik, Gary. "William Langer's First Administration, 1932–1934." Master's thesis, University of North Dakota, 1966.

Kleinegger, Christine Catherine. "Out of the Barns and into the Kitchens: Farm Women's Domestic Labor, World War I to World War II." Ph.D. dissertation, State University of New York-Binghamton, 1986.

Lantis, L. O. "Rural Socio-Economic Conditions in Ward County, North Dakota, and the Relations between Farmers and Townspeople." Ph.D. dissertation, University of North Dakota, 1935.

Perry, L. Martin. "The North Dakota Capitol." Unpublished manuscript, 1986.

Petry, Jerome. "Morality Legislation in North Dakota, 1920–1954." Master's thesis, University of North Dakota, 1967.

Pratt, William C. "The Farm Revolt on the Northern Plains, 1932–1936." Paper presented at the Northern Great Plains History Conference, Sioux Falls, S.D., 1987.

Ramsey, Ronald. "Emergence of the Architectural Profession on the Upper Great Plains, 1850–1920." Paper presented at the Northern Great Plains History Conference, Eau Claire, Wis., Sept. 1986.

Remele, Larry. "Public Opinion and the North Dakota Farmers' Holiday Association." Master's thesis, University of North Dakota, 1969.

Rylance, Daniel. "William Langer." Unpublished manuscript, 1987.
Sannes, Erling. "Organizing Teamsters in South Dakota in the 1930s." Paper
  presented at the Northern Great Plains History Conference, Sioux Falls,
  S.D., Oct. 1987.
Stine, Thomas Young. "The Development of Social Welfare in North Dakota."
  Ph.D. dissertation, University of North Dakota, 1944.
Stock, Catherine. "FDR and the Forgotten Class: Petit Bourgeois Culture
  and New Deal Policy on the Northern Plains." Paper presented at the
  Northern Great Plains History Conference, Eau Claire, Wis., Sept. 1986.
Wentz, Leonard. "The Nonpartisan League: A Quest for Community." Mas-
  ter's thesis, University of North Dakota, 1968.

INDEX

Atherton, Lewis, 230–31 (n. 4)
Autobiography of Theodore Friedrich Straub (Straub), 83, 84
Automobiles, 114, 116
Avery, Inda, 40
Ayres, Homer, 93

Baer, John M., 133
Baltimore, Md., 216
Bangs, George, 190–91, 192, 193, 198, 257 (n. 25)
Bankers, 13, 63–64, 95, 132, 139, 140
Bankers' Association, 132
Bank failures, 18, 130, 176
Bankhead-Jones Farm Tenancy Act (1937), 38
Banks, 38
Baptists, 59
Barley prices, 19
"Barnyard" sales, 137–39, 215
Barrett, Ben, 143
Bartruff, J. A., 145
Beaudry store, 50
Bechhofer, Frank, 217
"Beef cattle being loaded for market at Killdeer, North Dakota" (Harris), 105
Beers, Howard, 11, 25
Benedict, Ruth, 236 (n. 47)
Benson County, N.D., 145
Berg, R. D., 213
Bern, Enid, 116, 126, 217
Berry, Tom, 206, 230 (n. 104), 237 (n. 21)
Berthold, N.D., 176
Biddle, Francis, 98
Bird, Caroline, 215
Birth control, 150–51, 165–68
Bismarck, N.D., 11, 15, 185, 193, 196, 197, 258 (n. 48)
Bismarck Tribune, 75, 88, 198, 199–200
Black, John, 102

"Black Sunday," 24
"Black Thursday," 18
Bledstein, Burton, 78
Boese, J. H., 213–14
Bonanza farms, 43
Boosterism, 58, 60, 61, 225 (n. 40)
Borglum, Gutzon, 211
Boston, Mass., 24
Bottineau County, N.D., 27, 32
Boulding, Elise, 246 (n. 1)
Bowdle, S.D., 30
Boy Scouts, 174
Brain Trust, 108–10, 111
Bremer, William, 118
Brigham, Allen, 54
Brinkley, Alan, 6, 9, 142
Brookings, S.D., 158
Brunner, Edmund, 173
"Buffalo Commons," 209
Burdick, Usher, 44, 132, 137, 140
Bureau of Reclamation, 37
Bureau of Women and Children, 162
Burke, Walter, 64–66, 73, 75
Burleigh County, N.D., 37
Burr, Alexander, 184
Businesses, 46, 47
Businessmen, 42, 60; social standing, 13; depression and, 28, 76; "ideal," 53, 79; and farmers, 72–73, 132–33, 140

Campbell, Grace, 55
Canada, 181
Capitalism, 10, 42–43, 82, 242 (n. 2); and old-middle-class producerism, 4, 5, 6, 62, 189, 217; industrial, 5, 7, 155, 207; agricultural, 7, 73, 112, 118, 207, 209–10; and work ethic, 53, 179; and farmers, 72–73; managerial, 87
Capitol Commissioner's Act (North Dakota, 1931), 187–88
Capra, Frank, 216

Carothers, Ruth, 15, 45, 55, 56
Case, Francis, 259 (n. 5)
Cass, George, 43
Cass County, N.D., 93
Casselton, N.D., 139
Catalina, M., 113
Catholic Order of Foresters, 60
Catholics, 13, 66, 67, 71, 73, 174
Cattle raising, 23, 24, 25, 36, 117, 131
Cayton, Andrew R. L., 231 (n. 13)
Cedar County, Iowa, 130, 131, 132
Chain stores, 46, 155–56
Charity, 30–31, 55–56, 59, 75, 93, 113
Chase, Stuart, 100–101
Cheney, Benjamin, 43
Chicago, Ill., 24, 216
Childbirth, 29, 51, 152
Children, 58; photographic depictions of, 85, 103–4, 117; motherhood and child-rearing, 91, 149, 160–64, 248–49 (n. 70); health, 165–68
"Children of a Sub-Marginal Farmer in Pennington County" (Rothstein), 103–4
Chinook, 20
Christianity, 55, 59
Churches, 29, 58–60, 70, 71, 121, 122, 126
"Church on the Great Plains, South Dakota, 1938" (Lange), 123
Cities, 56, 210
Civilian Conservation Corps (CCC), 33–34, 38, 96–97
Civilian Works Administration (CWA), 32, 244 (n. 44)
Civil War, 5, 171
Clair, Eva, 160
Clark, William, 181–82
Class status, 7, 8, 13, 42, 225 (n. 46), 230–31 (n. 4); and political positions, 5, 6; denial of class conflict,

8, 56–57, 92, 189, 233 (n. 60); intraclass conflict, 13; social divisions, 74–76, 92
Clergy, 29; letters to Roosevelt, 120–26, 241 (n. 133)
Clerks, 47, 74–75
Cleveland, Ohio, 154
Clubs, 60–61, 75, 171, 173
Cold War, 215
Colorado, 216
Common laborers, 13, 47
Communism, 72, 174, 214
Communist party, U.S.A., 215, 242 (n. 2)
Community ideal, 5, 6, 42–43, 62, 217; pioneers and, 11–13, 54–55; men and, 14, 60; women and, 14, 60–61; Great Depression and, 29–30, 90, 92, 93, 175; premium on character and reputation, 47–48, 63, 65–66; work ethic and, 51; charity, 55–56, 93; rhetoric of classlessness, 56–57, 92, 194; "boosterism," 58, 60, 61, 225 (n. 40); religion and, 58–59, 66, 121, 122; ethnic divisions, 67–68; New Deal and, 112; Masonic lodges and, 174, 175, 176–77, 184
Community organizations, 29, 57–58, 60–61
Congregationalists, 58
Conitz, Alice, 48–49
Conklin, Frank, 193–94, 256 (n. 18)
Conservatism, 5, 8, 15, 206
Consumer goods, 19, 114, 168, 208–9
Consumerism, 75, 158
Cooper, Ed, 139
Cooperatives, 71
Corn, 19, 35–36
Corporations, 55, 133, 153, 155
Costain, George, 27–28
Cost of production, 133–35, 136, 141, 142, 146, 147, 245 (n. 51)

Eastern Star, 60, 179
Eastgate, Charles, 143
Eastwood, Lydia, 56
Eckman, N.D., 57
Economic planning, 100–101, 111
Edgely, N.D., 174
Edgemont, S.D., 86
Education, 78
Ehrenreich, Barbara, 158
Eisenmenger, Jacob, 45
Elections, 87, 112, 139, 206–7
Electrification, 31–32, 38, 154
Elliot, Brian, 217
Elton, Theodore, 173, 174
Emergency Farm Mortgage Act
    (1933), 37–38
Emergency Relief Appropriation Act
    (1935), 32
Employment: occupational distribu-
    tions, 4, 47, 99, 208, 210, 219–20,
    221; self-employment, 9, 42, 47,
    50–51; women, 14, 153, 168, 221,
    247 (n. 25); agricultural, 89, 208
Engels, Friedrich, 5
English, Deirdre, 158
Engsten, Ada, 55
Errington, Frederick, 122
Ethnicity, 67–68, 71, 92, 178–79
Eureka, S.D., 69, 71, 77, 78, 80, 81,
    84–85
Eureka Civic Club, 80, 84
Europe: class politics in, 6, 11, 56;
    World War I and, 18; immigrants
    from, 58, 68, 174
Evangelical Lutherans, 59
Evictions, 137, 138–39
Ezekiel, Mordecai, 102

Factory operatives, 47
Fairbanks, Arvard, 199
Faragher, John, 4, 59
Fargo, N.D., 60, 93–94, 158, 174, 178

Fargo Forum, 9, 94, 194
Fargo Tribune, 61
Farm Aid, 215
"Farm Boy near Dickinson, North
    Dakota" (Rothstein), 106
Farm Bureau Federation (FBF),
    102, 130–31, 143
Farm credit, 18, 19, 38, 110, 111
Farm Credit Administration, 37–38
Farm equipment, 114, 208, 209
Farmers, 2, 13; political radicalism,
    5–6, 38, 61, 71–72, 111, 129, 143,
    147, 185, 214–15; tenant farming,
    13, 17–18, 46, 74–75, 89, 206;
    foreclosures on, 17–18, 128, 140,
    206, 215; government price sup-
    ports, 18, 31, 34–35, 146–47, 209;
    incomes, 19, 25, 27, 132; Great De-
    pression and, 19, 28, 128; indebt-
    edness, 19, 130, 137, 207; drought
    and, 20, 23, 25, 26–27, 46; dust
    storms and, 24; in public works
    projects, 33; federal emergency re-
    lief, 34, 35, 36, 110–11; AAA pro-
    grams and, 34–36, 118, 129, 134,
    142–47; self-employment, 42, 47,
    50–51; migration to the Dakotas,
    43, 44, 45; land ownership, 43, 89;
    work demands, 48, 50–51; conflict
    with businessmen, 72–73; and chil-
    dren's occupations, 89; New Deal
    reformers and, 103, 110, 111,
    118–19, 142, 145–46, 209–10,
    245 (n. 70); protest movement,
    128–29, 130, 131–33, 147, 215;
    farm strikes, 132, 136–37, 139,
    141, 215, 243 (n. 14); taxation of,
    133, 139; cost-of-production move-
    ment, 133–35, 136, 141, 142, 146,
    245 (n. 51); domestic allotment
    plan and, 134, 135–36, 142, 144,
    145, 146, 245 (n. 51); antifore-

44, 210, 221; homesteading in, 45; churches, 58; Masons in, 60, 172, 174–76, 178, 183, 250 (n. 3); Ku Klux Klan in, 67; German-Russian immigrants, 68; support for Roosevelt, 112, 206; Republicanism, 112, 206–7; NPL in, 129–30; FHA in, 132, 133–34, 136, 137, 139–41; foreclosure moratorium, 140; AAA county agents in, 143; women's employment in, 153, 221; grocery chains in, 155–56; home economics programs in, 158; health care in, 211; "pioneer heritage" ideal, 217; railroads in, 225 (n. 40). *See also* Dakotas

North Dakota Agricultural College, 142

North Dakota Board of Capitol Commissioners, 187–88, 189, 190, 191–93, 194–95, 198, 255 (n. 7), 256 (n. 18)

North Dakota Capitol, 185–87, 196–97, 254 (n. 3); "Pioneer Family" statue, 15, 199, 200, 204–5, 208, 258 (n. 53); labor strike, 93, 193–96; fire of 1930, 185; architecture, 187, 198–99, 255 (nn. 5, 7); architects, 187–90, 257 (nn. 22, 23); building materials, 190–93, 257 (n. 25); cornerstone ceremony, 197–200, 258 (n. 48)

North Dakota Federation of Club Women (NDFCW), 200

North Dakota Federation of Women's Clubs, 61

North Dakota National Guard, 140

North Dakota State Relief Committee, 91

Northern Great Plains Committee, 25

Northern Pacific Railroad, 43

Norwegian-Americans, 44, 68, 71

Nye, Gerald P., 24, 212
Nye Investigations, 212

Oat prices, 19
O'Connor, Hugh, 91, 92
OddFellows, 60
Ohio, 221
Onuf, Peter S., 231 (n. 13)
Ore Tax bill, 139
Otter Tail County, Minn., 32
Out-migration, 17–18, 39, 208

Parkman, Helen, 72
Pearson, Jessica, 246 (n. 1)
Peek, George N., 102
Pells, Richard, 4
Pennington County, S.D., 47
"Penny" sales, 137–39, 215
Peters, C. E., 124–25
Peters, C. R., 53, 79–80
Peterson, Fred, 68
Philbrook, Mrs. L. A., 214
Photographers, 15, 84, 103, 105, 117, 119
Physicians, 29, 51, 90–91, 211, 248 (n. 56)
Pierce, Gerald, 197
Pierre, S.D., 11
Pillsbury Company, 35
"Pioneer Family" (Fairbanks), 15, 199, 200, 204–5, 208, 258 (n. 53)
Pioneers. *See* Settlers
Plankinton Herald, 110
Political clubs, 61
Politics, 42, 92, 226 (n. 47); class relations and, 5–6; farm radicalism, 11, 38, 61, 71–72, 111, 129, 143, 147, 215; newspapers and, 15; political resistance tradition, 46; and landownership, 46–47; election of 1932, 87, 112, 139; FSA photographers and, 105; Republicanism,

112, 206–7; women and, 168–69;
literature and, 202
Popper, Frank and Deborah, 209–10
Populism, 2–4, 42, 71, 215, 235
(n. 23)
Populist party, 5–6, 46
Postproducerism, 9, 87, 207
Poultry raising, 149, 246 (n. 3), 250
(n. 95)
Poverty, 25, 30–31, 93, 103, 210
Powell, John Wesley, 23
"Prairie Is My Garden" (Dunn), 204
Presbyterians, 58
Producerism, 15–16; historians and,
2, 4, 6, 42; new middle class and,
5, 9; cultural conflict and, 9–10;
community ideal and, 62, 80
Production control, 37, 102, 144
Professionals, 28–29
Progressive Era, 100
Progressivism, 6–7, 46–47
Prohibition, 70–71, 177
Proletarianization, 168, 217
Protest, 128, 130, 132, 147, 215
Protestant Reformation, 51
Protestants, 73; social standing, 13,
65, 68, 171, 178; churches, 58, 122;
anti-Catholicism, 66, 67; anti-Ger-
manism, 70; politics, 71
Public opinion, 153
Public schools, 70
Public Works Administration (PWA),
32, 34, 250 (n. 1)
Public works programs, 31, 32–33

Radicalism, 11, 38, 61, 71–72, 111,
129, 143, 147, 215
Railroads, 43, 45, 46, 133–34, 225
(n. 40)
Rainfall, 20, 23, 39, 206, 207
Ranchers, 36, 117
Ransom County, N.D., 143, 145, 146

Rapid City, S.D., 66
Reagan, Ronald, 209, 215
Real estate, 28
Rebekkah, 60
Reconstruction Finance Corporation
(RFC), 31
Redfield, Robert, 236 (n. 47)
Red Owl Stores, 155–56
Red River Valley, 11
Relief payments: reliance on, 30, 32,
95; county commissioners', 30–31;
necessity of, 31, 86; inadequacy of,
34; reluctance to accept, 91, 94,
216, 239 (n. 81); stigmatization of,
92, 93, 110, 113, 237 (n. 21); clergy
and, 125, 126
Religion, 92; political divisions, 71,
226 (n. 47); New Deal and, 124;
Masonic ritual, 172, 173, 174, 183,
184
Reno, Milo, 128, 130, 131, 132, 134,
137, 142, 147
Renville County, N.D., 144, 145
Republican party, 2, 112, 206–7
Republicans, 13, 71, 171, 226 (n. 47),
234–35 (n. 22)
Republic Steel Corporation, 114
Resettlement, 111–12
Resettlement Administration, 36,
103
Resource conservation, 37
"Revolution of 1906," 46
Rieder, Jonathan, 214
Riley, Glenda, 151
Ripley, Edwin, 172, 174
River, The, 215
Road construction, 155
Robinson, Doane, 47
Robinson, Elwyn, 41
Robinson, John, 175, 177, 179, 182,
253 (n. 59)
Rodgers, Daniel, 51